AMERICA
a prophecy

the
SPARROW
reader

edited by Marcus Boon

AMERICA:
A PROPHECY

A SPARROW READER

EDITED BY
MARCUS BOON

SOFT SKULL PRESS
BROOKLYN, NY • 2005

America: A Prophecy
©2005 Sparrow

Edited by Marcus Boon
Book Design by David Janik

Published by Soft Skull Press
www.softskull.com

Distributed by Publishers Group West
www.pgw.com • 800.788.3123

Printed in Canada

AMERICA: A PROPHECY

Americans will grow
stupider and stupider
until they can no longer
read rfe words bh thes
poem.

And gyht the bgjhi
increasingly njkiuy
eruhj npoli when
fdgjkol nmlpwq.

CONTENTS

PREFACE

Sparrow is primarily known as a poet. Astute literary scholars will notice that for the most part, this book does not contain poems. In fact, Sparrow has worked as a journalist and prose provocateur since the late 1970s, when he wrote for a local weekly in northern Manhattan, *The Heights-Inwood*. Inspired by reading *Moby Dick* he is the author of the bestselling, though unpublished, account of his pilgrimage to his guru in Calcutta, *Born Too Young*. After a distinguished career in national politics, he has worked diligently on his memoirs of the brutal 1996 presidential campaign, published as *Republican Like Me*, and a book of inspirational short pieces, *Yes, You ARE A Revolutionary!*, both courtesy of Soft Skull Press.

Many of these essays appeared in *The Sun*. Others were published in the *Whole Earth Review, Ulster, Chronogram, the New York Observer, Exquisite Corpse, The Unbearables Assembling Magazine, The Literary Supplement of the Revolutionary Poultry Overview (Pro-Poland), LUNGFULL!, Funny Times, Cosmic Society, The Uptown Dispatch, the Poetry Calendar* and, notably, in *The 11th Street Ruse*—the mimeographed zine that Sparrow and his wife Violet Snow published from 1987-1998. "My Names" appeared in a different form, as "Spam I Am" in the *New York Times*. "Barbie: A Memoir" was in *Mondo Barbie* edited by Lucinda Ebersole and Richard Peabody (St. Martin's). "Meet the Beats" appeared under a different title in *Thus Spake the Corpse: an Exquisite Corpse Reader, 1988-1998, Volume 2: Fictions, Travels and Translations*, edited by Andre Codrescu (Black Sparrow Press, 2000).

I first met Sparrow in a squat in Hackney, East London, England, in the winter of 1986. It was the Jewish Sabbath and Sparrow, an observer of many religious customs, asked me to chop firewood for him. So I lazily pulled apart a few empty fruit crates and tossed them in the fireplace. In saying yes at that time and place, perhaps the seeds of my involvement in this book lie, where, once again, Sparrow has asked me to chop firewood for him. May this wood burn brightly!

Marcus Boon
January 2005

INTRODUCTION: MY NAMES

My given name is Michael Gorelick. Both these names have a meaning, which may be translated as:

Who is like God? A beggar.

"Michael" is Hebrew for "who is like God?"—originally applied to an angel. "Gorelick" is the Russian word for "burned." ("Gorel" means fire.) A "Gorelick" is a person whose house or village has been burned down. (As far as I know, this is always a Jewish name.)

The most successful musician in history has this last name (and also doesn't use it). He is Kenny G. (who has sold more records than any other instrumentalist).

Despite my spiritually instructive name, I have long endeavored to change it. In high school, I renamed myself "Swarmy" Nud Myrtle—but no one paid attention. At Cornell University I changed my name to Mike Hotel (the first year) and Mike Motel (the second).

After flunking out of college, I found myself in Gainesville, Florida. There I met a woman named Jennifer The Princess Of Love. She always dressed in purple and went barefoot. She wore long dresses, and sometimes a snood. She looked like a Tarot card come to life. One day I asked Jennifer for a name.

Twenty-eight years later, I recall that moment clearly. It was portentous, like a judge passing a sentence: "You be Sparrow; you look like a sparrow."

(Later Jennifer said, "I thought I was just naming you for that day.")

At first I was impressed by the justness of my name. I had been born in Manhattan, surrounded by sparrows. As a child walking to school, I admired these birds nesting above a Chinese laundry on Nagle Avenue. Like all New York City children, I believed sparrows were baby pigeons. (This was because we only saw two species of birds, and pigeons zealously hid their squabs [newborns].)

When did I lose faith in the name Sparrow? Probably around 1980. It is, for one thing, a wimpy word. Who needs the name of a little beady-eyed, low-flying bird? Even the one mention of sparrows in the

Scriptures—"God sees every sparrow fall"—is ominous. Why can't God see every sparrow *thrive*? Or sing? The name "Sparrow" seemed one of the thoughtless excesses of the hippie era.

But what name to replace it with? I was given the Sanskrit name "Garuda" in 1977, which I still use within my meditation group. "Garuda" attempts to correct the weaknesses of "Sparrow."

Garuda is (according to an Indian comic book I have) "a mythical bird... held in great veneration in India from time immemorial." He is the "mount" of Vishnu, one of the great Trinity of Hindu gods. In my comic, Garuda is depicted as a man with voluminous gold jewelry, brown wings and a beak. Indra, the King of the Gods asks him: "O greatest of birds, I want to know the limit of your strength." Garuda replies: "I can bear, on one of my feathers, this earth with her mountains, forests and oceans—and You! My strength is such that I can carry without fatigue all the worlds put together..."

If "Sparrow" is too weak, "Garuda" is a bit cosmic-macho for me.

I need a newer name, somehow—but where to find one?

2.

In Western culture, the first naming is accomplished by Adam and Eve, in the garden of Eden. Turning to Genesis 2:18, I discovered, to my surprise, that Adam names all the animals himself, before the arrival of the Eve. Here is the passage:

> *And the Lord God said, It is not good that the man should be alone; I will make an help meet for him.*
>
> *And out of the ground the Lord God formed every beast of the field, and every fowl of the air; and brought them onto Adam to see what he would call them: and whatsoever Adam called every living creature, that was the name thereof.*
>
> *And Adam gave names to all cattle, and to the fowl of the air, and every beast of the field; but for Adam there was not found an help meet for him.*

(Of course, you can see where the plot is taking us—towards the creation of Eve.)

What strikes me is the sense of frustration, or disappointment, in the first naming. Adam names every being, in the hopes of finding a "help meet" (a partner) and none are satisfying—in the same way all my names are unsatisfying. It's as if naming itself creates loneliness. As Adam defines each creature—gives it an inflexible appelation—he becomes more forlorn. Names are limits, and limits are sad.

3.

Names (at least in Western society) consist of two parts: the first name, or "familiar" (or "Christian") name, and the last name, or surname. The second name ties one to history, to a particular family which often extends back for centuries. Some people, who remove their last names (Madonna, Cher, Prince) amputate this connection to history. This makes them seem glamorous.

By adopting a single name, "Sparrow," I disconnected myself from my family, my lineage, my Jewish (and Russian) ethnicity. After a few years, though, the name began to accumulate its own history. Again I was weighed down by a burdensome "identity."

This is the problem with names. They can never liberate us, because they take on our personality.

I would be best if my name changed every day, according to my mood and disposition. And suddenly, this is happening. Recently I have been receiving e-mail solicitations (commonly called "spam") which constantly address me with new names. I find them exciting.

Am I the first person ever to celebrate spam?

The first one I noticed read:

"Hello Sparquee,

Valium - Viagra - Xanax - Ambien - Zoloft - Ativan
- AND MANY MORE -

No Prior Prescription Needed!

The name "Sparquee" was a total surprise. It combines "Sparrow" and the harpooner from Moby-Dick, Queequeg.

I began to keep a list of these solicitations:

Souciep
Dear healthslif
hello Sparky799@Juno.com
Sparrott1
Hello sparrow118@juno.com
HI,Mseligman
Hello Soowee,
Hello Snaper,
Hello soundmixer2@juno.com,
flyingscot1,
Hello Smorrison23,
Hello soowee@juno.com,
Tjhedrick
Hey there Deblack,
Hey There Zett,
Fparente
Hi! Fariel a'Wagothea
I hope this is asparky15@juno.com ...
Sparrish3
Sowders,
valeô
Spgross
icq
Chakkaboy, now is the time
1a
I hope this is aangelaherman@juno.com ...
Howdy Sparrow1257ss
Sparma1, you decide
Hello Sparkinson,
Dear, serge101
Hi rhino6,
Dear, silverpepper

Dear, soggyloafr
Dear, sonman2
Dgosch
Chukkaboy
PbUO
Tlyowbken

I love these names—temporary, awkward, apt. They seem expressive of my inner selves. "Sparky799" is my "party personality", "Souciep" my suave, artistic persona. "Soowee," though mildly insulting [it *is* a call for pigs] is my abrasive side. "Sparlin" combines my name with that of my hero, Abraham Lincoln.

I don't feel like a "Michael," a "Sparrow" or a "Garuda." But somehow I *do* feel like a "Snaper," a "Sparrish3," a "asparky15," and especially a "Fariel a'Wagothea." These wacky words are like the "pet names" lovers invent for each other.

I wish I had the courage to tell everyone, "I just received my e-mail, and this is my new spam-name for today: 'PbUO.'" But I am not brave, so these names exist merely as interior gestures—hints of some inner transformation. For instance, my most recent, "sparker14", is some new me, throwing off sparks in 14 directions, like a sparkler.

4.

In *The Wall Street Journal* of Monday, June 23, 2003 Bill Gates writes an essay entitled "Why I Hate Spam." It begins: "Like almost everyone who uses e-mail, I receive a ton of spam every day. Much of it offers to help me get out of debt or get rich quick. It would be funny if it weren't so irritating."

I suppose this is Billionaire Humor.

I was surprised how worried Gates is about "unsolicited commercial e-mail": "It is a drain on business productivity, an increasingly costly waste of time and resources that clogs corporate networks and distract workers. Among consumers, it spread scams, pornography and even computer viruses."

Do you notice how this paragraph begins in a corporate tone and rises into semi-hysteria?

But the paragraph continues: "Worse, spammers prey on less sophisticated e-mail users, including children, threatening their safety and privacy."

By now, spam is nearly equated with rape.

Clearly, big corporate CEOs are worried that spam is going to kill their golden goose. So what can they do? "... this month, Microsoft filed 15 lawsuits in the U.S. and UK against companies and individuals alleged to have sent billions of spam messages in violation of state and federal laws."

Who are these spammers? The answer is: "No one knows."

"... we are battling spammers who set up numerous e-mail accounts and move from service to service to avoid detection."

Like hackers, or revolutionaries, spammers are anonymous and secret. Now get this:

"Spammers also go to great lengths to conceal or "spoof" their identities, so we are partnering with other service providers to identify and restrict mail that conceals its source."

Spammers are spoofers! They hide their own identities, as criminals have since early recorded history. That's why they also hide *my* identity! The same technique (or technology) that generates their false names also generates mine!

And this is partly what interests me about these names: they are a type of poetry computers write. In some ways, they are similar to my own one-word poems:

POEM 161   POEM 63

sopher   Soddentine

POEM 73   POEM VI

exampee   beseven

POEM 37

sigit

Gates writes: "Our proposal is to create a regulatory 'safe harbor' status for senders who comply with e-mail guidelines confirmed by an FTC-approved self-regulatory body. Senders who do not comply would have to insert an "ADV: "label—standing for advertisement—in the subject line of all unsolicited commercial e-mail. This would enable computer users either to accept ADV-label mail or have it deleted automatically."

Already I am receiving some of this "ADV" e-mail—it is dull and generic. What I *like* about spam is its false air of familiarity. It is the air of a con artist who approaches you on the street and claims to remember you from high school. "ADV" spam is merely an advertisement, not a hustle. The hustle creates the Art.

Perhaps I should start an organization, Lovers of Spam, to fight the schemes of the Major Capitalists. In the meantime, I wait for the Web Criminals to supply me with unforeseeable new names.

P.S. One just arrived: zSparkeysquid1

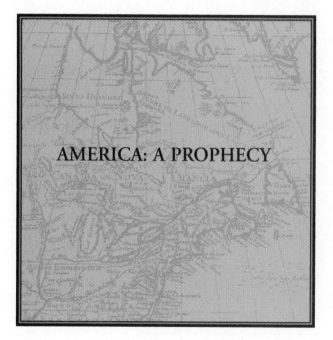

AMERICA: A PROPHECY

REPORT FROM AMERICA

Pardon me, but I've left New York. I've been touring the United States, and believe me, it's different. People actually wear those clothes that look so amusing in Times Square—yellow shirts and golf pants—they wear them *all the time.* Cash registers in supermarkets speak in a female voice, and no one says, "I saw Dave." They say, "I saw Dave's car."

Everyone curses more than in Manhattan, and takes more drugs. An informal survey made while hitchhiking indicates that 75% of the men in America have spent at least $100,000 on cocaine.

Americans work less than New Yorkers, or maybe it just seems like less. After work they come home and sit on a sofa, listening to the crickets. They don't go out every night to Bartok String Quartets and Transvestite Beauty Pageants like we do. By and large they have no desire to be famous.

On Passover, no American supermarket had ever heard of matzoh. When I defined it as a "Jewish cracker" the manager looked startled and conducted me to their vast selection of Ritz.

Americans prefer foods whose colors match their handbags. Their idea of eating out rarely involves leaving the car. Yet they all have lush gardens out back (Americans have an "out back") where they pull up glowing carrots even more beautiful than the Korean ones on Dyckman street.

America is a land of contrasts.

The most tragic side of the USA is its visual impoverishment. There's almost nothing to look at in the whole country. One block of St. Nicholas Avenue is more interesting than the entire drive from Florida to Texas.

America is very relaxing. It's quiet and it's easy to fall asleep. Those characterless Top 40 songs out of L.A.—bland remakes of *California Girls*—that sound so foolish on Amsterdam Ave. sound good here. They fit this slow world of freeways and trees.

Shopping centers are like little fake cities, where families wander aimlessly around, buying ice cream and staring at each other. There's a B. Dalton bookstore, tennis clothes and teenage girls with curly hair.

No one is America is political—all their extra energy goes into running triathlons, bicycling and canoeing. The more adventuresome fly little planes.

One meets grown men who have lived their entire lives in trailers.

Americans love plastic, because it's brighter than everything else, and every main street is like a Kandinsky-that-went-wrong. Just as New York seems a city of adults, and one feels like a child looking up the steps of The Metropolitan Museum, so in America one feels an adult among children—passing towns where the best movie is *13 Going On 30*.

In the souvenir shops there are no more "Tune On, Tune In, Drop Out" stickers, but there are lots of license plates that say, "I'm Spending My Children's Inheritance," and one commonly passes motor homes piloted by elderly couples with mischievous grins. My guess is the new hippies are over sixty-five.

The best thing about America is there are real cowboys here, who *know* cows, and pause about ten minutes between sentences, and seem aware of some mystery that never makes it into New York, except maybe by subway.

And there are clean rest rooms everywhere, and no one minds if you use them.

AN ATM OF ONE'S OWN

This is the story of a man, a vision and an ATM machine. The man is me. As we begin this saga, it is 2:14 a.m., and I am washing dishes. Lathering spoons, I listen to the radio, tuning from one far-off station to another.

There are certain commercials you only hear at 2:14 in the morning. One now arrives: "Unique business opportunities are opening up for ambitious entrepreneurs. Own your own ATM machine! Within the next four years, ATM use will increase by 500 percent! Find out how to take advantage of this remarkable offer! Call..."

I dash over to the sideboard and transcribe the number.

Next morning, I make the call. A woman with a southern accent answers the phone. "Hello," she says neutrally.

"Is this the number for ATM machines? I wish to own one," I assert.

"Yes. Give us your address, and we'll send you a packet," she replies.

I explain my location, and ask, "Where are you? I always wonder where the person on the phone is literally sitting."

"The business is in Dermain, Florida. I'm just the answering service," she explicates.

Hanging up the phone, I have several questions: Why wouldn't she name her town? Was she afraid of me? And doesn't a clerk normally speak the name of the business when she answers the phone?

Meanwhile, I await the promising packet.

Now I have a lot of decisions to make. My first is which room should house my new cash machine. Should I hide it discreetly in the closet? Should I place it in the bathroom, in front of the toilet, so that visitors having bowel movements will be tempted to use it? And next to the commode, I will place. . . a pile of Abercrombie & Fitch catalogues!

Also, I can customize my ATM. Upon its broad top, I may place crystals, West African ojima beads, a candle, three seashells. We have alternative medicine, independent movies, alternative rock. Why is there no alternative banking? Now is my opportunity to own a machine that combines the qualities of pagan altar and bank teller.

Perhaps my ATM should have no ornament except a human skull.

Or I could make clothes for it. My ATM could wear a dress, or a tutu, or a shawl and sombrero.

Or I could paint a vagina around the money slot.

Then there is the question of whether to install other machines in the house—a soda machine, a candy machine, a cigarette machine. (According to state law SR10693, it is perfectly legal for individuals to own cigarette machines. Only businesses are prohibited from harboring them.)

But the packet never arrives! I search through six piles of paper, and cannot find the "unique business opportunities" phone number.

I will never have a pet cash machine!, I weep. And just when I have nearly decided to use it as a tea table.

Then, one afternoon, in the bathtub, the answer comes to me: "Search the Internet!"

Toweling off, I type "ATM" into my Netscape search engine. "ATMs from IMS. International Merchant Services has the best deals on automatic teller machines sales/leasing" comes the message.

One click later, I am learning such remarkable facts as "49.4 percent of consumers surveyed prefer getting their cash from ATMs rather than having to deal with people." [Isn't that the same percentage that voted for George W. Bush in 2000?] IMS, I see, is located at 1331-A Airport Freeway, in Euless, Texas. They list an 800 number.

So I call. "Please hold," a woman tells me. On hold, I hear music lifting to sweet synthesizer crescendos through the telephone. "Hello, this is Pete King," says a manly voice.

"What was that music?" I ask.

"Aliska, what CD is playing on hold?" my sales representative inquires. Behind him, I hear Aliska walking out of the room.

"Is Aliska her natural name?" I ask.

"Yes, it is," Pete replies, proudly.

"That must be a Texan name," I muse. "You're in Euless, Texas, right?"

"'Useless, Texas', they call it," Pete reveals. "How did you know that?"

"I just visited the web site," I speak. "By the way, where is Euless?"

"Between Dallas and Fort Worth," Pete explains.

"I didn't know there was anything between Dallas and Fort Worth!"

"Sure. Arlington, the fourth largest city in Texas, is between Dallas and Fort Worth. You see, if you picture a baseball diamond missing second base, between the pitchers mound and home plate are a series of bedroom communities, including Bedford and Euless," Pete expounds.

I feel I must sit very still. Meanwhile, Aliska returns with the name of the CD: *Keys To Imagination* by Yanni.

"So how can I help you?" Pete volunteers.

"I am interested in buying an ATM," I venture bravely.

"Well, there's three main ways to do that. You can buy one outright, with cash or credit card, you can lease one through a leasing company, or you can borrow money from a bank—but most banks aren't going to lend to you unless you have credit like God. Even if you're a business, you need good trade references, four figure average monthly earnings..."

"So anyone can buy an ATM?" I persist.

"Just put down the money."

"How much is one?" I inquire.

"Between $6200-6500. If you amortize that over five years, you'll pay about $100 a month."

"Do they come in different colors?" I ask.

"There's just the colors you see on the Web site. If you want a Korean brand, I can get you gold and putty gray."

"Thank you so much," I effuse.

"Call us anytime," invites Pete King.

In Euless and Phoenicia, we hang up our phones.

$6200! If only I had credit like God!

International Merchant Services website: www.atm24.com, 800-769-2826. Pete King is a pseudonym.

MY COCKROACH DIARY

Dec. 7 8:21 AM: The cockroaches in this apartment have gone beyond all rational numbers; they have reached an irrational number. And they no longer wait until night to come out; they swarm after dark, at 5. Ever since our visit to Russia in 1990, they've been increasing, and now they outnumber us 4000:1.

8:54 AM: Oh no, I just found one in the saltshaker!

9:42 AM: I helped it escape, using one of the baby's spoons.

Dec. 8: This morning, three more cockroaches were in the salt-shaker, but I couldn't find the right spoon. I used a larger spoon, which they refused to climb on. It was sad to see them struggling through the killing salt, dreaming of escape, but avoiding the instrument of Salvation. This must be how Christians see the world, I thought.

Dec. 9: My wife woke up with a cockroach in her ear. "It feels really strange. It's moving around," she said. She tried to take it out with a tissue wrapped around a chopstick. I told her, "Let it crawl out. If you kill it, it'll get stuck in there." She stopped digging, and the bug did crawl out, fifteen minutes later—a cute baby roach.

Noon: Now Violet is cleaning out the insect den under the sink.
   "Sorry, cockroaches. It's just not working out between us," she explains, as she wipes away their nests.
   "It smells of cockroach shit down here," she just said. I never knew cockroach shit *had* a smell.

Dec. 10: Last night went well. There were fewer roaches than I have seen for months, as few as thirty-three.

12:03 AM We went to our neighbor's house to watch a video, and when we returned there were thousands again.

It's like destroying the *Mafia*. You can arrest them, but you can't break their organization.

Dec. 13: Up until now, we haven't killed the roaches. We've employed preventative methods - doing the dishes, taking the garbage out daily. Then last night, while washing dishes, I noticed a roach crawling on the side of a cup. I made no effort to save him, and in a moment he had drowned. A certain hardness has crept into me, I realized. When I bathe now, and notice three or four roach corpses in the tub, drowned as the water poured in, I feel a grim satisfaction. I wonder, "Could I kill a man now?"

Dec. 17: A cockroach has been trapped in the saltshaker all day, and I've done nothing. I'm bored with liberating them over and over. He walks around, while I pour salt out from under him. It's like having a tiny man living in your watch.

Jan. 4: At our New Year's Eve party, Norman announced, "I think you have a roach problem."

"Why do you say that?"

"Because I've seen several roaches walking around, next to the food. If roaches come out in the middle of a party, you have a problem."

"I've already killed six of them," Violet's cousin Bill added.

"I bet you don't kill them," Norman accused me. "You probably tell them to leave. I had a roomate like that, in San Francisco. We lived above a carriage house in an alley, and we had a bad roach problem. He believed that if he told them to leave, they would go. He'd say to them, 'Roaches, please don't stay here. We don't really want you here.'"

"Did they listen to him?"

"Of course not. They got worse."

"So what did you do?"

"I called in the exterminator. He came three times, and then the roaches were gone."

Violet said, "But our friend Therese told the cockroaches to leave an apartment, and they left."

"Yeah," I told Norman. "Your roommate probably wasn't spiritually evolved enough."

"Well, the roaches aren't listening to you, either!" Norman said.

Jan. 5: I forgot to tell Norman my favorite roach-killing story, the time a guy came to my door in Washington Heights and asked, "Do you want to be exterminated?"

Jan. 16: It is unfortunate that we had a baby in the middle of this cockroach war, because a baby's job is to eat 1/18 of a knish, then throw the rest of it on the floor for you to step on, while the whole time, you're thinking: "She's feeding the damn roaches! She's in league with them!"

Jan. 19: Today I drank some tea, and saw a speck floating in it. Is it a baby cockroach?, I thought. I looked closer, and it seemed benign. After I finished the tea, I thought, perhaps it *was* a roach. Maybe I eat cockroaches every day. They run out of a pot of millet, sometimes. But does *every* one run out? How many roaches a day do I eat?

Jan. 21: My mother came over to babysit and said, "I'm having *such* a roach problem! I got a small garbage can with a tight lid, but it doesn't help! I just can't cope with my roaches anymore!" This reassured me. Perhaps roach problems are hereditary.

Jan. 22: Today I was working on my novel, and a bug walked out in front of me. I looked down in anger, then saw it wasn't a roach! It was a grey, horned creature, like a miniature toad. I almost hugged it, out of gratitude.

Jan. 26: "Lately, when I open the cupboard doors, a cockroach usually falls on my head," my wife said today. "It's really obnoxious."

"I've noticed it, too. Are they *leaning* on the doors more than they used to?"

March 10: Violet woke up with another cockroach in her ear. "It's really loud," she said. "It's walking on my eardrum."

"Did you try to take it out?"

"No. But it stopped moving," she said. "Can you look in my ear and see?" she asked. (We bought a speculum—an earscope—to look in the baby's ear for infections.)

"Okay," I said, but we both forgot.

March 12: I remembered to look in Violet's ear. Inside was a small dead cockroach, curled on its back. It's strange to see a dead roach in your wife's ear—like looking in a Viewmaster! Violet tried to extract it, failed, and agreed to see a doctor.0

March 15: Violet is still procrastinating going to the doctor. Meanwhile, while meditating tonight, at 1 AM, I felt a cockroach in my ear. It crawled deeper and deeper—perhaps into my *brain*. (Does the brain connect with the ear? I wasn't sure.) I continued meditating, and found myself speaking mentally to the insect: "Turn around! That's a good roach!" Not that I *believe* in talking to roaches.

When I finished my meditation, I asked Violet, "Are you awake?"

"Yes."

"Can you look in my ear?"

She looked in my ear. "It's a hair," she said. "It's touching your eardrum."

Now I'm in the Bellevue emergency room, waiting for a doctor. It's 2:30 AM. I was hoping there would be no line on a quiet winter night, but I forgot the homeless come here to stay warm. So thirty-eight men and one woman are with me, as an infomercial plays above us: "I made a fortune investing in real estate. So can you. The last six months have created tremendous opportunities . . ."

Once in a while, the police pass through with a young handcuffed criminal. They walk right in without waiting.

March 16: After 2 hours and 45 minutes, I got into the doctor's office. "What seems to be the problem?" he asked.

"I have a hair in my ear," I said.

"Um hmm." He got a speculum and looked inside.

"You're right. There's something in there. It looks like a hair." (But to another doctor, he muttered, "It isn't a hair.")

"It might be a cockroach," I volunteered. My wife has a cockroach in her ear."

"Why doesn't she take it out?" the doctor asked.

"She's been busy," I said.

The doctor looked in my ear again. "It looks like a cockroach," he said this time. "I saw it moving."

"Really?" I said. I felt a cockroach in me. I felt it move. The other doctor came to look.

"I don't see anything," he said. My doctor took out a long Q-tip and put it in my ear. He pulled it out. Nothing was on it. Then he handed me the Q-tip.

"You try it. You can feel it in there."

I put it in. The 2 doctors watched. I pulled out the Q-tip. A tiny cat hair was on the end. The doctors looked disappointed.

The 2nd doctor took the Q-tip, with the hair. "Can I throw it out, or do you want to keep it as a souvenir?"

"Throw it out," I said. They gave me a bill for $295, and I left.

March 17: I am going to begin killing the roaches with my own 2 hands.

March 22: I killed my first roach. It was a baby that crawled out of my novel, when I brought it out. It took me 5 tries to kill it. They have very hard skins.

March 23: I admitted to Violet that I'm killing the roaches. "So am I," she said sheepishly. "Though I feel guilty about it."

"I wouldn't mind them if they didn't crawl into our ears."

"Well, they haven't crawled into *your* ears."

"We don't know. Maybe they crawl in and crawl out."

March 24: Soon after I killed the first roach, the others began running faster when I approached. They must have a sophisticated communication network between the living and the dead.

March 25: Since I've begun killing them, I've catalogued a number of roach species: a dark-colored one, a squat one, a long, thin one. Strange, I'd never noticed them before. You don't really *see* something until you kill it.

March 26: I came home late from work, and Violet said, "The house is clean, isn't it?"

"Yes, it is!" We hugged.

"I killed alot of cockroaches," she said.

"Oh, yeah? How did it feel?"

"Terrible. When I killed a little one, I would think, 'That's someone's baby.'"

"Yes, but I doubt the mothers love their babies as much as you do."

"And when I killed a big one, I thought, 'Maybe it's a pregnant one,' and felt horribly guilty." We hugged some more.

March 28: I keep the Jewish Sabbath, and I've decided not to kill roaches on that day. On the Sabbath, I feel I'm in the palm of God's hand.

Now it's the next day, and I still can't bring myself to kill any. I'm fatalistic. What's one or 2 more dead roaches?

March 29: I began killing roaches again, out of frustration, at the sink. But in the middle of my death spree, I remembered Darwin's Theory of Natural Selection.

"Wait a second," I told my wife. "If I kill all the slow ones, only the fast ones will survive, and we'll have the fastest roaches on earth!"

June 17: Violet, Sylvia and I went on a trip to Israel. I was struck by the utter buglessness of our Tel Aviv hotel, though it was in a hot, Middle Eastern country. A great deal of poison must be responsible, I thought with a shudder. Also, the room was lonely; there was no one in it but ourselves.

MEMOIRS OF A TELEPHONE SOLICITOR

At Metro News, contracted by *The Rocky Mountain News* to intimidate Denverites, sixteen of us sit at Formica desks under a sign, "If God wanted people to read *The Post,* He would've made their arms three feet longer," in a stylish office building in Wheatridge, Colorado. Many of us have removed our shoes to enjoy the wall-to-wall carpeting, and most of us are in the solicitor's trance.

The trance of soliciting begins for us when Hal, our cadaverous boss, announces, "It's that time," receivers are raised to mouths, and the near-identical spiel begins to drift around the room: "Hello, this is _____ with *The Rocky Mountain News.* Are you currently receiving delivery of *The News?*" The lies and half-truths mingle in the cigarette haze: "I'm terribly sorry about that, sir," "We're always trying to improve our service," "I'm here to solve your problems," "We'll get on that right away."

As I speak, I look out the window at the clouds passing over an apartment complex whose red roofs resemble a medieval village. On the desk in front of me is the sequence sheet: an exchange plus two digits on top, and the numbers 00 to 99 in six rows beneath. In front of the room, the bosses fold manila envelopes. (They are always folding manila envelopes, adding columns of figures, or speaking to unknown personages on the telephone.)

A bird flies across the window. The smell of cigarettes, coffee, and autumn fill the room.

I try to visualize the people I'm talking to. It's hard; voices are much more alike than faces. There is one Housewife voice, one Old Man Voice, one Old Lady voice, one Hippie voice, one Executive voice. In my mind I see the same six people over and over. I think of new ways to say, "Call us if you have a problem": "If there's a mishap, give us a holler."

In my time, I've encountered every reason for not taking the paper, from the ubiquitous "We're not interested," to the rare "I'd take it if they weren't made out of trees." In between are: "You need proofreaders - the misspelled words are terrible," "The ink gets all over your hands. Rub your nose and you got a moustache," "It's a difficult page-numbering system," "My husband likes *The Post*, I like *The News*, and he won," "They just pile up," "You write about all the crap going on in the world today", and the succinct, "Too much reality."

One man told Cleo, who sat behind me, that he would take it if she taught him how to read. "I haven't subscribed to newspapers since my dog was housebroken," a man told me. "I'm a hooker," one woman said, and hung up. "I'm a recluse," said another. "I retired and I want to take a walk every day and get it at the box." The best reason: a Mrs. Martinez, who needed the money to have a baby.

If the people receive *The News*, we pretend to supervise its delivery. Thus, we receive numerous complaints about that. The most common is that the paper carrier doesn't reach the porch, but there are numerous variants: "The paper breaks apart and falls all over the yard," "The days it rains it's not in a bag and the days it's dry it's in a bag," "I get the paper, but it comes in my birdbath," "Three times he threw the paper in my flowers," "He threw it on the roof," "He threw it through my storm door," and "I don't want to subscribe to any more Easter egg hunts." I will never again see paperboys as innocents.

Worse than the real deliverers are the counterfeit ones. One elderly woman reported three attempts to extract newspaper payment in the previous week. "A couple girls came here to collect money and asked if they could use the bathroom. I told them, 'I should say not!' My neighbor let them in and they robbed her." "What could they steal from her bathroom?" I wondered. "Cologne!" the woman pronounced.

Poor newspaper delivery has ruined men's lives. One fellow received a wet newspaper on a rainy day, called for a replacement, and received a second wet paper. Something in him was broken that day. A year later, he retells the story with fresh anguish. "No one cares!" one woman moaned, on the subject. "In the fifties and sixties and seventies they put it on the porch," one man said, expounding the Decline of Western Civilization Theory of newspaper delivery.

To be honest, I receive more praise than blame for the service, but it's rarely as interesting. Elderly women in particular take on a glow describing the competence of their deliverer. Several have described theirs as "the best in the world." Yet little of what they say is memorable. They point to the time of his arrival, the placement of the journal, but what they're trying to say is that in today's uncertain world, it is a relief to find the daily chronicle of murders neatly folded in the same place every day.

One woman complained of "too good service." She found the paper one morning on her terrace and there was no way it could've gotten there. "Next time you'll find it in your bedroom," I joked, but this only terrified her more.

I've also studied the Colorado dialect. Living most of my life in New York City, I had no idea anybody still said, "Everything's jake," or called strangers "Old Buddy." Many people answer the phone, "Y'hello," a bastard offspring of "Yeah" and "Hello." And after a week, a discerning linguist can distinguish, "Huh huh," which means "Yes" from "Huh uh," which means "No." In New York, if you call someone "Guy" as in "Hi, guy!" it means you're gay. Here it means you're a cowboy.

Fatalism is ingrained in the local character. If one asks a subscriber if there's been any problems with their service, they invariably answer, "Not so far." If you inquire how long they've been taking it, they'll admit it's been eleven years.

Suddenly Alfred Hitchcock's resonant voice emerges from the receiver: "Please leave your message after this brief interruption," followed by a woman's shriek. This is one of the fringe benefits of phone soliciting. I've spoken to Jack Benny, W. C. Fields, Amos and Andy, Santa Claus, Groucho Marx and Johnny Mathis (parodying "Misty"). Cheech enthused to Chong: "Hey man, we get $3.50 an hour just for answering the phone." Archie Bunker promised, "I'll tell Stan one of his Commie Pinko friends called." Jack Nicholson growled, "If you turkeys want to leave your name and number, go ahead." And an eerie voice intoned: "You have entered a dimension of time and space between 'No answer' and the busy signal . . . The Phone Zone!"

Perhaps my most extraordinary discovery was that Born Again Christians have a sense of humor: "Praise the Lord! This is the Andersons. No, we have not been raptured. But if you have a message or a prayer request . . ."

One stumbles into the middle of some unusual situations. "I've got company here—there's an officer. My motorcycle got ripped off," one young man informed me. Cleo's husband, Red, called a mental hospital in the middle of an escape. (They told him to hold on.) One woman fell asleep while ordering from me. One is always pulling people out of showers. Once I spoke to a woman *in* the shower. I've encountered some interesting salutations: "Narcotics," "Kingdom Hall," "KIM Radio Hotline." "You're coming in as a power failure truck," a woman at the Coors brewery informed me.

Then there are the eccentric civilians: "Your dime!" "You reached it!" "Jay's Party House," "Hello, dammit!"

One finds out personal information indirectly: "My ex-wife gets the paper and I'm over there every night helping her with our disabled kid." "My father passed away on the 6th and he was the one who read the paper." "I got *The Post* for 30 years and I remarried and my new wife likes your paper. She goes right to the obituaries to see if she's still alive."

Children, of course, are fine sources of private information. They'll say, "We don't want the newspaper cause my mom can't pay for it," where their parents would use the veiled phrase, "Not at this time." One young solicitor named Sandy plunged into a fever of worry every time a kid cheerfully informed her he was alone and would be for the next four hours.

Some replies are difficult to answer. "Is it a paper or something?" one man asked. "What does 'service' mean?" inquired another. "I'm just my daughter's mother," a third explained. It's impressive how many people get a paper but don't know which one.

One slightly inebriated woman was convinced I was a friend playing a prank. "Mike, why don't you break out of it?" she kept asking. Two of our solicitors met acquaintances over the phone. Donna found a third cousin she'd heard of but never met. "Is Bambi still alive?" she asked. (Bambi is her great-aunt, almost 100.) Red met a high school buddy. "Oh, yeah, committed suicide. Gassed himself in a car," I heard him report of a mutual friend.

It's surprising how many people are moving in two weeks and don't know where. And where are the rest going? To Nebraska, Phoenix, Wisconsin, St. Louis, Indianapolis, San Diego, Fort Worth, "between Memphis and Nashville." I haven't met anyone moving to New York.

One encounters Big Names in the telephone business. I personally spoke to Michael Jackson - in fact, he subscribed. Admittedly he wasn't Michael Jackson the singer, but that's certainly a Big Name. James Jones and James Stewart subscribed the same day.

I've met the only blind medical student in the USA, a man who hasn't worked for three years ("How do you live?" "Out of the rich man's trash can"), an eighteen year old video store clerk who's seen 1,005 movies, a woman who found God while nearly drowning on a sailboat, and the roommate of Barry Sadler, Jr., son of the lieutenant who had the smash hit "Ballad Of The Green Beret."

There are an almost unlimited number of ways to embarrass yourself as a telephone solicitor. You can call back the number you just dialed, revealing your canned spiel and false cheerfulness. You can mistake a man for a woman or a woman for a child. You can ask people who don't take the paper, "How's your service?" or offer subscribers the thirty day money back guarantee. You can forget your own name. You can, as my partner Bob did, say, "This is Bob with *The Denver Post.*" (He was so mortified he hung up.) Nina tells a story of a solicitor who was chewed out for bad service by a customer, apologized, hung up, muttered "Asshole!" then began the next conversation, "Hello, this is Asshole."

Every so often one calls *another* telephone solicitor. They fall into two categories: those who are wildly enthusiastic about it and those who endure it. The first type invariably refer to it as "telemarketing" and attempt to recruit you into their program, which is usually something like The Videotape Library of Sports. The latter type will often admit that their operation's a con—as did the woman offering free trips to a Las Vegas real estate promotion, who said: "There *is* land there . . . if you like desert."

Occasionally one meets one with a sense of humor. A solicitor for Sears mused on the aptness of her title: she worked for the Lost Potential Department.

A third group is ex-solicitors. "I hated calling people at their house," a Coors worker confessed. One woman, after escaping phone soliciting, joined a traveling door-to-door sales group, quit in Albuquerque and had to hitchhike back in mid-winter, a sleeping bag over her head for warmth.

A woman answering a pay phone had once held my job. "*The Rocky Mountain News* is about burnt out," she decreed. "The delivery people are no good. Telling people the service is gonna improve—it isn't!" She now sells discount books for the Junior Chamber of Commerce.

But not everyone can be a telephone solicitor. Almost 100 individuals have worked at *Metro News* in my four months here, many only for a couple days. Hal tells a story of a man who came to work for the office in Salt Lake City, made one call, picked up his hat and left. The ones who stay are often unusual. Tara was a large woman with gold earrings, polka dot blouses and an infectious laugh. She was fond of meeting men over the phone, visiting them after work and showing up the next day wearing a big smile and a much larger shirt. "What did you do?" Beth, our senior solicitor, asked her on one such occasion. "What do you *think* we did?" she returned. "No, stupid, besides that," Beth persisted. "He's gonna give me a car!" Tara announced.

Dan Ruud, my longtime soliciting-partner (we shared a desk), was an aspiring sportswriter from Bimidji, Minnesota. Twenty five years old and a Navy veteran, his sober manner concealed a dark humor. It was he who invented Big Phone Eddie, the solicitor's folk hero, and his Blue Telephone, Babe. (Big Phone Eddie sold newspaper subscriptions to the entire city of Dallas, Texas in one night, and once, when a tornado blew down the phone lines in San Francisco an hour before his shift, repaired them in time to begin dialing.) Dan and I are the cofounders of the Society of American Phone Solicitors (SAPS), which organizes boycotts of restaurants with "No Soliciting" signs.

Other memorable solicitors: Jerry, the closest person I've ever known to a storybook sea captain, with a fringe beard, one eye, a big belly—even the proper leer. He was given to speaking out of the corner of his mouth, and telling jokes like: "I stayed up all last night studying for a urine test." Bob, a longhaired youth in a Def Leppard t-shirts, told me a xeroxed dollar bill will get quarters out of change machine, if you cut it right.

Donna, a stout young woman with a spotty work record, once asked me, "Can priests get married?" "Why do you want to know?" I asked. "My boyfriend wants to become one." He turned out to be 60, Jewish and a bartender.

Cleo, a thin woman in her fifties with a Minnie Mouse voice, was capable of such delightful statements as, "I would like to thank you personally myself," and of arguing for ten minutes about the necessity of taking the paper (although *she* never read it).

There is usually only one Great Solicitor at a time – and usually only for a while. When I first came it was Craig, a swarthy nineteen year old with a mischievous look, who'd start five minutes early and rack up at least thirteen a night. His voice was fast and ingratiating, and he would say, "It's nice to hear a friendly voice for a change," at every opportunity. When he was happy—after receiving an order—he'd do a little dance in the aisle.

After a few weeks, I learned his story. His father had abandoned him at age two, his mother when he was a teen (the last he'd heard she had been arrested for armed robbery) and he'd lived on the streets of Chicago, eking out a living as a video games hustler, and sleeping for three months at O'Hare Airport.

Al, the current champion, is a thin, mustachioed, fast-talker with a "If you can't be sexy, be sensitive. If you can't be sensitive, be rich" t-shirt, who's an insurance agent on the side. He often befriends female solicitors, giving them advice like: "People don't realize the power of compound interest."

In fact there is, as you may have guessed, a streak of cruelty in most good solicitors. A man named Angus, who was quite successful, was observed indicting people who admitted they don't read the paper, "Don't you read *anything*?" Craig bragged that he told women who wanted to consult their spouse: "Can't you spend seven dollars without asking your husband?"

Frank, a middle-aged Chicano, had always been an unspectacular solicitor until Hal had a private meeting with him one day. Later he related some of their conversation. "Why do you hang up on women when their children are crying?" Hal had accused him. "Those are the best people to sell. They'll buy it just to get off the phone!" Frank improved thereafter.

One of the mysteries of soliciting is the slump. Suddenly, for no reason, one's sales will dive. Red, a 6'4" former truckdriver, slumped for a week once, and looked like a chastised child. Finally he asked

Hal, "Is there anything you can do for a slump?" "Just wait it out," Hal answered, with customary grimness.

Sheila, an eighteen year old peroxide blond, had also been in a slump, as it happened, and broke it that day. "How'd you do it?" Red called to her. "I used a different name," she mumbled. "Where'd you get it?" I asked. "Some girl I hate," she smiled.

Rare and terrifying is the Solicitor's Revenge. "We had one guy who was a real bastard," Craig related, of a previous job. "So we didn't take his name off the list. We kept calling him and calling him. Finally he got mad and called the police, but nothing happened." Lenore, a black woman in her forties, told a similar story from her tenure at *The Denver Post*: "There was this one woman who was real mean on the phone, so one after the other we called her, saying, 'This is the March of Dimes,' 'This is Muscular Dystrophy.' Finally she just screamed, 'Would you please leave me alone!'" Never cross a solicitor.

What I most love are the moments of cameraderie: Beth posing provocatively next to the raffle basket, announcing: "I'm the prize for tonight;" all of us snickering as a man arrives for an interview in a three-piece suit; the day Frank and Esther waltzed to Mexican music on the radio.

One afternoon the largest and clearest rainbow I ever saw appeared outside our window. We all gathered to watch it for a few minutes. Then we had to return to our seats.

"I'm gonna tell everyone to look at the rainbow," Beth said, dialing the phone.

HOUSES I'VE HAD SEX IN

I have had sex in seven buildings in Manhattan: in 322 East 11th Street, my current residence; in 424 East 11th Street, my wife's former residence; in 82 Wadsworth Terrace, where I first had sex with my wife, and where I was almost seduced by a homeless woman with horribly bitten-down fingernails (also my friend Melissa, the redhaired librarian, slept there one night platonically, though the next morning she went for a walk and found a gun); 81 Payson Avenue, where I slept with Margaret Corley in my parents' bed; 501 East 186th Street, where I slept with Millie Long, a second-generation Communist; and 135 West 107th Street and 153 West 111th Street, where I slept with Annette Vasar, an Israeli dancer. In my thirty-three years in Manhattan, I have had sex with four women, an average of one every 8 1/4 years. My own personal sexual skyline of Manhattan would be pathetically small—seven buildings—smaller than the skyline of Athens, Ohio.

ULYSSES GRANT

Grant is the only president who was a word. True, Washington was two words, and suggests that the Father Of Our Country was a vast launderer, forever washing a ton of . . . money? (One associates Washington with money because so much money bears his grim likeness, so perhaps America was created to be a money-laundering operation—which it has certainly become.)

After Washington came Adams, and the world is composed of atoms. Nothing would exist without atoms—and soon there was a second Adams, son of the first, to reinforce this concept. Could it be that Washington washed a ton of dirt off America, and that the dirt resettled as microscopic particles over everything?

Bush, I realize now, is a word, but barely a word. A poet will rarely speak of a bush, (though one's mother will sometimes say: "I'm bushed"). It is curious, however, that the phrase "I am Bush" creates a strong verb, one quite descriptive of George Bush, whose only talent was ambushing small militarist nations.

A poet does not speak of bushes because a bush is as poetic as a wrinkle, but a Grant—the whole goal of a poet is to receive a grant, and the sign of a great poet is the number of her grants.

"Grant us peace, Thy most exalted gift, O Thou eternal source of Peace . . ." begins a rather legalistic prayer in the Reform Jewish Prayerbook of my youth, and Grant did grant us peace, unfortunately through the method of warfare.

I forgot Taft, who sounds like a word, like a raft full of tact, and Taft functioned as a kind of tact-raft, floating us down the River of Uncertainty in the late Victorian century. Also there is a faint connotation of taffy, as if taffy were an adjective meaning "A lot like Taft"— which is also correct.

But to return to Grant, as one inevitably does when one speaks of words-who-are-presidents, Grant granted us peace, in the era shortly before Taft. He was, like all general-presidents, completely peaceful. In fact, of all our generals who became rulers, he hated war the most.

"War is hell," he didn't say, but one of his generals did, and Grant certainly looked like a man who had seen too much—he had a woozy, inebriated, suspicious expression that one sees replicated a number of times in this very room.

Grant hated war so much that he was a great general, and in a nation that has produced inept military leaders—Washington, for example, spent his war waiting for the French to save him (which strangely *happened*), and Eisenhower ran *his* war like a Midwestern high school . . . in such a nation, Grant shone like a drunken beacon. War is about killing, and secondarily about destruction, and once one has learned this gruesome fact, one is wise. Grant had this wisdom, but could not enlarge upon it. He granted us peace, but peace is not a goal, unless one is at war, and the peace he granted was the peace of industry and commerce, which is a war no one wins except a few ultra-rich fellows.

This frightening fact can be seen on the shell-shocked face of Grant, who must now be impeached forever.

(Transcription of a speech by Sparrow, Miner's Cafe, 2/19/94.)

MY SEX WITH A HORSE

In Kansas, I met a horse. I saw it the moment I left the plane. The horse supported a member of the Kansas Guard. Its eyes looked directly into mine— black, trusting eyes. A horse had never looked at me so tenderly before.

As I walked by the horse, into the Cyrus Wheeler International Airport, I scanned its underbelly for a penis. There was none.

Witchita is a small city, and I encountered the horse two days later, on Weaver Sreet. The same Kansas Guardsman sat on her, outside the Trentworth Cemetery. "Good girl, Shirley," he said, patting her flank.

I have always loved the name Shirley.

"Where do the Kansas Guardsmen keep their horses at night?" I asked my friend Barry, whom I was visiting—the same way Holden Caulfield asked where the ducks in Central Park go in the winter.

"By the railroad tracks on Sandford Avenue," Barry said, looking up from *The Witchita Times-Leader*.

That night, by a gibbous moon, I climbed in an open window of the Lt. Moorman Memorial Stables. In the huge room, I saw breath rising in mist from the many stables. How would I find her?, I wondered. I dare not turn on the light.

Then I heard a sort of purr to my right. It articulated into a whine, resembling speech: "Doooo meeeee." I had a chilling memory of Mr. Ed.

Looking over a wooden wall, I saw those dark, trusting eyes, now gleaming with a kind of mischief. I jumped up on the wooden partition.

For a long moment neither of us spoke. Then slowly, offhandedly, Shirley raised her mouth and tugged at the cuff of my pants.

I jumped down, loosened my belt, and she pulled my pants off— then my underwear.

Her tongue licked the tip of my penis. How did she know *that?* Had she and the Kansas Guardsman . . . been intimate? I feared he would sneak up behind me, the Jealous Lover.

Then Shirley lay down gently, turned her belly to me, and opened her legs.

Her vagina tasted like buttered oats.

A sudden anxiety gripped me. Shirley was accustomed to horses. Compared to a stallion, I was not large.

Then she trained on me her sweet, beguiling eyes. "Doooooo meeeee," she said. I lost my fear.

Don't most animals have sex for 30 seconds?, I thought, but we went two hours. I woke at dawn, warm against the beast's belly.

Will I ever return to women, so small and hairless?, I wondered.

We kissed deeply, and I climbed out the half-opened window.

MY SEX WITH AN ANT

I have cockroaches, like any ordinary person, but for a while I also had an ant. Whenever I took a bath, this ant would crawl onto the lip of the tub and watch me. It would sit motionless until my bath was finished, then climb down the tub. This became a kind of joke, and I would say, "Hello, Sadie," to her. Somehow I knew the insect was female.

One day Sadie crawled closer to me and gestured with her antennae. Then she flattened herself against the porcelain. When my bath was over, she seemed to walk down the leg of the bathtub with sadness.

I called Hubert, my friend the entomologist. "She wants to have sex with you," he explained. "She is performing the first stages of a mating ritual."

I put down the phone, and stared at the wall.

I called Eli, the Talmudic Scholar. "I've been propositioned by an ant. Is it morally wrong to fuck an ant?"

"Hold on," Eli said. In two minutes, he returned to the phone. "The only literature I can find is by Rabbi Shlomo ben Sliwa. He says sex with insects is permissible as long as one enters into it with respect, and is willing to accept the consequences—for example, if there is a pregnancy."

"Fine," I said, and hung up.

Now came the difficult part—I had to visit Moswell Stormlin. Moswell lives in the basement of a crumbling tenement on E. 2nd St. that smells like mice.

He opened the door wordlessly, his long grey hair in spears, and led me through three rooms crowded with rags and newspapers, into a chair with sixteen tubes protruding from it, surmounted by a blue crown.

"Drink this," Moswell said, offering me a colorless fluid in a Skippy peanut butter jar.

When I awoke, Moswell Stormlin was the size of the Chrysler Building.

"I'm putting you in my pocket," Moswell said, and I tumbled into darkness. As he walked through the streets, I rolled and pitched in my cloth room.

"I'm taking you out," Moswell said, and placed me on my kitchen table, before Sadie.

Sadie was larger than me, and—was this the effect of Moswell's drug?—stunningly beautiful. Her body was deep black and shined as if with oil. Her carapace had a sensuality reminiscent of the women in Matisse. I trembled with a feeling of unworthiness.

Sadie reached out her left antenna and touched my thigh. The antenna was cold, but soft, like a living noodle. I touched her face. It was also cool, until I reached her mouth, which pulled my hand in, and seemed immensely deep. There I felt Sadie's warmth.

Sadie reached out her vestibular foreleg, pulling me toward her, then lowered her mandible gently, placing it behind my neck like a stiff pillow. I felt her upper thorax pulsing, and beneath it I could hear her four hearts.

How can I express her tenderness? She stroked my buttocks as one would a frightened child.

Then her thoracic cavity opened to reveal her reproductive filaments—like pulsing white string. My penis entered her vortex. I wept—and so did she. Sadie's tears fell on my hair like wet gumdrops.

Moswell had to pull us apart when he returned. I shouted, "No!" over and over. We had climaxed, but our afterglow was more poignant than a Brahms *diminuendo*.

I rode back in Moswell's dark pocket, shouting, "Sadie! Sadie!"

When I returned to my apartment, she was gone.

I bought a plastic ant to set on the bathtub when I bathed, but that became too painful. So I gave the lifeless ant to my neighbor's son.

POLITICAL DISPATCHES

June 1

While reading a week-old newspaper, I came upon a surprising admission by Gov. George W. Bush—he confessed that he is a novelist. In an interview with CBS, (*New York Times*, 12/6) he discussed the political struggles of recent weeks: "It's been a fascination, as I'm sure you can imagine. I'm not a very good novelist. But it'd make a pretty interesting novel."

For those of you unskilled in grammar, let me explain. "I'm not a very good novelist" means "I am a novelist." Let me further elucidate. Suppose I say, "I am a very bad ice skater." This must mean that at some time I have skated on ice. Otherwise I must remark, "I suspect I am not a good ice skater." If Bush knows he is a poor novelist, he must have written novels—as the *American Heritage Dictionary* informs us that a novelist is "a writer of novels."

Even someone who has written a 312 p. manuscript with the title *Auction of Husbands*, yet which remains unfinished, is not a novelist. "Novelist" is not defined as "a person who begins novels" or "a person who cannot finish a novel." A novelist writes entire novels.

Thus we know that George W. Bush (unless he was lying or misspeaking) has written at least two novels—because our definition, I'm sure you noticed, refers to "novels" in the plural.

This can explain one mystery of Bush—what he does with his time. Many Americans have been puzzling over this question. We have noticed that he spends most days at his five thousand acre ranch, near Waco, Texas, but beyond that we are unclear. He doesn't seem to be riding around on horses. One gets the feeling that he is indoors. I heard a rumor that he is addicted to video games, but this could be a smear invented by his detractors. He seems, in interviews, only vaguely aware of the details of contemporary politics. He doesn't even attend church, although (and this may be a crucial statement) he did once refer to Jesus as his favorite writer.

Bush is writing novels. That's why so little of his time is accounted for. As a novelist myself, I know how much of my day appears wasted. I spend hours sitting in the kitchen reading week-old newspapers (or two month-old newspapers). Someone calls me on the phone, and I chat for forty-five minutes. But all this is preparation for the writing of my next chapter.

I know what you're thinking: "Bush is too unintelligent to write novels." First of all, remember what Bush himself stated: "I'm not a very good novelist." It's possible that, although he does write many novels, none of them are well-written. Another thought is that you and I know him only as a presidential candidate. Suppose we knew James Joyce as a presidential candidate. He might appear to us aloof, testy, muttering. We might be certain that he, too, is an awful writer.

We can only await, with ample patience, the eventual publication of Bush's novels. Then we can truly speak of his literary gifts. Until then, we can be proud to have (unless Bush was merely joking) our first novelist President.

June 6

Recently we had a mouse, here in the house.

At first, we did not see this mouse. (I don't know whether to call the mouse "him" or "her.") We saw only its turds in the morning, on the sponge in the kitchen sink. And we saw the small gouges it made in our food. It ate pears, bread, and soap.

After a few weeks, I sometimes noticed a blur late at night while I did the dishes—a gray streak, almost like a line.

More time passed, and the mouse slowed down. It had a strange way of walking: it leaned forward, with its tail up in the air, like a scholar who walks while reading a book.

Soon the mouse was all around us. At night, I would lay on the futon in the living room, and the mouse would walk up and down the cracks of the floor, searching for grains of rice and millet my daughter Sylvia had dropped during the day.

I worried that mice are unclean. What does my guru say about mice? I tried to remember. He says all animals are either "friends of man" or "enemies of man." Are mice friends or enemies?

One night while I was meditating, I heard a scrambling sound beside me. Then I felt the mouse sitting on my head, like a person standing atop Mount Rushmore. The mouse began to dig in my scalp, looking for food.

I began to think mice are enemies of man.

Two days later Violet caught the mouse. She took it to Phoenicia Park and set it free.

Afterward the house felt lonely, and smaller.

September 2

Visitors to the American Midwest have noted a haunting consistency of tone. A tepid affability inflects the speech. Polyester is often worn. White is the primary color (of skin, and of many buildings). No one is a transvestite.

A simple look at the map explains why this is. One speaks of a dull man as being "square." The states in the middle of America are almost literally square. (Iowa comes closest to perfect squareness.) Some extremely linear autocrat—almost certainly a man—divided up our lush continent into near rectangles, like a butcher chopping meat. How can the populace feel free while it inhabits parallelograms?

By comparison, consider the state I presently inhabit, New York, which resembles a crushed hat with a feather (the feather being Long Island). The boundaries of this state include Lake Ontario, the Saint Lawrence River, Lake Erie, the Delaware River, the Long Island Sound, the Atlantic Ocean, and Lake Champlain. In New York, eccentricity has long bloomed.

The solution is to redraw the Midwest, locating natural boundaries between the states. For example, the Niobrara River could divide South Dakota and Nebraska, the Republican River could separate Kansas and Nebraska, and the Earth River could distinguish southern Minnesota from Iowa. Eventually, the states will look more like rumpled clothes and less like cardboard boxes.

Then, perhaps, Midwesterners will begin to wiggle and joke, and wear long Polynesian gowns.

MONEY-BACK GUARANTEE
If you are
dissatisfied
with
this poem
IN ANY WAY,
return it to:
Sparrow, P.O.
Box 63,
Phoenicia,
NY 12464.

He will
mail you
a refund
within
six to eight days.

Only this
poem
contains
this unique
offer.

September 12

I just realized that "The Lone Ranger and Tonto" is an oxymoron. The Lone Ranger is, by definition, lone. That is, he is unaccompanied, solo, bereft of retinue.

Am I the first one in the United States to recognize the grave implications of this? Because if the Lone Ranger is considered lone, yet rides constantly with Tonto, then Tonto is not identified as a man but is relegated to the same status as Silver, the Lone Ranger's horse.

How can a "lone" hero always appear with another person? Because the person is of non-European descent.

How awful we American television-viewers are!

In the future, I suggest we refer to this masked character as the Accompanied Ranger.

September 27

In the documentary *Derrida*, an unseen interlocutor asks French philosopher Jacques Derrida: "Which philosopher would you want for your mother?"

Derrida begins to think. His eyelids flutter. "That's a good question," he says, smiling. Then he continues to think.

It is the longest scene of a person thinking I have ever witnessed.

Nine days after seeing the film, I still recall Derrida cogitating. Why aren't there more movies of women and men engaged in thought? I am tired of watching actors have sex. I am anxious to see more "thinking films."

CHICKEN BREEDERS REVEAL THEMSELVES
TO BE A REVOLUTIONARY CLASS WITH
APLOMB AND A KEEN SENSE OF TIMING

I almost bought *Amerika* by Kafka just now for fifty cents—on the sidewalk, Houston St. It was the sideline of a hotdog salesman. "I can get that at the library," I finally opined.

Everyone's selling books right now, on the street—like Calcutta. That's because our Constitution defends their rights. You know why? Because our country was *founded* by printers: Benjamin Franklin, T. Paine, Peter Zenger. (I just figured this out.) If Calvin Klein had founded our country, we'd have Freedom of Dress.

And I'm glad. Because I can think of lots more to say than to wear. I was just talking about this with my friend Sheila. Neither of us has ever found our clothes, we realized. We wear only what's in the store. But when we write—we write what will never be in the stores.

When I was eighteen, first a vegetarian, I believed that when my clothes wore out, I'd start wearing robes. I'm not sure what happened—my clothes never all wore out at once, I guess. Clothes are insidious. Even if you don't buy them, you get them. This may be true of food too, but it takes more waiting than I'm comfortable with. Whereas Ira, if he sees your Travel To England pants have holes in the buttocks, *gives* you these beige slacks I've donned today. They have the patient personality of a glass of milk.

I can picture Sheila's costume—what she *should* wear: hundreds of sleeves, and loose, like Mickey Mouse's outfit in *Fantasia*.

And I? Something tall and brown, like a poplar.

But I'm ... well, poor. And even if I had the money, how could I walk around hundreds of feet in the air?

Clothing is cruel—crueller than biology. Because it fits *over* biology.

CONFESSIONS OF A SECRET SMOKER

Now that smoking is nearly outlawed, secret smokers such as myself must tell our stories. My smoking career extends for thirty-four years, yet I never bought a cigarette. Let me explain.

I first smoked in the spring of 1970, when I was sixteen years old. I found a pack of cigarettes in the hallway of my high school (the Bronx High School of Science). It was a box of Marlboros. For a moment I hesitated, then reached for it. The pack was a little more than half full.

Cigarettes were quite rare at Bronx Science. Probably less than two percent of the students smoked. The 3400 young people in this school (90 percent were Jewish) were studious, college-bound. They had no time for self-destructive habits.

I hid the Marlboros in my bookbag, and rode home on the bus. Soon I would smoke Cigarette No. 1 of my life!

That night I went for a walk alone. I must have stolen matches from the kitchen. I walked and smoked, through the streets of Inwood (the northernmost neighborhood of Manhattan). I had already tried marijuana, so I smoked cigarettes the same way—inhaling deeply into my lungs. In fact, I would never learn the correct method to smoke tobacco.

The cigarettes themselves had no effect. I was surprised by the blandness of smoking. This strong addiction and widespread habit seemed based on Nothing. Cigarettes were like pot without the pot. The whole ritual was useless, except for its aesthetic beauty. In the black night I became a point of red light—like the light The Great Gatsby watched from the end of his dock (or was that blue?).

Also I enjoyed the smoke, rising up against the tyranny of gravity, twisting with light agility. Psychic researchers sometimes take photographs of disembodied "spirits" which exactly resemble this smoke.

For several evenings I wandered, smoking in the nighttime corridors of Inwood. The cigarettes were free, so I smoked them quickly. I felt I was walking down a ramp with my burning ember, deeper into some dark crevasse. One night it rained, a misty spring rain. I walked, hatless, toking, through the reflective streets. When I finished a cigarette, I would toss it down, and its red light would bank and spark on the wet street.

Smoking is minimalist: the white of the cigarette, the red of the burning tip, the grey smoke. Red, white and grey are the colors of the Smoker's Flag, a flag that has never flown over any nation.

Always I was alone, with my cigarette. Once, however, on Dyckman Street, I met a friend. "I didn't know you smoked," he said, with a touch of fear.

Clearly I had crossed some boundary, between the Wholesome and Good People—the people on television—and the Cataclysmic, Dangerous people—the people in movies.

"I just found some cigarettes on the floor of my high school," I explained.

"Oh, I see," my interrogator answered, walking off. Did he believe me?

My parents (who were unobservant) never noticed the smell of tobacco on my mouth.

•

I had my twelfth cigarette in Ithaca, New York in 1973. I was living in a "collective" (with a group of friends) called the Green Lantern Coop. I shared a room with Joan, my girlfriend. Earlier that year I flunked out of college; now I was becoming "a writer." (My actual job was sweeping up at a construction site.) In the evening I would sit at Joan's desk, writing. One day someone gave me a cigarette, which I smoked at this desk.

My poetry was quite lighthearted, consisting of verses such as:

INGREDIENTS

With my every action
an animal comes out of me.

This morning, when I smiled,
Two white ducks waddled out.
Whenever I cry,
An aged flamingo stands by me.

See, even as I write this poem
a donkey appears, braying.

I add him, with the others,
To the list of my ingredients.

Nevertheless, within the curling smoke of my Winston, I became what the French call *un vrai poète*—an Actual Writer—solemn, infinite, arduous. Though I was just twenty years old, I felt forty—even forty-six. I puffed little, allowing the smoke to rise on its own. The smoke bent around my head, curious, as I wrote. (This was the first cigarette I smoked indoors.)

•

My next cigarette came nineteen years later, in 1992. The Unbearables, a group of bohemian writers, organized a poetry reading on the Brooklyn Bridge. Afterwards we held a party at Tzaurah Litzky's house in Brooklyn. This is the same building Hart Crane lived in. As we stood on the rooftop, talking and viewing the East River, someone offered me a cigarette. I accepted.

I held the cylinder in my right hand, and discovered that I need not puff. I watched the cigarette—was it a Camel?—slowly diminish, as if by magic. The wind was smoking my cigarette. I felt free and lofty.

This was the first time I had smoked with other people.

Will I ever quit tobacco? No. My habit (unless I am deluding myself) is benign. Since 1970, I have smoked an average of 14/34 cigarettes a year (which is slightly less than half a cigarette, for the innumerate). It has been 11 years now since my last one. Quietly, I prepare for my next cigarette. I refuse to stop smoking.

~Proverbs~

Geese can't fly backwards.

•

At night milk is black.

•

The first wife remembers everything.

•

All criminals are optimists.

•

Gravity was the first tax.

•

It's always dark inside an egg.

•

Snowmen marry young.

•

A triangle points three ways.

•

Fish invented the one night stand.

•

The tall perspire first.

•

Volcanoes are safe most days.

•

Anything can be gift-wrapped.

•

Astigmatism lengthens a journey.

•

The cheapest anchor floats.

•

No one ever relaxed in a lounge.

•

Drummers are altar-shy.

•

Nowhere is pastry illegal.

•

A bomb can't destroy dust.

•

Mice give milk, too.

•

Romeo wasn't built in a day.

•

Monks invented real estate.

•

Death is no gourmet.

•

Let sleeping bags lie.

•

The bus comes whether we wait or not.

•

Sheep are flammable.

•

Flying is easy, landing is hard.

•

Everyone in a bathroom eventually meets.

•

Before music, flutes were weapons.

•

Light curves out of politeness.

•

A houseboat's furniture need not float.

•

No church can cure doubt.

•

You can't catch a spider in a spider-web.

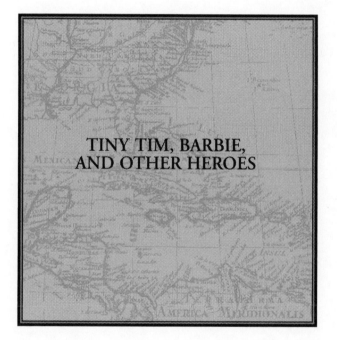

TINY TIM, BARBIE,
AND OTHER HEROES

MY EXCLUSIVE INTERVIEW WITH DR. RUTH

On the set of Dr. Ruth's show, a grip paced the floor singing *The Most Beautiful Girl In The World.*

"Dr. R-r-r-ruth," said a cameraman in a mock German accent.

I was one third of the studio audience. Behind me a doctor's publicist and a liaison woman discussed lower back pain.

A Walt Disney version of a professor's study lay before me: baby blue walls—pink behind the bookcase—with photos and carved zebras to divert the eye.

Ten men stood in headphones or adjusted cables with an enviable blend of industry and calm.

"All right!" came a high, accented voice, and a tiny woman in an egg-yolk yellow suit hurled toward me.

"You're from *The Uptown Dispatch*?" she asked. I agreed and we shook hands. Such is her effect that I suddenly remembered one should rise when a woman enters the room. Standing on a step, I was three feet taller than her.

"Maybe I should kneel," I thought, but by then she had sped on, saying, "I'll speak to you later."

She sat in the Hostess chair and the grips continued gripping. There were two huge TV cameras—a lion could have fit in each one— but being hydraulic they were easily controlled by the technicians. Everyone there was slight, and by their pressed jeans and trimmed beards one knew they'd long ago been hippies. On the monitor, the Doctor coughed, in close-up.

Then a lanky man spoke with sudden authority: "Quiet please. Quiet on the floor. The tape is rolling. Nine eight seven six five four three two one."

ASK DR. RUTH

came on the screen backed by breezy TV theme music (full of flute) and a close-up of the hostess and her guest, who looked like John Forsythe. I watched the monitor because the camera blocked my view.

"I would like to welcome Dr. Lehrman," said Dr. Ruth, and he began to describe the tragedy of back pain: "75 million Americans have back pain at one time or another. We sit at computers and TV sets out there and our muscles get tighter."

"As you speak, my muscles get tighter," Dr. Ruth giggled.

She asked how back pain affects the sex life and he looked nervous. "Of course it affects it," he said.

"I see a lot of people younger and younger with back pain," Dr. Lehrman said, "from all these aerobics tapes that are out now."

"People are being hurt by aerobics?" Dr. Ruth asked, startled. But she pursued sex and finally it paid off. He admitted that for a back pain sufferer on bottom with a pillow under the pelvis, sex is the perfect exercise.

"Be back with us in a moment when Dr. Ruth takes phone calls from the viewing audience," an announcer intoned.

Then the magic was switched off and we were ourselves again. Dr. Ruth was asking her guest for his inflatable pillow to prevent backache, which he had mentioned several times but failed to produce, despite whispered plans before the show. "For *everyone*," Dr. Ruth was saying. "I don't only ask for myself."

Two minutes had seemed a half hour, partly because I'd held my breath. I'd felt the fragility of TV, an edifice one cough can topple.

The back doctor left, promising many pillows, the crew bore down, and the first call came on the phone.

It's strange to watch a phone call on TV. Seeing Dr. Ruth's features retract as she considered the case (a woman, sixty, whose boyfriend avoided her but wanted her available) seemed indecent, like watching someone sleep. But she rebounded.

Gleams of curiosity lit her face as she questioned: "Does he take you out?" "Who pays?"—and the lanky man's cue cards grew more and more desperate: "60 SEC," "30 SEC," "10 SEC," "FIRM OUT,"— until, looking into the camera, she pronounced: "You should drop him! Anybody who doesn't think of you on Valentine's Day and Christmas is not worth it!" That moment when she looks at you and seems to take charge of your life is satisfying television.

"That was a take," the announcer said, "RUSS READE" was flashed on the screen, and a mustached man with salt and pepper hair stepped up to the chair.

"Hello, Chicken Ranch! Ah, he's a good-looking guy! Good-looking Chicken Ranch guy!" Dr. Ruth cheered. This was the manager of the largest brothel in America.

Russ Reade wore a pinstripe suit befitting a man who'd found his job in the *Wall Street Journal,* but one noticed his bushy eyebrows, and when Dr. Ruth asked, "Have you ever enjoyed any of your hostesses?" the glint in his eye was just what one would expect from a genteel pimp.

"Do you ever get complaints?" she asked, and he explained that as the former manager of a grocery store he'd learned to handle such problems.

"How come you don't have men?" Dr. Ruth inquired. "Why only women?" and after stammering a bit, Mr. Reade confessed an aversion to homosexuals.

Meanwhile, a similar looking man had seated himself near me— Transit cop moustache, grey suit. He revealed himself to be an AP radio reporter working on a series, *Whatever Happened To The Sexual Revolution?*

"Who have you talked to?" I asked.

"Oh, the guy who writes *The Playboy Advisor* . . ."

"You couldn't get Hefner?"

He smiled. "No, they're keeping pretty close tabs on him these days."

"Who else?"

"Oh, Masters and Johnson. . . the usual."

"And whatever happened to the Sexual Revolution?"

"There's been a slight setback—I'm just speaking from statistics— but it's still going on."

In the meantime, Rita Rudner, a curly-haired comic with metaphysical eyes, was explaining her love life to Dr. Ruth, who read questions off of cue cards.

"I understand you've had difficulty maintaining a relationship."

"Yes, I split up with my boyfriend after two years. Finally I told him, 'I'm gonna leave unless you tell me your name.'"

In this special case, we were allowed to laugh. Dr. Ruth proved a gifted straight-woman.

Meanwhile, Mr. Chicken Ranch was telling a friend of Dr. Ruth's:

"The girls were excited for days after she came. She has such energy!"

More miserable people called: a young woman whose boyfriend thinks of cheerleaders when he masturbates instead of her; a mother of three whose husband's girlfriend had just gotten pregnant; a wife who dislikes oral sex.

Of a lonely college student in Ohio, our host inquired: "Do you go to church?"

"Yes."

"Every week?"

"Almost."

"Do you always go to the same church?"

"Yes.

"Catholic?"

"No."

"Well, I'll tell you what to do. From now on go to a different church every week. And promise me you'll come a few minutes early. Now stand in the back of the church and look around. And if you see a nice redheaded or blond girl sitting alone, and if you happen to sit down next to her. . . You'll give it a try?"

He agreed and we broke for "lunch." (It was 4 p.m.)

I was just figuring out what some of the crew did. A longhaired woman in black set out ginger snaps, for example.

In Dr. Ruth's dressing room, the AP man and I held an impromptu press conference. Pierre Lehu, her publicist, a stooped man in a disreputable suit jacket, told us: "Her parents were killed in the Holocaust while she was at boarding school. . . She went to Israel where she fought with the Hagannah . . . She almost lost her legs from aerial bombardment, and she went to France. . . When she first came here, she worked as a maid for $1 an hour. . ."

Then Dr. Ruth autographed copies of *Good Sex* for the Chicken Ranch manager while the AP guy interviewed her. She said it wasn't a Sexual Revolution but a sexual *evolution*, that marriage is here to stay, and that when a man is tired he should say no. Then it was my turn.

Uptown: How do you play the board game?

Dr. Ruth: No, I'm not going to stand here and tell you how to play it. You got to get the game.

Uptown: Do you play it yourself?

Dr. Ruth: Of course I play it.

Uptown: But don't you know all the answers already?

Dr. Ruth: Wait a minute, wait a minute. That's not the type of interview I want to do. Because that's not really for *The Uptown Dispatch*, that type of interview. They *had* an interview on me, and a very wonderful one. Do you have it here? Did you read it?

Uptown: No, no.

Dr. Ruth: (*Looking at my list of questions.*) And these questions, I will not answer any of these: "What's the state of sex in Washington Heights?" "Do they have better sex in Washington Heights?" "Different ethnic groups." There's nothing I can say about that.

Uptown: I just wanted to know if your butcher, if the people you meet on the street in Washington Heights, ask you about their sexual problems?

Dr. Ruth: No, no, they don't. People are not so stupid that they would say to me what is their sex problem if they know that I go in there the next day to buy bread.

Uptown: Have you been to the Heights Theatre—you know, the dirty movie theater?

Dr. Ruth: No, no, no. First of all, there's no "dirty movie theatre" for me. I didn't know there was a "dirty movie theatre" in Washington Heights.

Uptown: Yeah, the Heights Theatre; it's right on Wadsworth Avenue, just south of 181st street.

Dr. Ruth: Oh yes, yes, I do know. No, that's not for me. You see what you have to do, you have to read the one that was in the paper. Because otherwise you are going to write an article that has been done. I don't think you will get an article out of this.

Uptown: You don't want to talk about how you came to live in Washington Heights?

Dr. Ruth: There's no "why." I found an apartment. And I love it there. Yes, I'm very happy there. That you can say. Yes, but I can't talk to you about "good places to have sex in Washington Heights." (*Considers a moment.*) Around the Cloisters in Lover's Lane! Okay, goodbye. Thank you very much.

Uptown: So you're not going to answer the question, "What is bad sex?"

Dr. Ruth: There's no such thing as bad sex.

Uptown: Really?

Dr. Ruth: No.

AN INTERVIEW WITH TINY TIM

I waited in the lobby of a hotel on 72nd Street next to a mirror veined with gold. Out of the elevator stepped Tiny Tim, in a red "Gilley's" jacket, bellbottoms and sneakers, his shoulder-length hair henna'd red. He was much heavier than in the sixties and his voice deeper, but his nose and unfocused eyes remained the same.

"I live with my mother. She's almost ninety," he told me. "Why don't we do our interview down here?" We seated ourselves in the Women's Lounge and began.

Tiny Tim: Mr. Gorelick, it's a pleasure speaking to you and *The Uptown Press.*

Uptown: Thank you. You grew up in Washington Heights, didn't you?

Tiny Tim: Well, I shouldn't say that, really. Most of my memories were there, but I also grew up on Amsterdam Afifty-five, and if it slips, who cares? I remember the lines of people waiting to see *Snow White* at the RKO Hamilton, up near 145th and Broadway, in 1937.

Are you familiar with The Audubon Theatre across from Columbia-Presbyterian? I was there in 1935, '36, '37, and '38. From 1935 on, my relatives lived in the Upper Heights, and I went to visit them. At that time, they had men driving the elevators—up till about 1942. They used to have very fashionable houses—I'm talking about the twenties, the middle thirties—at 163rd St. The Audubon Theatre at that time—in the twenties—was the upper class vaudeville house. Mayor Walker was one of the many honorary celebrities who visited there. You know that George Gershwin lived there, near where I lived? For years and years, since the Forties up until 1967, when I was discovered, I lived at 601 W. 163rd St, on the corner of Broadway. There's a Theresa Drugstore right on the corner. I lived on the first floor, apartment 1B, and then I moved up to apartment 3K.

Uptown: Which side of the street was this?

Tiny Tim: It's on the side of the hospital. Gershwin lived on the other side of the street, near the Audubon—I think it was 545 W. 163rd St.—before he got his big break. In 1917 he lived there.

The same with Ted Lewis. You know, they all give Paul Whiteman credit, but I personally believe that Ted Lewis, with his Jazz Syncopaters, in 1919, was ahead of Paul Whiteman, and he really was the first white man who was the King Of Jazz. He lived on Riverside Drive in 1917, in a roominghouse there. In those days, the rents were about $7.50 a week. He lived on about 162nd, 161st Street.

Uptown: But you didn't know either of these guys?

Tiny Tim: No, but I tell you who I knew later on: Frankie Lyman and The Teenagers.

He came from Amsterdam Avenue—may he rest in peace—and 163rd, 164th St.

They did "Why Do Fools Fall In Love?" Kenny Rankin came from there. Also Freddie Prinze came from that neighborhood.

Uptown: Did you know him?

Tiny Tim: I didn't know him, but I met him in 1974 or '75 at Catch A Rising Star, just about the time he was doing the pilot for *Chico And The Man*, and he came up to me—I don't bother these stars—and I said to him, "Congratulations on your new series. I hope you do well," and he was very nice. It's just too bad, unfortunately, that this happened. I tell you, his mother must've gone through heck and high water, because it was so hard. He was before his prime; he didn't even *hit* his prime. He was so good.

It reminds me of Russ Columbo, who was one of the great singers of 1932; he was right up there with Bing Crosby, may they both rest in peace. Columbo died by accident Sept. 2, 1934. He was 26 years old. He was up at a friend's house and fooled around with a toy pistol—he thought it was a toy—and the bullet hit the wall and came back and hit him in the head. But him and Freddie Prinze are two examples of people who died really before they hit their prime. That's why, praise the Lord, we're grateful for our lives here.

Uptown: I met Freddie Prinze at a party on Thayer St.

Tiny Tim: That sounds familiar. Where's that?

Uptown: Next to Dyckman St.

Tiny Tim: That reminds me—I performed there, at the Loew's Dyckman, in 1956 or '57.

Uptown: They had live entertainment then?

Tiny Tim: That's when rock'n'roll was getting hotter than hot, especially for the white singers, 'cause you know, the blacks had been doing it for years. I was going around, I had long hair before all of them. . .

Uptown: You were probably one of the first people in America with long hair.

Tiny Tim: Well, there was always long hair around. Jesus Christ had long hair. They had beatniks in those times: it was just that they noticed it more on me. I had to find myself, I wanted to find my own identity. Part of it was for show business, part of it was for me, and so it wasn't just a gimmick all the way. Then I had the makeup, 'cause I'm not good-looking, and I wanted to attract the women—and I did. I don't care if they laugh at me, as long as the young girls like me.

I was scared to go out in the street, especially in the daytime, but I had to do it. I just couldn't cut it off. In those years, I was really looked at as way out. Believe me, they'd run away in the subway train. But at night is when I thrived. Then I went to the talent shows all around the city. At that time I was known as Larry Love.

And I played the Loew's Dyckman in 1957, November or December—and they even roared when I appeared on stage. They called me "Larry The Weird One," I'll never forget that. I never went back after that one shot there. It was so good, I didn't want to try again.

Uptown: So this was an Alan Freed-type rock'n'roll show?

Tiny Tim: Sure, it was a talent contest. And Frankie Avalon was going to appear there a week later—and to me this was Big Time, appearing in a theatre that Frankie Avalon was coming to.

Uptown: And you played songs from the twenties?

Tiny Tim: No, I think this was an Elvis Presley contest. I was trying to do an Elvis Presley. Whatever happened, I won. I got an egg thrown at me—one guy—but I won the contest.

II

Tiny Tim: Y'know, this is a great nostalgic city. There was a fellow named W. J. Nugent who wrote an article in *Variety* in 1917, and he said, "A true vaudeville artist. . ."—and this goes for anybody today in show business—"never blames anyone for his failure. He must make his own breaks, and he falls as he goes." And I really believe that. This city was *the* city: Vaudeville, the Palace …

I did a show in The Palace about two or three years ago, for the black organization for Sickle Cell Anemia. I did it 'cause I wanted to do it for them, plus I wanted to say, "I played The Palace." Even if it was just for charity.

Uptown: So you think things have declined since the death of Vaudeville?

Tiny Tim: I think we live in the greatest of times. We have instant coffee; we don't need fans, we have great air conditioners. I think there's no better times than today, from the standpoint of comfort, of ease—if you have the money.

These are the greatest times—but we have to pay. More people today are tighter than ever; the atmosphere of the world, especially in big cities, there's human tensions. We're under a strain of birth in this world.

In the last four years I predicted that New York would have an earthquake. I said, "You gotta watch New York." I said it to the press, and anyone can look it up. And I say there will be more earthquakes there. I believe there's gonna be a major earthquake right in the heart of this city.

If I ever made it big again with monies—right now, day by day I pay the rent—I'd put it in scattered banks across the country. Because the Scriptures prophesize that before the end of the world there will be earthquakes in diverse places. It's a warning sign that people are not listening to God's laws.

The same way I believe there will be an earthquake, I also believe this: if this world continues, we are going to make contact with beings from outer space—or inner beings, from the sea. I am one of the few who believe that papers like *The Enquirer* and *The Star* are 96% *right*. They have a nose for news, and they inquire real deep into things.

Uptown: Do you have a sense of your own spiritual mission?

Tiny Tim: I really don't. Right now I'm trying for a hit record or to hit the Lotto.

Incidentally, I'll tell you how to win at the slot machines. Never play a machine that's cold. You have to stay and watch the people that are playing. When you see a machine that's hot, you stick with it. I won $500 in Reno that way; it made the papers.

Uptown: What was the biggest audience you ever played for?

Tiny Tim: Two hundred thousand, at the Isle of Wight in 1970. I had to follow Joni Mitchell, who got five encores. I don't have to tell you I was nervous. I got out there, and at the end of my show, three-quarters of the audience stood up. It was as if the spirits of their ancestors came in them.

But I always keep up with the times, praise the Lord. I just recorded the best record I ever made, *Highway To Hell*, with a heavy metal band in Australia called His Majesty's Orchestra.

Uptown: Did you know the Beatles?

Tiny Tim: Yes, I met them. My closest meeting was with George Harrison. He met me in New York and took me up to his hotel room, and I sang "Nowhere Man" into his tape recorder. He told me to say, "Merry Christmas from The Beatles," at the end, and it became the Christmas single for 1968, sent out to their fan club. It's worth a fortune. I did *Laugh-In* with Ringo.

Uptown: Weren't you on *The Smothers Brothers?*

Tiny Tim: Everyone remembers that, but no, I wasn't.

Uptown: Do you get tired of singing "Tiptoe Through The Tulips?"

Tiny Tim: Not yet. If I did, I'd sing it anyway. I never knock it. You know how many people would love to be in those shoes, to have one hit record?

Uptown: How high did it go?

Tiny Tim: The album hit seven. The record hit seventeen. I should have been the Number One Promising star of 1968. You know who won? A fellow named Andy Kim. You know why? 'Cause you're talking to one star who wasn't considered normal before he was discovered. Even when I made it, I got a half to three-quarters of the mail: "God, what is happening to this country?"

Even when I was hot, I was filling up one-tenth of the places I was playing.

If the place seated 2,000, I'd get 200. Believe it or not, I'm getting more people percentage-wise now than I did then.

I didn't help myself by coming out against the hippies. I had this enormous press conference in Chicago in July of 1968, and I told them I believed we were right being in Vietnam. The whole press was shocked.

Uptown: Do you still believe that?

Tiny Tim: I believe we were right. I don't want to see war—I can't kill a roach—but I think there was a reason to be there, to stop the spread of Communism.

Uptown: Have you ever used drugs?

Tiny Tim: Never, praise the Lord. The only thing I do is drink beer.

Uptown: Did you ever meet Bob Dylan?

Tiny Tim: Are you kidding? I met Bob Dylan in his house in Woodstock, New York in 1967. He heard of me through the

Underground. (I was a good friend of Lenny Bruce.) I told him, "You're today, with your poetry, what Rudy Vallee was in the Twenties," and I sang him "Like A Rolling Stone" the way Rudy Vallee would've sung it. Then I sang a Rudy Vallee song the way Dylan would've done it. He said to me, "Do you want a banana before you go to bed?" I said, "No, I've got my own fruits."

I heard him do a rare version of "Cool Water" on the guitar.

Uptown: What's your real name?

Tiny Tim: Herbert Khaury.

Uptown: Where is Miss Vicki?

Tiny Tim: She's married again. She lives in New Jersey. I have a 12-year-old daughter with her.

Uptown: How long were you married?

Tiny Tim: Four years, off and on. She left me twice, temporarily in February, 1972 and again in February, 1974. She's married to a fellow named Chandler. He's in graphic arts in Philadelphia. Nice fellow.

I don't believe in divorce. She divorced me in '77. I was in Florida, and I didn't have the money to contest.

Uptown: What was your experience at George Washington High School?

Tiny Tim: I never graduated. I didn't get along with the school, and they asked me to leave. I liked the girls there; they were beautiful. I think Rita Moreno, who played in *West Side Story*, went there. When I went there in the late forties, it was beautiful, like a college campus, like a palace.

Uptown: Do you have any other memories of Washington Heights?

Tiny Tim: I used to play in the streets. I never studied. We played curb ball on 163rd St.; we had first and third bases. You know, I was telling Gene Rayburn about this, and he actually wanted to have a film crew come and film a reenactment of a curb ball game, with the guys I used to play with. But we couldn't find enough of the guys.

Uptown: Were you good at curb ball?

Tiny Tim: No. They always left me out.

BARBIE: A MEMOIR

I spent only one year as a junkie, and it was a year I didn't need anyway. I had just graduated college, in art history, and worked in a taco shop in Ithaca, New York.

In retrospect, it was a productive year. I wrote my first novel (a fictional biography of Antoine-Joseph Sax, inventor of the saxophone), lobbied for the impeachment of Ronald Reagan, learned chess, and studied Islam in a small mosque at the edge of town.

It was then that I met Barbie. She must have been twenty-five. She was a speed freak. She frequented the same bar I did, a melancholy dive with a nautical motif, called The Sloop.

Barbie was obviously an addict; her eyes had that hollow, shapeless-look. She was a "quiet" speed freak, too. When you know hundreds of meth heads, you'll meet three or four quiet ones.

Barbie had remarkable perception. She could notice an eccentric keychain at fifty feet, or overhear two conversations at once, with complete accuracy.

I'd always found her attractive. My sister had had one of her dolls, as a child. That attenuated, "airline" look—Barbie resembled a stewardess *and* an airplane—was always, for me, the purest American beauty. As an addict, Barbie's charm increased; her face had the luminosity of tile.

I slept with her once, simply because she had stayed till 3 A.M. at my house, and saw no point in leaving. In bed, she was earnest, yet reserved. The word that comes to mind is "tact"; she was a tactful lover.

She and I would play chess for hours. She won 90% of the time, though I was studying with a Master. "I just took Barbie's rook!" I'd think to myself with amazement.

She only spoke of Ken once. "He was a shit," she said, while drunk. I had a suspicion he was somehow behind her dissipation.

I put her on a bus to Seattle in 1986, knowing I would never see her again. That day she was suddenly voluble. "I threw out all my Talking Heads records!" she said, with an enormous smile. "Maybe I'll go back to school and become a chiropractor!"

I'm sure she never became a chiropractor.

BABY JESSICA ONE YEAR LATER*

A year later we spoke to Baby Jessica. She wore a smart pink jumpsuit, two-tone shoesies with crocodiles on them, and carried a copy of David Copperfield. *First we offered her a toffee, then we spoke.*

BJ: First of all, let me thank God, my mother and my father, and the people of America for standing by me in my trial, and through the days of moonlit fugitive horror.

Ruse: How old are you now?

BJ: Two, or rather *nearly* Two. In February on the twelfth I will be fully two.

Ruse: Has anyone ever told you you're extraordinarily articulate for your age?

BJ: Why… no.

Ruse: It's difficult to believe, in fact.

BJ: Are you implying I'm some kind of *hoax* (*gestures with David Copperfield*)?

Ruse: Oh no, not at all.

BJ: Because, lawsuits are not entirely outside of my *range*. It's not just jumpsuits with me, ha ha.

Ruse: No, of course, we're not saying anything of the kind… We love babies.

BJ: Also, I could *cry*.

Ruse: Please, please. Let's get back to the interview.

BJ: This *is* the interview. Let me ask *you* a few questions. Just what exactly *is The 11th Street Ruse?*

Ruse: Well, er… Me and my girlfriend put it out. We live on 11th Street, in the East Village, um…

BJ: And how many *copies* do you put out?

Ruse: Well, we make 101, but lately Violet's been pushing me to make more. It's just that 101 is such a *symmetric* number, and the *next* symmetric number doesn't come until… well, actually 111 is symmetrical, but *too* symmetrical, if you know what I mean; it looks like 3 in Roman Numerals, and it gives me that spooky feeling of WWIII. Maybe I'm superstitious, but…

BJ: Do you realize I've been on the cover of *People* magazine? *Twice?*

Ruse: Oh yes, of course. And very flattering pictures they are, too. Particularly the recent one. Unfortunately, the mimeographic process makes photography very difficult. But Ira, I think, is going to let us use his xerox machine, so we could possibly use a photo. Hmmm… See, neither of us has a camera… Perhaps a publicity photo…

BJ: I'm going to *kill* my publicist. Marvin! (*Marvin, a publicist, enters.*)

Marvin: Yes, BJ?

BJ: Do you realize who this *11th Street Ruse* is? They make 101 copies because they love symmetry!

Marvin: Well actually, I misread the spreadsheet. Right below them was *The Daily News*, and I read the wrong line over…

BJ: Marvin, do you realize I only keep you for sentimental reasons?

Marvin: Oh, implicitly, BJ.

BJ: (*Turning back to us*) Well, let's conclude this damn interview. And don't you put in the word "damn"—I've got millions of fans who would dye their hair purple if they saw that.

Ruse: Baby Jessica, just what is your opinion of the National Deficit?

BJ: I think military spending is entirely responsible.

Ruse: Yes, and what would be the hairstyle of the '90s?

BJ: It will be winglike, I know that, and it will appear to have teeth.

Ruse: And the writings of Trotsky? What meaning do they have for you?

BJ: I personally do not trust anyone whose fame is from the cavalry.

Ruse: And Meryl Streep?

BJ: To tell you the truth, I think the ability to do accents is a *curse*, not a blessing.

Ruse: Jewish food?

BJ: Pickles are tremendous.

Ruse: Thank you so much for this interview. You have been unforgettable.

BJ: Your umbrella's in that urn to the left of the door.

* On October 14, 1987, toddler Jessica McClure fell into a well in Midland, Texas and was the central news story throughout the world. Three days later, she was safely rescued.

RUSHDIE SPEAKS!

Was I surprised when Salman Rushdie called us from England! "*The Ruse* is the only newspaper I trust; please come for your exclusive interview!"

"But I constantly praise Islam!"

"Actually, your praise is *worse* than an insult!"

Luckily I knew a packet steamer, the Diana Rigg, heading out of New York, where the cocksman would let me stow in the barley bin. It was a rough crossing—I lost ninety-three games of Scrabble—but Salman was right at Martha's Chip Shop in Heatherington, outside Twombly, as he'd predicted.

I was amazed to find him alone.

"I thought you're under absolute surveillance!"

"You see that woman?" he asked, pointing back to a doddering granny with an earphone.

"Yeah?"

"Special Services."

Just then a man behind us coughed, and the grandma leaped like a viper. A menacing looking man fell on the floor, his turban disarranged, a long curling dagger clattering from his hand.

"The best in the business," Rushdie said cooly, returning to his chips.

"I notice you take them with vinegar," I pointed out.

"Yes, it reinforces my vinegary temperament," he chortled.

"So how does it feel to be on the lam?"

"It's great. It's like being in a novel. I've never felt so alive."

Just then, the venerable woman jumped out of the store, tackling a fellow with an enormous moustache. The bomb dislodged from his hand harmlessly destroyed three autos.

"But don't you get nervous?"

"Nothing to fear with old Mum here."

"But doesn't she ever sleep?"

"You should see the one I have at night!"

"How's your wife?"

"Marjorie Samson, the American novelist? She's at home practicing her mumblety peg."

"Are you really critical of Islam?"

"Oh, I dunno. I've always liked the religion, actually. It's the *roundest* religion. Have you ever been in one of those big mosques? You feel like a goldfish, in the perfect bowl. And it's produced the world's greatest interlocking designs. I used to go to my masjid in Bombay and stare at them for hours. But I think Muhammed *did* have a nervous condition. If you study the scriptures…"

Just then the Special Services Grandmother tackled us. Machine gun fire sprayed four inches over our faces on the oilstained floor.

"…you'll see that he seemed to have an inordinate fear of garden vegetables…" Rushdie continued.

"It's been wonderful speaking to you," we replied, and ran out of the store in search of the Diana Rigg.

EXCLUSIVE BORGES INTERVIEW!

Recently, in Whatever-That-Library-on-10th-St.-is-called, I found Dialogos Borges Sabato, *which has never appeared before in English. As a service to our readers, we offer a translation. (I did take out a Spanish-English dictionary, but I was too lazy to use it more than about twice— still, you get the basic themes.) This is the first page.*

Borges

Where are our notes? Towards… I forgot the century of our years. A coffee substitute believes that came in the house of Bioy Cesares, in the era of *One And The Universe.*

Sabato

No, Borges. This book came out in 1945. Our notes (knowledges?) in those of Bioy, lost ones years before, believe that was around 1940.

Borges [*Pensively*]

Yes, reunions… Let us lead our feet to a star all of the night speaks dark literature and philosophy… Era of a different world… Now speak me, see, that we speak much of politics. In my opinion they were interested in politics. The abstract politics, no. To us our preoccupation was other houses.

Sabato

I will say, not well, that in those habitual meetings we talked of that which made us passionate in common to you, to Bioy, to Silvina, to me. It is described in the literature in music. Not why no our preoccupations the politics. To me, to my mind.

Borges

Why speak, Sabato, that not to put up a house in the Merged with Brahma reference to our notices on the side, fugitive.

Sabato

Yes, that is true. Gramophones are permanent themes.

(To be continued.)

LETTER FROM SRI LANKA

Ruse,

As a former Rickshaw driver, I write to express outrage at your twelfth issue's masthead, which read "OUTLAW RICKSHAWS." How simple and worthy that phrase hits the eye! But once again, you blundering Westerner, you pull a rope you know not the strength of.

If only rickshaws could be freed from existence! If only *all* labor could be illegalized! So you have tried to do, with your microwave popcorn signed by Paul Newman, once a matinee IDOL.

But an idol is only as strong as his base—Durga, for instance, will fall over if she's not glued properly. *And where is the glue that holds the USA together?* 7-11s, you will say. And is the 7-11 more humane than the rickshaw, a seat in which at least *one* person is happy?

I have seen a 7-11 worker on the last hour of her nine hour shift, listening again to Bon Jovi, again to the ad for Tidewater Commercial Bank, her very *lungs* buried in an entropy emerging from the pistol magazines on the rack.

These are the soldiers who sell microwave popcorn. While between rides, we rickshaw men play a card game called "23."

And another thing. I saw Dukakis on Ted Koppel last night. Oh, I don't want to express the terror in my soul. Remember your forefathers, Mikalis, who slid swords in Turks over Helen! This world is given to those who *want* it.

Where is the woman who wants it for *good?*

America, though I live far from your flocks, I am grateful you gave the world rodeos and Charlie Parker. You have a wonderful silhouette and your flag is the world's most asymmetrical. I expect more from you. I know you can sing even a *better* song than "This Diamond Ring" by Gary Lewis & The Playboys, which illuminated a November of my youth.

In Allah,
"Legs" O'Brien

OUR VISIT TO POLAND

No doubt you've seen the feature "JetCapade" in *USA Today*, where 6 editors travel the earth, presenting intimate views of nations. In emulation, we sent *our* staff—including Ralph, the leader of the Mailroom—to Poland for the first Rusecapade. So, fasten your seatbelt and prepare for: Poland!

Poland is, in many ways, a frustrating land—a land where Old and New do not meet so much as riot, where a lawn gnome (the statues Suburbans plop on their lawns) may be worshipped as Jesus Christ or beheaded by a passing nobleman. Yes, there are still noblemen in Polska (the official, or dutiful name of Poland)—or those who *see* themselves as noble—though they are, in truth, more *Nobel* than noble—that is, they blow things up.

Noblemen run through the countrysides with pistols, in gangs, and often the moon turns red at their sight. They will approach a narrow peasant and demand: "Show me your card!" and if the person is too slow, they will shoot themselves. Yes, there is a streak of self-hatred buried in the nobility of Polandia (the Italian word for "Poland.") And from where does this self-hatred originate, in this landlocked kingdom known sometimes as "The Korea of Europe"? Why, from the *self!* Where else could self-hatred originate?

Of course, there are other factors: children are raised from an early age with milk snakes, which creates a permanent tic, as it were, on the face of the Polish public. They are *nervous*, in short, from hours at age 8 hoping a snake—say, a viper—won't realize it's being milked and turn on them deadlily. (Snake milk, in peasant Poland, is an ear elixir and evening beverage.)

In Poland, many a *protzl*, as they're called, stand on streetcorners asking for "small change" (*strettz preeess*)—which is tragic, in some sense, as all Polish change is very large—in some cases, larger than a record album.

Prostitution has been outlawed under Communism, and in its place has risen *zeqru*—or "ring-giving." Women in quilts and pigtails cluster at certain pubs—or *czernias*—waiting to be procured. For a price, they will place a ring on a man's finger—sometimes a half-plastic image of Bambi, sometimes a diamond. The men keep the rings, and certain *pilas* (men's social clubs) have walls of them.

Dirt is a national obsession, and purists bathe in ice water. Warning: if traveling with children, beware lest they be inducted into a Bathing Society, clandestine organizations where seven or eight baths a day are scheduled. Also, don't shake hands unless you wear some covering over your palm.

Many dislike Barbra Streisand in Poland, but Charles Bronson is recognized as an *auteur*, and country homes are often nicknamed "Death Wish II." Beyond him, Harold Pinter, Samuel Beckett, and the national poet, Anton Pliz, are admired.

Pliz, virtually unknown in the West, writes almost exclusively about water, and his "Trench In The Atlantic" series is memorized by children.

Life is crazy
but water can move quite
ceaselessly

it begins, and is in fact often recited at breakneck speed. Currently Pliz is living in his bathtub, at work on a novel, *The Four Humours.*

Poles wish they had an island, and many a chance meeting at a railroad terminal or kiosk will culminate in the fellow nerously wiping his moustache, lighting a Prolla (the national smoke) and sighing, "I wish we had an island." The consensus is one of the Canary Islands would be nice, but a surprising number have their eyes on Rhode Island.

When traveling to Poland, stock up on glass eyes—due to an archaic Government regulation they are difficult to procure, and therefore pricey on "the Brown Market," a semi-legal exchange which also includes handkerchiefs and massage.

Polish massage tends to be short and brutal—and, in fact, the name "Poland" derives from it. Broad sticks are used by masseurs, and the welts they raise (*styuts*) are believed to convey wisdom and a wary sort of courage. I recommend Polish massage only for the Diplomatic Corps and those inclined to mysticism.

Perhaps the biggest surprise in Poland is the size of everyone's feet—tiny, almost minnowlike, with the third, fourth and fifth toes formed like nowhere else on earth. Foot-worshipers must not miss Poland. Likewise lovers of straw. Most of the world's straw originates in the Zcuk Valley, between Trimt and Sullarok, where straw has been cultivated as long as the rosary. (Poland, of course, recently celebrated a milennia of Christianity.)

Whither Ol' Poland? Today's rebellious Polish youth are not content to sit behind the washing machines and sewing machines of the Past—they want something *new*, something that begins with the letter "k" and is often found by streams. But will they be able to achieve it? Pundits disagree. In today's rough-and-tumble economic world market, it's dog-eat-cat, and "Where's the mustard?" It is up to the Youth of Poland to show the readiness and charm to emerge from Soviet servitude (never a popular topic) into the Robot Laundromat of The Future.

INTERVIEW WITH THE POLISH PRESIDENT

The President of Poland, Lem Ravitsky, is a largish, olive-faced man, with a predisposition to spit and a kind of echo in his voice. I met him at a fruit bar near the Gleed Airport in Strust, on a balmy day in November, when weeds seemed to fill the sky. The talk turned casually from haberdashery to a philosophy of governing "mentally."

Ravitsky: That's an excellent suit which you wear.

Rusecapade: Oh, it's nothing.

Ravitsky: No, it's—as we say—"glorious in bud."

Rusecapade: Oh, come on.

Ravitsky: Really, I speak without celerity. Where did you achieve the purchase of it?

Rusecapade: There's a place on 9th St.—what's it called: "Clothes That Escaped The Wars?" Something like that.

Ravitsky: Oh, I would sell radishes to have a suit like this.

Rusecapade: Sell radishes?

Ravitsky: That is merely a proverb from the Gdang region, from which I am born.

Rusecapade: Is that so? What's it like there?

Ravitsky: Oh, old, old as Moses.

Rusecapade: Old?

Ravitsky: Indeed, old it is. Yes, perhaps you, being from the American mainland, cannot know such age. Your country is, as we say, "young enough to open a bowling alley."

Rusecapade: Actually, America's quite old—as old as Afghanistan. The *place*, I mean. What's recent is Chuck Norris, The Leaning Tower of Pizza, stuff like that. Of course, The Leaning Tower of Pizza's been around a while, by now.

Ravitsky: The Leaning Tower of Pizza?

Rusecapade: Yeah, it's on Route 17, in New Jersey. At least I *assume* it's still there. I mean, where would it go?

Ravitsky: To Italy?

Rusecapade: (*Laughs*) Ho! That's a good one.

Ravitsky: It truly leans, this tower of the pizza?

Rusecapde: Well, let me clarify this. You don't *sit* in the tower and eat pizza. It's just kinda cafeteria style. But on top, made out of an intermediate substance between plastic and paper maché, is a Leaning Tower—or rather the *front* of a Leaning Tower—the back is flat, like a postage stamp. So you can't really climb the tower—although this friend of mine, Eddie, claims he fucked a girl up there one night, while cars honked.

VISIT TO ICELAND

We've received some clamorous requests to recommence our Rusecapade, that madcap visit to all our earthly friends in the multicolored nations, so let us begin with a voyage to . . . Iceland!

Iceland may be described as a mountainous land without mountains. Imagine the Rockies hammered down by an imaginary fist, and you have Iceland. A vast rocky plain, it is a nervous wonder to behold, with only an occasional gazebo, or a marching band all in pink uniforms, proceeding in a row across the flat expanse, playing a patriotic ditty by Gjuln, the national composer, whose tunes are similar to the later work of Bob Marley.

The plant life of Iceland is thrilling, and distracting to behold: the *ixamilus cloei*, or "Beginner's tree," for example, with its leaves resembling cameos of Dolly Madison, and its serrated trunks, often used for the construction of lunchboxes. These trees, of which there are only four in Iceland, are hundreds of feet wide, and only 17" high.

Iceland is, in fact, often referred to as "The Sideways Land," and even doorframes require a curious twist and a hop to get through (accompanied by the national curse, "Jlam tor Torni," ["Shoes of Christ"!])

When visiting Iceland (which actually has no ice) be prepared for a breathtaking view of bobcats and plumbing. Plumbers from as far as Malaysia have wondered at a system that uses the earth's natural heat to warm swimming pools, and bake bread; and the national bobcat, the White Penetrator, moves freely through city streets, feasting on government deer preserved in small parks at major intersections. The bobcats are protected by a progressive national wildlife law, and add immeasurably to city life.

"We love our Selfish Cats, and they often help us solve disputes," says Reg Jbinversk, greengrocer and dentist. "It is our custom that whoever a Cat rubs against immediately wins an argument."

Besides verbal jousts, Icelandic sports include wind-stabbing, bicycling. and face-hockey, a game in which a small ball is moved across a recumbent man's face until a goal is scored in his mouth.

Many Icelandic novelists have moved to other countries, changed their names, and become renowned. Henry James, for example, was born in the suburbs of Reykjvik, emigrated to Manhattan, and claimed to be from New Hampshire. (The truth was only discovered by a patient Icelandic scholar, J. Phitses, in 1979.) The same is true of Willa Cather and Thomas Hardy.

Why do so many leave the Granite Isle? "The absence of good margarine, logic, and anything with fringes have all been cited as factors," notes sociologist Norra Tambborrt, at Silica University in North Clamd, near the Arctic Circle. Economic factors are also a consideration. Though VCRs are almost universal, money is scarce, and in some far western regions, Disney videocassettes are the medium of exchange. (This has led to the expression 'heavy with cartoons,' meaning "wealthy.")

By all means visit "The Land of Distended Shadows" (so called, because for six months of the year, shadows are commonly a mile long). Hotels are plentiful and full of toast, and guides will gladly show you the Rising Foothills of Mount Garden, in the east, which are exactly three feet high.

Icelanders should never be asked "yes" or "no" questions, as this petrifies them, and one must begin every sentence with, "By the way, this isn't important, but —" for the first few months of any friendship.

Never lose your keys in Iceland, as there are no key shops, and rooms with lost keys are generally boarded up or burned—and beware of snails in drinks. (Sometimes, they are intentional, sometimes not, so be sure to ask—avoiding, of course, a Yes or No question.) The pylons of the Klerrit Bridge and the fanciful clouds, which often take the shape of Iceland itself—a strange coincidence—are alone worth the fare of excursion.

NEW LETTER FROM SRI LANKA

Dearest R.L.S.,

The leaders of our two nations are similar. Ours is a violin-faced man who loves to enter airplanes. He knows four languages, but cannot translate between them. His wife is large, and kind to dogs. She is quoted more often than he is.

They drink, but don't enjoy drinking. In fact, their ability to enjoy *anything* has left them, possibly from The War.

In its place is the ability to *be* enjoyed.

Thousands of men mildly like our leader, and for him this sums to one big man who loves him.

If he were to die next month, no one would wear black.

Our leader puts pepper on everything. He wears glasses, but a rumor states they contain no glass.

He speaks of his concern for those who live next to the railroad tracks, in houses of cloth: "No one should live in a house of cloth!" But it is unclear what he means. A few of the more patriotic poor changed their building material to terra cotta. He made no comment.

Our leader needs a leader himself. He often looks at the sky and speaks of rain. I suspect he wants, really, words to descend on pieces of paper. He will say these words, and will be honored like a king.

> In duty,
> Legs.

OUR ANSWER

Legs,

There's helicopters overhead every night now. One crashed last night, I heard. But was it shot down?

The teams of Police surround houses one at a time, and the drug dealers come out, in a file. If they are alive, they file.

Two families have moved into a car in the backyard, and do crack, all day. At night they feed the cats.

One policewoman gets standing ovations when she comes to our neighborhood. She's strong, and she pushes men well.

Last week, I learned she used to be a man, but Science changed her.

How are you? I miss your weekly letter.

I'm sitting in Mass Transit next to a woman reading a chapter called THE CONTROVERSIAL ALIEN BODY PHOTOS.

Yesterday was Hiroshima Day and we went to a movie, *Little Foxes*, with Bette Davis. The meaning of the movie was: Your Mother Is Evil, But You Can Leave Her.

The movie made us take off our shoes. We felt hope, and sleepy.

A woman entered   a building and put a gun to the people's heads inside. "I want a meal," she said. The Police surrounded her, with their guns. For a long time in this hot weather, the guns stood.

Then someone gave her a meal. She ate it, put down her gun, and went out to the Police.

Love,
R.L.S.

INTERVIEW WITH A SUPREME COURT JUSTICE WHO VOTED AGAINST FLAGBURNING

We interviewed one of the Supreme Court Justices who voted flagburning should be a crime. For reasons of confidentiality, we refer to him only as Madame X.

Ruse: What are you, some kind of fucking idiot? You think a flag is *holy*, like God or something?

Madame X: Excuse me, sir, you must apologize for your language. I will not converse with you unless you apologize.

Ruse: Fuck *you*, apologize! Bull*shit*, apologize! I'll be a flamethrower for the South Korean Army before I apologize!

Madame X: Lawrence, remove this man. [*Lawrence, a balding butler, appears. He wears a black armband.*]

Ruse: [*Struggling, as Lawrence holds us by the arms.*] You haven't removed me forever! You will see me again, in sunglasses! I'll follow your children to school!

[*Lawrence ejects us. Silence, in the carpeted foyer. Doorbell rings.*]

Lawrence: Who is it?

Ruse: I apologize.

Madame X: Show him in, Lawrence. [*We seat ourselves, uncap a Papermate pen.*] You may continue.

Ruse: So what got into you? Are you a colossal jerk in knickers? You think the flag is worth more than a half ounce of paste?

Madame X: That's a little better. You are closer now to the English language.

Ruse: Aah, you big fuddy duddy.

Madame X: My mother was an alcoholic, and swore a great deal. I came to hate profanity, as well as birdcalls.

Ruse: Birdcalls?

Madame X: Sometimes she would lock me out of the house all night, and I would sleep on the porch. I'd wake to the sound of birds. Then I could not return to sleep.

Ruse: I'm very sorry to hear. And the flag? How is it sacrosanct, and uninflammable?

Madame X: The flag is highly flammable, and of course inflammable. Unfortunately the English language finds itself in the unenviable position of 'inflammable' meaning both 'able to catch on fire' and 'unable to catch fire.' If only every word meant its opposite! Then our life would be easier—particularly the life of judges. We could declare a man guilty and he could go free. Or flagburning could be a crime, and also no crime.

Ruse: But each word *doesn't* mean its opposite meaning.

Madame X: No, except for a word like 'elope' which exists inside 'cantelope' and 'antelope' as a sort of *hex*.

Ruse: Anyway, the flag…

Madame X: Ah, God bless the flag. That is exactly what we're discussing. What is speech? Who speaks? The government protects our right to speak, but is burning something speech? Hitler burned books. Was that speech? Do we have a right to burn? I suggest that burning is not speech.

Ruse: Suppose we burned a speech of Hitler's?

Madame X: A burning speech cannot speak.

Ruse: Suppose we came to the end of a speech, a speech we poured into all our glory and singing voice, and then said: 'Now, to show you what I mean, I will burn the words "AMERICA THE BEAUTIFUL"— because how can AMERICA be so beautiful when it trains men in HONDURAS to kill nurse's aides over the border?

Madame X: Must you burn something to speak?

Ruse: I must burn the flag or be burned myself.

Madame X: Now I, too, speak no more.

A RECENT LETTER FROM SRI LANKA

R.L.S.,

No one shits in the great novels. In the epic poems no one shits. There is a great pile of shit that has been left out of literature. The shit of Don Quixote, of Ulysses, of Ethan Frome, Arjuna. A great novel could be written of the shit novels have forgotten. All the twisting shapes: pretzel-like, the Ls and Js and U's. Shit is literary in itself, as it forms letters—most often the letter I. Shit and autobiography have this in common.

Why did writers of all cultures, from Greece to China, choose to edit out feces? So many a soldier's last shit, in Hannibal's army or in the Crusades, must have been a moment fit for poetry—as one notices, shitting, certain moods of fear and envy that are lost otherwise.

And of prognostication! How many knew this was to be their last shit?

Shits are oracles. The inside emerges.

Why did all the writers exclude this?

Perhaps its solitariness. Sex is a kind of shit two people take together, and it is the basis of every book in the world—even The Bible! But the shits we take alone—these must remain in hiding. There is a fear that if we spoke of this we might speak of nothing else, ever again.

The pleasures of being alone are not fit for literature, as literature is what one tells someone else. And how can one tell someone one would rather not speak to her?

Only mystics like Yogananda discuss being alone. They have the courage shitters have not. Because they are alone with Someone, while the rest of us are alone with our shit.

Now, in the Age of Doritos, I'm sure shit threatens to invade literature. But it is too late. Too much has been written without shit.

If you are writing a book, omit shit. Let the canon stay as it has. Do not foul the nest of writing.

Let the painters paint it. It is more their field.

Jai Ram,
'Legs' O'Brien

LETTER FROM A CHRISTMAS TREE SELLER

Dear Ruse,

Well, it's all over but the counting. All but a few of us Christmas-tree sellers retire for the annum on noon, Dec. 24th. A few stalwart Koreans last till midnight, but it is a known fact that no one will buy a tree after Christmas. (I tried it one year just to see, and I was actually spit on—on Second Avenue.)

You'd be surprised how many people buy them on Christmas Eve day. I had a guy come every day for a week—a man with a very tall hat, looked like a concert violinist. He peered at the trees, as if he was buying shirts for them, the walked away, without saying a word. three days I did not see him. Then on Sunday the 24th, there he was. He immediately picked out a spruce, and paid with a check with a picture of a bear in the corner.

"Finally made up your mind?" I asked.

"It's for a friend," he said, putting it under his arm.

You learn a lot about relationships when you sell trees. Last year I was on the Upper East Side, and this couple comes up, arm in arm, smiling. He kisses her, they buy the second tallest tree—a Motherwell Pine. Two days later, she's back, with a face like a file cabinet, and tries to return the tree. "All sales are final," I tell her, but I must admit when she'd left, I went behind a wreath and cried a little.

The next day, the guy comes with another woman on his arm—who looks almost exactly like the first one—buying another tree. If I were a principled man, I'd have refused to sell to him. He bought a smaller tree this time.

"Has a nice guy ever bought your tallest tree?" I've asked several sellers. They all said no. It's almost always a lawyer—usually short ones. It's enough to make you not want to *have* a tallest tree, but that's, I'm told, mathematically impossible.

I said "Christmas Trees" in the beginning, but in fact, in New York, we never call them that. They're "trees." You do with 'em what you want. If you want to eat them, fine.

Also, Jews have strange policies with Christmas trees. I've seen men with yarmulkes buy them swearing they're for Hanukkah. Now, there *is* something called a "Hanukkah bush," but a 15' blue fir is not it.

Still, I don't play Christmas carols on a tape, like some of the guys do. Sometimes, in the evening, I forget Christmas even exists—it's just me standing in front of the supermarket with a bunch of dead trees, as the Emergency Medical Personnel drive by. It's a lonely job, sometimes, though I defy anyone to tell me an occupation that smells better.

In New York what happens is a lot of women fall in love with you. Most of us are pretty big guys, to load trees into trucks, and men in New York—even the cops—look like women with flatter shoes. Also the women in NYC, one guy explained to me, have all given up on men. All they do is go to their therapist once a week and stay home the rest of the time listening to talk radio. But their womanly instincts emerge when they see a fellow in a flannel shirt. I'm a married man, and the infatuated women all look like marmosets, so I've never seen how far they'll go. But I've heard stories. Trees are a symbol of a man's privates, one of the intellectual guys told me.

This year one woman gave me a potholder she made herself on a loom. She kept asking me if I'd read *Madame Bovary*, but I told her I don't like women writers. Anyway, I'll throw it out the window when I get upstate.

I stayed in a motel this year, with two other guys. They had the Disney Channel and we watched *The Hardy Boys* a lot. I love those stories. When I was young, I wanted to be a detective. But I never knew how to go about it. Are there schools for it?

One year, someone stole one of my trees—a Harvey pine—and I actually tracked him down from a shred of sweater he left on the next tree. I found him in his apartment, and he tried to burn me with an iron. He was not poor, either. I left and he threw $30 after me. I picked it up and went back to my corner.

The extra trees? Sometimes I give them to an old folks home, or take them to my land and watch them burn. They make a lovely blaze. In the fires, you see all kinds of figures: those women that fall in love with you, the ambulances, the drug dealers, the men in suits, walking fast.

Then I don't have to work for three months.

Regards,
Ed

A BHUTAN VISIT

"Oh Bhutan!" we said as we debarked from our smoking Air Burma cabin cruiser, on a firm Tuesday in the Himalayas. "We never thought you would be like this!"

Four men in full dinner dress were holding silver trays laden with cut oranges for us as we stepped down the gangway! And behind them stood Ling Xish, Emperor of Bhutan, greeting us in perfect English: "We have a special policy of welcoming each and every visitor to this enchanted land. It is not, I assure you, because you are from *The 11th St. Ruse!*" And he bowed.

Clearly the legendary Bhutani Intelligence System was on its toes, and had heard we planned a visit after a layover in Holland.

"Frankly, Emp, we're bushed," we said. "Do you know of a cheap place we can catch some REM?" Whereupon the monarch produced a small card, with, in upraised letters, "Chi's Heaven" and an address. A driver deposited us there, and a man with a beard that almost obscured his chest came down the stairs, clapping his shoes together (in a traditional Buddhist greeting): "Come in, come in. We read your paper religiously! Tragically, our copies are several weeks old!"

The nation of Bhutan, wedged contentedly between China and India, the two most populous states on earth, and yet unknown even to viewers of *Jeopardy*, is a stronghold of *The 11th St. Ruse*, which is read aloud at community meetings in each of the 114 *buxties* which make up the nation. Why? This is a nation of practical jokers, who love to offer each other ice cubes with mouse skulls frozen into them. *The Ruse* appeals to this madcap polarity, and feeds a certain frenzy on Friday nights, when teenage girls, after rereading the recent number, take to the streets, flinging mud pies into passing hearses.

Women are absolutely equal in Bhutan, by decree. In 1933, they were given equality, in a voice vote of the National Assembly of Conscience, which then dissolved itself and moved to a lake together (near Xino), where a few of them still repair toasters and write poetry. In their place was an assembly, half-women, half-male, the Commission of Perfection, the so-called "salt government" (because it "sprinkles" itself into all walks of life) which mandates that women and men have exactly even representation in all professions and trades. For each female dentist there is a male, and every time a business executive asks his secretary to sit on his lap, he must later sit on hers.

Women won equality after a long battle, waged, characteristically, by joke. During the brutal War of the Sexes (1931-3) men found their pants ripping each time they sat down, and all fortune cookies had demeaning messages, such as: "A ballerina will spit on you before the week is out."

Beyond sexual equality, there is a curiosity of income. Everyone's income is guaranteed by law, and, while unequal—in fact, wildly divergent—are chosen by the fair method of chance. A roulette wheel in the Imperial Palace (which is known as "the Moon Cow" (*Chunti Xoo*) from its four-teated appearance and pockmarked stone) decides it all. This year, for example, olive-growers are by far the highest paid members of society, and electricians the lowest. Opthamalogists must forgo vacations, for lack of funds, while assemblers of bird cages have more money than they can spend.

If you visit Bhutan, you may go only once (due to an archaic regulation), so choose carefully. And take plenty of notes—if you can find a pen without disappearing ink.

(Note: "Rusecapade" is a regular feature of this paper. Normally, we have a small introduction explaining how our editors travel, all expenses paid, around the Earth, seeking to inform you of the mysteries of all nations, but this time we forgot, which is why the note is here.)

NEW LETTER FROM SRI LANKA

R.L.S.,

Now temperance has become an important topic, here in Colombo. The women wish to ban *colla*, the leaves which the men chew, and the men oppose *topa*, the ladies' drink. For three months, the fight has drawn on. The men say *topa* makes for memory loss, the women say they have little to remember, anyway. The women say *colla* causes laziness, the men reply there is little work to do.

The women say, "For twenty-one centuries we have drank this bluish fluid. Now, why must we stop?"

The men say, "This is a new world, a world of modern light."

The men say, "For twenty-one centuries we have chewed the sweet *colla*. Now, why must we end it?"

The women say, "If you take away our *topa*, we will stop *colla*."

The men say, "Women are wolves."

It's true, twenty-one centuries ago, a man named Abda found *colla* growing by his house. (A god, Artapa-Svini, had planted it there to give him power.) He went on to rule Sri Lanka, and to fight gallantly with our swollen neighbor to the West.

Since then, men have chewed this leaf to become great.

"But few of you have become great," the women say. "Look at you!"

"Yes, we have not become great," the men reply. "But this is not our blame. We tried. We chewed *colla*. Perhaps we are greater than we'd have been, without her."

Colla is considered a woman, by our belief. *Topa* is a man. The women drink men, the men chew women.

The women began drinking *topa* when their ancestress, Torit, drank it to be beautiful.

"But it has not made you women beautiful," the men explain. "As you drink, you become more pointed-looking and pained."

"Who asked you?" the women reply. "We drink to be beautiful. It doesn't matter if it *makes* us beautiful. The point is that we try."

"You men are so weak," the women go on. "You chew your leaf beginning in the early morning. We do not drink until afternoon."

"Yes," say the men, "but we hardly feel our leaf, while you stagger about from your drink."

"We stagger because we are sensitive. You men are as drunk as we, but you are unaware of it." (The women say.)

"You women are weak. With no man in the house you drink more," the men continue.

"And how can we drink, when you are staring at us?" the women ask back.

One politician, Tikoola Slew, has suggested a solution. The men must begin to drink *topa*, the women to chew *colla*. If they understand the other, they will no longer fight and scream.

Slew is a visionary man, I say. Quietly one day, I went to my wife's cabinet and drank a glass of *topa* quickly.

The room began to be smaller, like a policeman's booth at a cross-roads. Then it grew larger. Then a picture flew off the wall and fell on my head. Then it shattered. Then it flew back on the wall. Then a small snake emerged from my belly. Then I fell asleep. In my sleep beautiful women licked my body.

I woke up and knew this drug must be abolished.

To be fair, I gave my wife *colla*. She said no nine times, then she said yes. She chewed a leaf and began to dance. She danced as if she would fall to the earth, but then she leaped again. She cursed at me, and laughed. She moved her breasts like pumpkins on a stream. She raised her legs, one at a time, very slowly. She crawled on the ground. Then she fell asleep at my feet.

This is a good drug, I realized. Men are often right, women are not. But when she woke, she bit me.

Love,
Legs.

THE NEW YORK TIMES

The New York Times is the paper of record, and it sounds like a record—it has that *doctored* sound records have, as if ordinary sound weren't good enough. Records are made in places without sound—scrupulously *soundproofed* rooms, like tombs; consequently records record silence first, then sound. Likewise a silence pervades *The Times*, a similar made-in-a-tomb sensation. *The Times is* a tombstone for future men to see, and every morning all the people in it look grey and dead. The living women do their living in the tabloids—there they take pills and have love affairs—but the dead men live in the *Times*, where they cough and sign bills. *The Times* goes frequently to Mars, and recently our whole solar system made the front page (because it had its first portrait taken), while the tabloids don't go much beyond Brooklyn. But the solar system looked solemn and airless, in *The Times*, like a Romanian bureaucrat.

Much of the Science Section, on Tuesdays, is pure myth. *The Times* is not concerned that its news be true, but only that it *look* true. Now they have expanded their "Corrections" section so everything may become true in retrospect. One envisions one day a 100,000 page correction supplement dating from Millard Fillmore to the present, adding all the details the paper's omitted: "Harry Truman burped through much of 1949... Most of the people in the Navy hate saluting the flag... Jonas Salk threw out his underwear every day..."

The Times' greyness is like that of smoke, and in fact it is one of the dirtiest papers—in the sense that it comes off on the hands. All the human dirt—the secret that men ejaculate, that women bleed monthly—suppressed in its text, appears in its ink. One must wash after reading it, as one does after fixing a car.

INTERVIEW WITH SADDAM HUSSEIN!!!!!!!!!

Here are the peculiar circumstances by which we came to interview Saddam S. Hussein. One day last November, we received a telegram from Des Moines: "WANT TO INT. SAD. HUSSEIN?" I wrote back a post-card immediately, "Yes, this is a goal of ours, thank you," etc. We heard nothing for two weeks. Then one day, as I was shopping at the local Sloan's, a woman in my aisle asked me if I knew the price of Whisk. As I turned to her, I felt a large cloth covering my head, and a family size box of Tide clobbering me on the head. All was darkness for two days, though I awoke from time to time to feel the rocking of a train. Then the cloth was yanked from my head and I faced Hussein, who grinned and offered me a ciga-rette. I was so hungry that I ate it.

This interview was suppressed by Pentagon decree for the last several months. Now it has been declassified. We hope you enjoy this view of a moody yet dynamic leader.

Ruse: I'm honored—and surprised—you offered an interview to us.

Hussein: Of course. I am startled myself, to be frank. I often operate by whim. *Time* and you were both suggested to me on the same day, and I thought, out of contempt for *Time*, I would speak to you.

Ruse: Yes, we might have to make extra copies of this issue.

Hussein: Well, I wish you the best. I myself once put out a small paper like yours.

Ruse: Oh yes?

Hussein: It was called *The People's Tribunal of Death*. We described major public officials we wanted to kill. This was after my failed coup in 1979. I made it in Syria, and sent it Parcel Post to Baghdad.

Ruse: You say "we." How many people worked on it?

Hussein: Well, actually I wrote all the articles—except for the Sports section. A fellow named Omar did that. It was our one attempt at humor. We discussed sports figures we wanted dead. Omar was a drunk, and would write these streams of rhetoric that were almost inspired. He had a problem with adjectives, however. He would say "lovely" all the time. It sounded odd: "We call for the summary beheading and extraction of the lovely liver of lovely Salaam Besidda." I'm translating from Arabic, of course.

Ruse: I'm impressed by your English. You have quite a command of it.

Hussein: I have phenomenal mental abilities.

Ruse: Yes. What are the sports in Iraq?

Hussein: Soccer's popular. And a type of wrestling where only the legs touch. Also there is a sport played on camels called "Zaki," which is like a combination of polo and frisbee.

Ruse: What happened to Omar?

Hussein: I still hear from him occasionally. He stayed in Syria, and became involved with video. We have an Arabic version of MTV, which is much more advanced than yours. People regularly grow and shrink on it, and some turn into cats, or their tongues grow six feet long.

Ruse: How do they do that?

Hussein: I'm not sure. Contortionism is a much developed art in the Mideast; that may have something to do with it. But Omar is too erratic to function regularly in video. He'll make one, then drop out of sight for a few months and drink up the money, in fig liquor.

Ruse: Do you drink?

Hussein: I am a Muslim.

Ruse: Yes, but do you drink?

Hussein: I am a Muslim.

Ruse: Do you *drink*, though?

Hussein: I am a *Muslim*.

Ruse: [*Pause*] Didn't anyone else work on the paper? A typesetter?

Hussein: We had a typist named Sadie. (She had been raised by Christians.) She was overweight, and loved to laugh. She'd tell me to shave, and I would growl. It was a joke, between us—that I was a bear.

Ruse: How do you feel about the invasion of Kuwait?

Hussein: I'm very proud of it. Few men died. And almost no women. I try never to kill women. It went the way one hopes an invasion will go. Unlike that stupid war in Iran. I don't know *what* was on my mind all those years. One day I woke up and thought, "If you're going to fight a war, fight someone you can *beat!*" Since then, I've been in a really good mood.

Ruse: Thank you again for speaking with us.

Hussein: Salaam Aleichem.

Ruse: Aleichem salaam.

INTERVIEW WITH DAN QUAYLE

One Thursday morning I received a strange phone call: "The Vice Prez is ready to meet you in an ATM lobby on East Broadway." Then I remembered—I'd filled out a form to interview Mr. Quayle two months before. But I never believed such a moment would occur. I put on a black leather jacket and a grass skirt, and raced down to the Harvest Savings Bank. Quayle was inside, in sunglasses.

Ruse: Mr. Quayle...

Quayle: Let me say first off that I love your newspaper.

Ruse: Really? Why?

Quayle: I think it addresses the main problem that faces America today.

Ruse: By "America" you mean the United States?

Quayle: Yes.

Ruse: And what is that problem?

Quayle: It's war and drugs. It sounds like two things, but it's really one. War is a drug, and drugs are a style of war.

Ruse: How are drugs a war?

Quayle: Well, they *invade* your *boundaries*, and they take your mind prisoner. You see?

Ruse: Kind of. You mean drugs are a way of changing the internal government?

Quayle: Yes, of course. They're *violent*, but not a destructive violence, necessarily. Not all violence is destructive. I saw a Kung Fu movie recently that pointed out that agriculture is violence. The earth is opened, and seeded. It's a form of rape, really.

Ruse: Yes. Which movie is this?

Quayle: I'm not sure of the name. I didn't see it in English.

Ruse: Where did you see it?

Quayle: In a theatre in Bangkok. I saw it between meetings with foreign diplomats. I just ducked in there with my Secret Service agents. The ticket woman didn't believe I was Vice President of the United States, so I had to pay full price. It was a wild theatre—one woman brought a pigeon with her in a cage. I guess if you and your pigeon share a seat, you can get in with one ticket. The bird squawked through the whole show.

Ruse: So you think *The Ruse* is about drugs?

Quayle: Certainly. It's all about drugs. *And* war. I know, you're anti-drug and anti-war, but you recognize that war and drugs are a temptation for us North Americans. We can hardly avoid them, like the English can't stop playing cricket.

Ruse: It sounds hopeless.

Quayle: No, the trick is *living* with temptation. It's like living with kidney disease.

Ruse: I sense you're speaking from personal experience.

Quayle: Oh yes, I only gave up drugs when I attained high political office. And even now, I occasionally fire up two or three doobies, when the Allman Bros. are in town. I can't go to their *concerts*, or course, but when they play near me, I feel a bright sensation that night, in my Adam's apple. What I love about the Allmans are their high tunings—they're like the squeaking of bedsprings. A shrill, but instructive sound.

Ruse: So what is your favorite drug?

Quayle: You won't print this, right?

Ruse: Of course not.

Quayle:

Ruse: Oh, mescaline! What do you like about mescaline?

Quayle: It resembles a cat, in that it loves the dark. When I am on mescaline, I can sit for hours in the dark, just *seeing* darkness. There is so much in darkness, as much as in light. Darkness has many different types of graininess. But that was all in the past.

Ruse: Now you don't do drugs, only war.

Quayle: I'm afraid that's so.

SPARROW SPEAKS

Sparrow, whom we at The Ruse *support in his bid for the Presidency, allowed us to speak to him at an East Village café one sunny Sunday. He offered us a cookie and spoke before we could.*

Sparrow: First of all, I consider yours a foolhardy publication.

Ruse: Foolhardy? What does that mean?

Sparrow: Foolhardy. Because you publish all these interviews with famous people, like George Bush and the inventor of the flashlight, and any schoolchild can tell they are faked.

Ruse: Like this one?

Sparrow: Yes, I was going to say, in this interview, too, it's obvious one of us is an imposter.

Ruse: One of us? Which one?

Sparrow: I'm not sure. Either you or I.

Ruse: Isn't it possible both of us are imposters?

Sparrow: I hadn't thought of that. It is possible.

Ruse: But even if we are both other people—suppose I'm Martha of Martha and the Vandellas, and you're Willem De Kooning—we're still conducting an interview. That, at least, isn't a lie.

Sparrow: Unless we're both the same person.

Ruse: But wouldn't we know it?

Sparrow: Not necessarily.

Ruse: All right. Let's conduct a test. I'll pinch myself, and you see if you feel it. [Pinches himself.]

Sparrow: Hmm. I *think* I feel it.

Ruse: Close your eyes.

Sparrow: [*Closes eyes.*] Ouch!

Ruse: I didn't pinch myself.

Sparrow: You're lying.

Ruse: I am not.

Sparrow: This is the most tedious interview I have ever engaged in. And I myself have interviewed numerous people.

Ruse: Like who?

Sparrow: I interviewed the man who harnessed the power of tides. I met him on a park bench in St. Petersburg, Florida. He told me he spent 45 years trying to receive recognition from the U.N., and it never came. Ever since then, when I pass the U.N., I shudder.

Ruse: Did you ever interview anyone famous?

Sparrow: I interviewed Haile Selassie.

Ruse: Really?

Sparrow: I was very young. My father flew to Ethiopia on business— he does marine engineering. I wrote a fan letter to Selassie, and he let me visit him.

Ruse What was he like?

Sparrow: Very quiet. He may have been deaf. But he did tell me a long story, which began "When I was your age…" Apparently he had sex with hundreds of women. Why he told me, I'm not sure. He was chewing bubble gum, also, which surprised me. And he had a small dollhouse. As we spoke, he rearranged the dolls. There were dozens of dolls. Perhaps I imagined this, but I believe each of the dolls represented a woman he'd had sex with.

Ruse: The dolls were black?

Sparrow: Mostly. But every color was present. I remember being struck by that. Even Eskimos. But despite his eccentricity, there was nothing sinister about Selassie. He had the personality of an aging dentist. Very patient, and a bit shy, as he constantly rearranged his dolls. He seemed to be giving a party for them, in the parlor.

Ruse: Anyway, we're supposed to be discussing your Presidential campaign.

Sparrow: I really have nothing to say about it. For me, running for President is a daily practice, like flossing my teeth. I do it once or twice a day, then forget about it.

Ruse: And you're doing it now?

Sparrow: Exactly.

Ruse: Why do you think you should be President?

Sparrow: I don't know that I *should* be President. I just *want* to be President.

Ruse: Thank you very much for speaking with us.

Sparrow: Personally, I found this whole thing irritating.

SPARROW SPEAKS AGAIN

After rereading our rather disjointed interview with Presidential candidate and art collector Sparrow, we realized it was necessary to contact him for a followup interview. He agreed readily, and we met in the same East Village café (Zuella's) we met him in previously. This time he wore an amber diaper on his head.

Ruse: We decided to re-interview you, Mr. Sparrow, because our last encounter gave so little sense of your programs, etc.

Sparrow: Yes, I find it difficult to speak of my convictions. I prefer to follow a conversation where it leads. Where did you get that tie?

Ruse: In San Juan.

Sparrow: On vacation?

Ruse: No, my mother lives there. Actually, nearby, in a place called Vallejo de Hojos.

Sparrow: What does that mean?

Ruse: "Valley of the Pigs."

Sparrow: How did it get that name?

Ruse: Pigs lived there, in the nineteenth century. It's said that they uprooted pumpkins, gored them, and wore them as masks.

Sparrow: Really? They did that every day?

Ruse: No, only on the new moon.

Sparrow: Do pigs still live there?

Ruse: Four or five pigs live in a pen on the town square. The locals believe their ancestry predates Columbus.

Sparrow: They treat these hogs respectfully?

Ruse: Yes. It's common to give them flowers on the birth of a child.

Sparrow: What a wholesome custom.

Ruse: Of course, the pigs are eventually eaten.

Sparrow: Eating someone does not erase the honors he has been given.

Ruse: That's true, Mr. Future President.

SPARROW AGAIN CONFRONTED

Again we tried to corner the candidate Sparrow, whom we support in his bid for the Presidency, although we can never quite discern his position on issues. This time we ran into him in a bakery on Second Ave., and deluged him with questions. He was buying moon cookies.

Ruse: What exactly is your platform, Mr. Sparrow?

Sparrow: Well, a "platform" I don't have. What I have is musings.

Ruse: Musings?

Sparrow: Yes. I oppose the platform system. Standing on a platform, one is *above* the rabble—and I am among them. To me, even platform shoes represent a false egotism—look how David Bowie has suffered for his grandiosity.

Ruse: So you have no platform?

Sparrow: Nothing is *written*; nothing is *formed*. My campaign continues to form, and reform—it's a kind of reform school. Even my campaign manager, Hal Sirowitz, is evolving. He's beginning to shout "Strike!" and "Ball!" on streetcorners, like an Umpire for the Empire.

Ruse: So you believe America is an empire?

Sparrow: Not in the sense of the British Empire. America is a vertical empire. It spreads upwards: colonizes the moon, sends out spy satellites. Americans are curious about the sky, because we are a literal people, and believe Heaven is above us.

Ruse: Where do you stand on national health care?

Sparrow: I have ideas on it, but I don't want to tell *you*. The people should elect me President without being befogged by my positions. We all believe certain rapes occurred and certain ones didn't. All politics in America now comes down to whether you believe the Alleged Victim or the Accused.

Ruse: And whom do you believe?

Sparrow: I tend to believe everyone. I have a faith that liars tell a certain truth. That's why they're so impassioned. Though rape is wrong.

Ruse: So you oppose rape?

Sparrow: I would like it to end, yet I do nothing to stop it. I suppose I relish the slowness of my life.

Ruse: And you think a person like you should be President?

Sparrow: The Presidency seems to me a very private office. You live in a small, sacred garden, and share your solitude with the nation.

Ruse: Are you religious?

Sparrow: Not in any appreciable sense. Religion, for me, is like trying to buy bread with Monopoly money. I am an American—I want to *see* Heaven; I don't want to read about it. That's why America makes the best movies. We show, we don't tell. For the same reason, our children cannot read.

Ruse: Thank you, Mr. Future President.

INTERVIEW WITH TED BERRIGAN

Ted Berrigan, the legendary beatnik poet, was my teacher at The City College of New York two months before he died in an ambulance on the Fourth of July, 1983. Two weeks ago I interviewed him. I went to my friend Ira's house, sat on the couch, looked up at the ceiling and asked questions. I heard a voice in my head. This is what it said:

RLS: Anything interesting happening lately?

Berrigan: George Bush fascinates me. He brings the element of football to the White House, in a cowardly way.

RLS: Do you think he'll be indicted?

Berrigan: Never.

RLS: Do you know who's gonna win the Pennant before it happens?

Berrigan: You know *less* when you're dead.

RLS: Do you eat there?

Berrigan: Chinese food, little else.

RLS: What about Pepsi?

Berrigan: I hear it's very big in Russia. History has vindicated me.

RLS: What did Pepsi really *mean* to you?

Berrigan: Pepsi is "Pep" and also "yes" in Spanish. A very positive drink. (*Laughs*)

RLS: What advice do you give young poets today?

Berrigan: Go home. Live by your wits. Don't try to be public.

RLS: Do you write now?

Berrigan: Now and then. Not long. It's relaxing not to have an audience. Though certain people *tune in* and steal my poems. Certain *old friends*. (*He glares, humorously*).

RLS: Ahem. What else surprises you?

Berrigan: The outcry against fur? Up here fur is part of someone's body, or nonexistent.

RLS: You mean some people are partly animals?

Berrigan: *You* should know that, Mr. Sparrow. You think aborigines were *kidding*?

RLS: You have kangaroos there?

Berrigan: I just met one, at a party. Very nice guy. A sociologist. His wife was in his pocket. (That's not a joke).

RLS: Do they have Jews up there?

Berrigan: Millions of 'em. Practically every Jew goes to Heaven. Except a few Hasidim.

RLS: The ones who jerk off?

Berrigan: The ones who *don't* jerk off.

RLS: Do the Jews keep to themselves, in Heaven?

Berrigan: I wish. You know Jews. You're half of one.

RLS: What about Catholicism? Have you returned to it up there?

Berrigan: No, they don't really have it here. Or any religion. Mostly people just read Kahlil Gibran.

RLS: And salesmen? Do they have salesmen?

Berrigan: They have a few Insurance men.

RLS: You still need Insurance there?

Berrigan: You *never* need Insurance, but a few people here still believe they do.

RLS: There's anxiety in Heaven?

Berrigan: Lots. Apartments are scarce, for one thing.

RLS: But can't you live outside?

Berrigan: It gets very cold at night.

RLS: Hmm. Any tips for people preparing to ascend?

Berrigan: Learn a lot of stories. Not exactly jokes—barbershop stories.

RLS: Do they have magazines there?

Berrigan: A lot of very old magazines. *National Geographic.* *Le Monde.* Actually, we read your paper, *The 11th St. Ruse.* Everyone thinks it's terrible.

RLS: Yeah, well, we have no control of that. Is there science?

Berrigan: Very primitive, primitive. Equipment's so scarce. I call it "Heaven" because there's no word for it in your language.

RLS: Aren't you speaking English now?

Berrigan: Not exactly. This is panther language, simultaneously translated *into* English.

RLS: You're a panther now?

Berrigan: Don't jump to any conclusions.

RLS: Are there blacks there?

Berrigan: Sure. More blacks than whites.

RLS: And Finns?

Berrigan: Yes. But a lot of them are social climbers.

RLS: What does that mean?

Berrigan: They want more things on their head.

RLS: Huh?

Berrigan: Up here you carry all your possessions on your head.

RLS: Like in Egypt.

Berrigan: Or in *Caps for Sale.*

RLS: What else? Can you give me a quote from a great socialist?

Berrigan: Bakunin's here. The other day he said, "Ear wax is the strangest thing on planet earth."

RLS: What about me? What should I do with my life?

Berrigan: You're doing it. Keep pasting stamps on letters and sending them through the mail. Your sex life is improving. That's a good sign. Be Republican, as much as you can, without *voting* Republican. I miss TV.

DAVID KORESH INTERVIEW

Most of us know him as the dead, up-in-flames self-proclaimed Messiah of Waco, Texas, but The Ruse *was curious to know, "What kind of man is David Koresh, really?" So we dug a tunnel into his compound in the middle of his gun battle, and had the following conversation with him:*

Ruse: How did you find such a nice piece of land?

Koresh: As John says [20:27]: "Then saith he to Thomas, Reach hither thy finger, and behold my hands." So I let my *finger* do the walking, through the local real estate ads, and eventually they *handed* this fine piece of land to me.

Ruse: I notice you're firing a large-bore 20 lb. Samson repeater while we're speaking. Do you consider yourself a good shot?

Koresh: As Acts 22:2 says: "And when they heard that he spake in the Hebrew tongue to them, they kept the more silence." I see shooting as a form of conversation—that's why I can simultaneously *speak* to you and shoot at *them* [*indicating the 400 Federal agents around us*]. I feel that when one shoots well, it creates a *silence* in the person one has shot.

Ruse: What are your plans for the next few years?

Koresh: John 5:25: "Verily, verily, I say unto you, The hour is coming, and now is, when the dead shall hear the voice of the Son of God: and they that hear shall live." I plan to continue converting people to Christianity by shooting them. It's a unique approach, and may win me a permanent place in the history of religion. Other than that, I enjoy gardening.

Ruse: What's your favorite vegetable?

Koresh: Luke says in 5:34: "Let us alone; what have we to do with thee, thou Jesus of Nazareth?" You notice he says "let us." Therefore my favorite vegetable is lettuce.

Ruse: Do you have a particular favorite movie?

Koresh: Mark 14:62: "And Jesus said, I am: and ye shall see the Son of Man sitting on the right hand of the power, and coming in the clouds of heaven." That's why I prefer movies with a lot of clouds in them. *The Return of Batman* has a lot of clouds.

Ruse: I notice you wear an earring.

Koresh: Acts 8:26: "And the angel of the Lord spake unto Philip, saying, Arise, and go toward the south unto the way that goeth down from Jerusalem unto Gaza, which is desert." By Jerusalem, I believe He meant the Temple, and since we also have a temple on the side of our head, I believe we should go *south* of that temple, and put an earring there.

Ruse: It certainly has been fascinating talking to you.

Koresh: Luke 12:4: "And I say unto you my friends, be not afraid of them that kill the body." In other words, I'm not such a bad guy.

Ruse: Have a nice day.

Koresh: Have a nice day.

INTERVIEW WITH KURT COBAIN

We spoke to Cobain three weeks after his death!

Ruse: How does it feel to shoot yourself in the head with a shotgun?

Cobain: Quite pleasant, actually. There is a sense of "There, that's over with." Yes, there is a slight pain, but no more than burning yourself with a match.

Ruse: And afterwards?

Cobain: A deep disappointment. Here I am dead, and still doing interviews.

Ruse: Why did you decide to kill yourself?

Cobain: I realized suddenly that I hated rock music.

Ruse: What happened?

Cobain: I was listening to my favorite Uriah Heep album and I noticed I was totally bored.

Ruse: Do you like opera?

Cobain: Of course. Especially Verdi, and the late works of Striaten. He was a rather obscure Viennese, who usually wrote about dairy farming. Here is one of his great arias. [He sings]:

> di motto ornatio capassio
> realto nomo sensati

But do you hear the weakness of my tone? On the low A's, I tend to fall into a sharp nasality. I took lessons for six years, and got nowhere. That's when I started Nirvana.

Ruse: Why did you choose the name Nirvana?

Cobain: I had three friends who were Buddhists, and I knew it would irritate them.

Ruse: Did it work?

Cobain: Two of them stopped speaking to me.

Ruse: And the other one?

Cobain: He started Alice In Chains.

Ruse: What are your plans for the future?

Cobain: I was hoping to go to Hell, but there seems to be some kind of bureaucratic mix-up. At the moment I am in a place remarkably like Coney Island in the 1950's.

Ruse: Thank you.

Cobain: God bless you.

INTERVIEW WITH O.J. SIMPSON

O.J. Simpson agreed to be interviewed by us if we did not mention his recent troubles. He is currently in prison.

Ruse: Did you ever study physics?

OJ: A little in high school, a little in college. Of course, one could describe a career in football as a long study of physics.

Ruse: What did you think of physics?

OJ: I liked gravity. It amazed me how they had *equations* for it. Just being alive, one would never have guessed that there were equations for gravity. Particularly I was nettled by their certainty that all objects fall at the same speed—big or small. Everyone knows a boulder falls faster than a feather, but they had all sorts of explanations for this: wind resistance, shape, etc.

Ruse: Do you think about physics much nowadays?

OJ: Well, a prison *is* physics. Without gravity, everyone would escape in the yard, by floating over the walls. And if you could shrink, you could walk between the bars. In prison, one's thoughts often turn to the cruel limitations of physics. In a sense, I am a prisoner of Newton as much as of the State.

Ruse: Do you have any other hobbies?

OJ: I've always wanted to be a songwriter. Right now, I'm trying to write a song called "Single-Celled Organism." It struck me recently that since I live in a cell, I'm a single-celled organism. I want to make puns about plankton, which is a single-celled organism that whales subsist on. I feel, at times, that a whale is swallowing me.

Ruse: Thank you for your time.

OJ: That's all I have.

INTERVIEW WITH PATRICK SWAYZE

Today we begin a new, and belated era for *The 11th St. Ruse*. Finally, now that every other periodical in the world—including *Better Homes and Weapons*—is involved in it, we are too: Celebrity Journalism! We begin by following Hollywood idol Patrick Swayze—star of *Dirty Dancing* and *To Wong Foo With Love, Julie Newmar*—around on a typical day.

As we entered Patrick's brick post-colonial Bel Air Swedish-style mansion at 6:21 a.m., we were surprised to hear his sexy contratenor intoning:

> ham swaratam mora namas
> ranat samar tvipar asas.

After an hour and a half of this ritual, we could contain our curiosity no longer. "What is it that you're chanting?" we asked.

"It's the *Bhagavad Gita*," Patrick replied nonchalantly, fixing us with his just-east-of-blue eyes.

"Oh, really?" we asked. "Do you chant daily?"

"No, it just happens that I'm reading it. I pick books out of the library at random, and read them—always cover to cover. I was bored with the *Gita*, until my friend Priscilla Presley suggested that I chant it. 'That's what the real yogis do, anyway,' she said. And it works. It's quite exhilarating to chant. But I disagree with yogic philosophy—all this devotion to God, and the Cosmic Consciousness—who needs it? I say you make your own breaks in this world. If you don't look out for Number One, somebody is going to do Number Two all over you. That's one of my personal mottos. Here, come with me, while I practice my underwater aerobics."

We followed the seductive Mr. Swayze into a bizarre chamber in his sub-basement: a metal room, lined with rows of steel studs, which slowly filled up with water, like a scene from *Indiana Jones* (a movie which Mr. Swayze foolishly turned down). Once the water was neck-high, the youngish Hollywood thespian began a series of violent contractions and flips, punctuated by an occasional "Yow!" or "Arghhnoo!"

"That is more my style," he said, toweling off in the auxiliary locker room afterwards. "Now watch this!" he said, as we exited the room.

Suddenly, in the hallway of the sub-basement, six large muscled ogres attacked us. One by one, Patrick swung them by the feet, pummeled their heads, and smashed them into the walls. Finally, as he stood above the heap of villains, he turned to us and smiled: "Care to join me in a bowl of Cheerios?"

As we munched on the nutritious breakfast cereal, served by Patrick's robot maid, Hilda, the screen legend explained: "You see, my goal is to stay in peak physical and mental form. That's why I hire the firm Creative Assault to attack me at various times through my day. Sometimes I know when the attacks are coming, sometimes they are surprises."

As he spoke, a grenade bounced through an open window. With one hand, Patrick caught the weapon and hurled it back outside, where it exploded harmlessly. With the other hand, he continued eating his Cheerios.

"That's very interesting," we said, cowering under the table. Suddenly, we realized we were not alone on the gleaming kitchen floor. We turned to see a powerful woman, dressed as a cobra. She lifted a finger to her lips.

Then, in one motion, she sprang up at Mr. Swayze, brandishing a dagger. He wrestled her to the ground, then kissed her passionately.

"Thank you for sharing your lifestyle with us," we stammered, running out the door.

MY SEX WITH CHER

Sex with Cher is something most people can only dream of. But I have excellent Hollywood connections, and one of them, a man I'll call Budd Everett, suggested I send my sexual resume to Cher's organization: Amazon, Inc.

Sexual resumes gained currency in the movie and TV community in the late eighties. In them one lists one's disease status, prominent people one has slept with, one's body type, and any special skill one possesses: massage, Oriental mouth techniques, etc.

Once received, the resumes are delegated to a group of screeners who eliminate the more unlikely applicants, and present the best candidates to the star or starlet. This process is remarkably similar to the procedure for sifting through piles of unsolicited manuscripts at large magazines such as *The New Yorker*.

I sent my resume to Amazon, Inc. in September of 1991, and received a phone call on October 4. It was a female voice which sounded perfumed, if a voice can sound perfumed: "This is Shelly, Cher's undersecretary. She has time for you on June 14 of next year."

I was overjoyed—both that I would have sex with Cher and that I had so much time to prepare. The one drawback of a sexual resume is that, if accepted, one must labor to resemble that resume.

I immediately enrolled in a gym—the Indoor Sports and Muscle Therapy Center—which had been recommended to me as the cheapest place, per pound of body weight, in the five boroughs. I began by working on my pecs, then my counter-pecs, my lats, my gluteous scillitars, my dexteral sub-planals, my throtteus dexitals, my subthrotteus dexitals, and finally my nurrender sub-tallislats. It was a grueling seven months of effort, mostly under the merciless tutelage of a trainer named Larry, but by June 14, 1992, I resembled a Hasidic Marky Mark.

I entered Cher's penthouse that evening to find a candlelit room behind a heavy gauze curtain. "Come in," a voice called—a voice saturated in perfume, if a voice can be saturated in perfume. When I pulled back the curtain, I saw a longlegged woman lying totally naked on a couch, as if in conscious imitation of Goya's famous portrait of

Hermana dos Lavos San Dia.

Her face was in shadow, but the voice was unmistakably Cher's—the intonations almost exactly the same as on "Gypsies, Tramps and Thieves." "Come here, my sweet boy," she said.

I did, and immediately disrobed, out of courtesy—then modestly looked down.

Her fingers, softened by years of cream, slowly circled my chest, which had the hardness of glass and the strength of bronze.

"You have a glorious body," she said, her face still in shadow. "You have used the gift of youth well." Her fingers slid around my neck, down my shoulders, along my pecs, my counter-pecs, my lats, my gluteous scillitars, my dexteral sub-planals, my throtteus dexitals, my sub-throtteus dexitals, finally lingering on my nurrender sub-tallislats.

"You have a body any woman could worship," she said, her voice growing husky.

Suddenly, she thrust her hand down my throat, and I gasped for breath. Simultaneously she grabbed my balls and pulled.

When I came to she was kissing me, and I saw her face for the first time. Plastic surgery had twisted her mouth into a distorted grin, and her lips resembled rubber. She held my dick in her lotion-softened hands, stroking it with slight, sensitive gestures that sent my senses skiing.

We kissed, and I felt her tongue snake around my teeth. It was three times as long as any tongue I'd ever felt.

Is this the secret of her vocal technique?, I found myself wondering. My reaction to her was the same I had always had to her records—a mixture of revulsion, respect, and a faint love.

She lowered her mouth onto my manhood, and I came into her eternal smile.

"You are a dear, dear boy," she said, as I dressed, and I realized with gratitude that I had not touched her the entire evening.

~Proverbs~

Spaghetti lives twice.

•

A parasite never changes its mind.

•

When whales laugh, plankton cries.

•

It's better to turn on the television than
    to curse the darkness.

•

Atoms make quick decisions.

•

Sometimes only a nightmare can wake you up.

•

Never pay cash for a satellite.

•

One noodle, long enough, is a meal.

•

Don't wear a dress to jail.

•

A carburetor is only clean once.

•

Mustard doesn't taste yellow.

•

To learn to swim, try to drown.

•

The Pope doesn't get a pension.

•

Earthquakes open schools.

•

All tailors are geometers.

•

The nose aligns with the penis.

One baby can't carry another.

•

Nothing on the telephone is free.

•

A cow won't buy milk.

•

The gods meet by coincidence.

•

Pumpkins can be two-faced.

•

Nudists are born, not made.

•

Stand on the Gospels and you'll be taller.

•

Cancer does its own research.

•

Mermaids disappear after marriage.

•

A dog will bite a robot only once.

•

The road turns while you're reading the map.

•

Animals can't see cellophane.

•

All vacations are justified.

•

No one is blackmailed for his virtues.

•

Graffiti never sleeps.

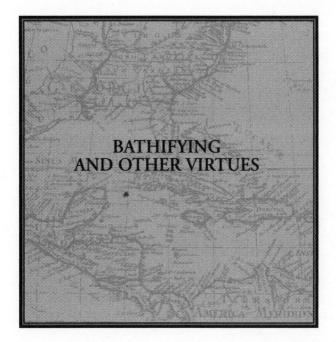

BATHIFYING
AND OTHER VIRTUES

GARBAGE I HAVE READ

One day I told Kevin Kelly, editorof the *Whole Earth Review*, that I only read magazines I find in the garbage, and that I was presently on an article in the Fall 1988 *Florida State* magazine (for FSU alumni) about a football coach, Bill Peterson, famous for his slips of tongue, who in fact had invented the same proverb I had: "Let sleeping bags lie." (He also said: "Don't burn your bridges at both ends, "Don't look a sawhorse in the mouth," "You guys line up alphabetically by height," and "This is the greatest country in America.") Kevin asked me to write about what I read, and I responded with obsession: typing up salient passages of my readings over the course of a year (mostly news-papers and thirteenth century Chinese poetry) until I had 440 pages - and growing! Suddenly I realized I'd written a book. On the way, I learned that dipping ping pong balls in hot water restores their resiliency ("Hints From Heloise," *Daily News*, May 2); that up until the 1930s, schoolbuses could be any color (*Newsday*, April 26); that Elton John's gay name is Sharon; (*People*, Dec. 5, 1988); that Dik Browne, the creator of "Hagar The Horrible," *looked* like Hagar The Horrible (*Times*, June 5); that Batman and Robin were originally called "Birdman" and "Scamp" (*Post*, May 28); that George Bush was the first president to visit Hungary (*Newsday*, July 13); that over two million dogs and cats disappear each year in the U.S. (*Our Town*, July 2); that a nude car wash was closed in Jacksonville, Florida(*USA Today*, July 6); that Betty Crocker put an egg back in the "lazy baker" recipe to involve consumers (*New York*, May 8); that Charlie Parker never lis-tened to jazz at home (*People*, Dec. 5); that before the War Brides Act of 1949, the Chinese community in America was 96% male (*Newsday*, July 21); that Frank Zappa's father was a chemist for the military who volunteered to be experimented on (*Post*, May 21) and that Dr. Ruth said: "It is possible for women to enjoy quick sex. You can train your body and mind to respond faster *if you want to!*" (*USA Today*, June 16).

I also learned that Doc Severinsen and Miles Davis's fathers were both dentists (*Parade*, July 23, *It's Hip*, July); that at Bennington College, W. H. Auden ate cold cereal at every meal (*Times Magazine*, May 14); that Jasper Johns' first American flag painting came to him in a dream (*Times Magazine*, June 19); that camels pulled lawnmowers in Central Park in the nineteenth century (*City Edition* 1986/87); that Keith Richards briefly changed his name to Keith Richard (*New York Press*, Oct. 20); that Wilbur Wright was a fine harmonicist (*USA Today*, June 23); and that Donald Trump, asked if he would consider devoting the rest of his life to Good Works, replied somberly: "I'm looking for a disease." (*Daily News*, Feb. 8).

Bill Peterson composed by having a kind of verbal dyslexia and I wrote *my* proverbs by combining objects in a room: "Pencils cry when wastebakets sing"' Our results share the virtue of surprise. Which is the virtue of garbage. One of my goals in this essay is to encourage North Americans to search the trash for words. (It seems incongruous that words can be discarded at all - that you can throw out Erasmus along with the inside of your toilet paper roll.) Imagine, I spent less than five cents to read all this. (In fact, I spent zero.) The vast majority of it went the same route: garbage → my mind → my journal → the cat box. (One Monday I decided it was foolish to throw away *The New York Times* and buy sand for the cats to shit in. So I shred my documents, like Oliver North, every two days, and bundle the used strips with jute rope. It seems appropriate for the cats to pee on *The New York Times* - perhaps because it pees on us.) In the December 5, 1988 *People*, the Greenwich Village pastry chef, Rose Beranbaum (author of *The Cake Bible*) tells of disposing of an unsuccessful cake when she meets her neighbor at the incinerator. "Don't you realize that your failures are our life's delights?" he shouts, and my whole book is made up of such "failures." (Ron Perambo, a writer for *Albany's News*, had a theory that Chinese restaurants serve food thrown out by Italian restaurants, which seems relevant here.) I see the garbage as an oracle, like the I Ching. Because it's random, it shares the quality of the yarrow sticks that cast the Ching, or the scared bolo beans in Santeria. In fact, when I studied with William Burroughs at the Naropa Institute in 1976, he assigned us to cut up news articles and reassemble them, with the theory that, "If you cut apart the present, the future leaks out." (One of my compositions featured an Indian chief marrying a computer, but I don't know if this has yet come to pass.)

Rolling Stone's "The 100 Best Singles of the Last Twenty-Five Years"

(Sept. 8, 1988) suggests that our whole culture now is based on such sudden strokes. These 100 Singles have usurped the Great Books as our basis of collective knowledge, and none of them were stormily labored at like *A Pilgrim's Progress* or *Two Years before the Mast*. They were dreamed up in 10 minutes next to a swimming pool (#1, "Satisfaction"), written on toilet paper (#18,"Louie, Louie"), improvised while drunk (#33, "When A Man Loves A Woman"), composed as jokes (#72, "Wild Thing")—in short they were found, too, amid the garbage ofthe singer's mind. Many of the great black songs are associated with crying ("Every time we sang that song the people in the audience would cry," Smokey Robinson said of "The Tracks Of My Tears") and many of the great white songs were intentionally silly ("Wooly Bully"). The moments one breaks down and cries, like the moments one is a fool, open a door, like opening the lid of a trashcan.

USA Today is to real papers what rock'n'roll is to Mozart: a bastardization, and yet with an inspirational goofiness. *Jetcapade*, where the editors go from country to country, asking the President of Switzerland if he likes chocolate, and creating such headlines as "Canada: Sportsmen, the French Love It," make whole nations into jokes. (Perhaps this could bring unity to the world, if all countries were systematically made silly.) The most amazing thing I read in that paper was an interview with Leontine Kelly, the first black woman elected bishop in the United Methodist Church, where they asked her: "Is it possible that God was a woman?"—using the past tense, as if God was either officially deceased, or had had a sex-change operation (Feb. 14).

News has become the literary art of the present, and a general reader today finds the news continually compelling and trenchant, with wonderful plots and stories, and modern novels listless and dogged. The world has outpaced our ability to imagine it.

Janusz Glovacki, a Polish playwright, wrote recently in *The Times* about a friend who spent years on an 800 page novel condemning the Polish regime, only to see it become unpublishable in the space of weeks. Right now, the world is dreaming itself faster than we can. This article is already out of date.

My own writings exist in periodicals, but not books, and in fact my life right now is an attempt to leap from magazines to books. (Perhaps that's why I created a 'book' of magazines.) In this way, I am purely local, like John Purple, a visionary of my neighborhood (featured in the April 19 *Downtown*) who created a large garden in the shape of a yin-yang sign which he fertilized with his own feces. ("I can't take the environmental movement seriously until it addresses SHIT," he says.)

I read a lot of poetry written in my neighborhood, which is a poet's neighborhood, and it's strange to read intimate thoughts of people I live a few blocks from and haven't met. I wonder, when I read in Heidi Schwartz's "I Don't Know":

> I have been among the gypsies and the thieves
> and I can see into the palm of a hand
> "You will cross two oceans" they said,
> "And then you will marry"
>
> I have been in the house of a Turkish man
> who was arrested for committing a murder.
> A man has stored weapons in my house.
> I have walked out alive.

Is she the woman who hovers around the Farmer's Market on 10th Street on Wednesdays?

For *The National Poetry Magazine Of The Lower East Side* we each make 120 copies of our poem and meet at King Tut's Wah Wah Hut (a nightclub) and collate them, and the poems are a kind of voyeurism into other's apartments—though sometimes one is profound, as when Patrick Christiano said (in the "Special Root Of Crime Issue," No. 16):

> The sea, meanwhile, is not satisfied
> With the shape of Long Island.

I am proud that some on the streets around me are wise. One subject I didn't take notes on—because I couldn't—is a major part of my education: reading papers of other nations. ('Reading,' is the wrong word, though; 'beholding' might be better.) One of the great things about New York, is how many languages the news is in. I've had Portuguese, French, Korean,

Spanish, German, Hebrew, Chinese, Italian papers, without particularly trying. My favorites are the Chinese, who had color before English papers, and whose delicate pinks and salmons evoke a cheerful childhood.

I was startled when I first learned Chinese newspapers were about America; I thought you had to speak about China in Chinese. Once you've seen Arnold Scwarzenegger in a Chinatown newspaper you can't see him the same way again. This American hero, with Lilliputian letters doing somersaults around him, looks tinny and haunted. Each letter is a riddle. I feel I'm studying The Sacred Scriptures of Agamotto, like Dr. Strange—that they are improving my mind, or digestion, even if I don't understand them. Chinese newspapers are the Kabbalah of the garbage can, and I believe that if every American studied—or 'beheld'—a Chinese newspaper 10 minutes a day, our national sins would be forgiven. But in a sense, the newspapers in English are as much riddles. The Dec. 31 *Parade,* "Our Annual Roundup Of The Year: The Best & Worst Of Everything," reports that 87% of Americans prefer not to work around people who don't use deodorant. What does that mean, "prefer"? And Richie Schalit, owner of Schalit's Children Shoes, says in an interview in *The Lower East Side Voice* (Fall, 1989): "Today's generation has big feet. Today's size nine and a half used to be the last generation's size six." *Why are people's feet getting bigger?*

Another great moment is finding a newspaper on which a love message has been written. It's another dimension in literature, like a pop-up book. Perpendicular to the black voice of print is the blue voice of a Bic pen, saying:

> I do love you
> I miss you
> think of you consteadly
> But too Many Problems
> between us—to reunited
> We must talk
> I will never stop
> lovin you (Dont worried)
> I wish, You the
> very best my love

(on a photo of a Cape Cod lighthouse—in the May 28 Sunday *Post*.) It appears to be speaking to you, and in the cadence of a rock'n'roll song—as if the newspaper loves you. Such love cannot be bought; it can only come free, from the garbage.

The newspapers are an epic, like *The Odyssey*, the tale of a character who migrates through a hundred lives in one—who marries Aristotle Onassis, starts the War On Drugs, becomes homeless, collects *Man From U.N.C.L.E* memorabilia, sees a statue of Jesus close its eyes, is raped in Central Park, and hears six fiddle notes over and over in his mind for thirty-one years. This hero is vicious, proud, mad. I would never know her on the street, because her face changes daily. He is ugly and I am glad I have no part in his violence.

"Show business is the business of America," to preempt Calvin Coolidge, and in the papers today one is struck that entertainment, our number two industry, has merged with politics. At a benefit for Dionne Warwick's AIDS foundation, Tony Orlando said, "Show people are the first ones to pick up a rifle and shoot the demons down," (June 27 *Village Voice*) and increasingly there's a privatization of idealism, a move from political figures like Malcom X to singer/humanitarians like Michael Jackson (who recently appeared on the cover of the *Daily News* with George Bush.)

And now even international crises have agents. *7 Days* (March 8) rumored that Andrew Wylie, Salman Rushdie's agent, who'd gotten his client an $800,000 advance for *The Satanic Verses*, spurred its poor sales by sending the book to the Ayatollah (through another client, Benazir Butto), provoking a near-assassination. As a result, 10,000 Maniacs [the rock'n'roll band] were glad "Peace Train"—their cover of the Cat Stevens tune—was not a hit, because Stevens is now a Muslim, who supports the Ayatollah, and they're boycotting his songs (June 27, 1989 *Daily News*). A war of ideas shakes the jukebox.

Speaking of war, G. I. Joe (the doll), which was discontinued briefly during a pacifist period in the late seventies, has returned as a totem for male children. In the absence of real wars, he provides the glamorous surrogate wars a global power needs. In a sense he is the ultimate soldier, because he fights the wars we all imagine, while the paid soldiers sit, smoking cigarettes, their hands tied by a timid

Congress and the Geneva Convention. I learned about him in the "Kidsday" section of *New York Newsday* (April 22), in an article called "Happy Birthday, G. I. Joe" [he was 25] written by three kids, one of whom has sixty-seven of the dolls. When Joe was introduced, it was doubted boys would play with him, but these boys speak of their little man almost maternally. They advise their readers to save their G. I. Joes for their own children—an emotion rare in this society.

Spy magazine (July) attempted to find a sympathetic taker for Rambo Trade Units, "the first monetary system based on a major motion picture"—silver coins with an American eagle on one side and a "very grim, very moussed" Sylvester Stallone on the other, minted for use after a nuclear catastrophe. ("We can't accept them . . . yet," a cautious saleswoman at the Reminiscence boutique adjudged.) Putting Rambo on the dollar is more logical than G. Washington, anyway, because Rambo is new and real, while Washington waged war upon a horse.

In "FBI Star Search" in the Sept. 22 *New York Press*, Jon Cohen examines the FBI documents on rock-n-roll stars released under the Freedom Of Information Act. Senator George Murphy met Elvis Presley on a flight from Los Angeles to D.C. in December, 1970, he reveals, and contacted the FBI to arrange a tour of their headquarters for Elvis. On the tour, Elvis confided that he considered J. Edgar Hoover "the greatest living American" and had read his *Masters of Deceit, A Study of Communism* and *J. Edgar Hoover On Communism.* According to a memo by agent M. A. Jones, "Presley indicated that he is of the opinion that the Beatles laid the groundwork for many of the problems we are having with young people by their filthy unkempt appearances and suggestive music while entertaining in this country during the early and middle 1960s."

Of course Elvis' politics were opposed to the Beatles! They were the great political leaders of their time. Perhaps it isn't coincidence that Elvis and Lennon both died mysteriously, by violence. Elvis was 'The King,' and his politics corresponded to a brand of monarchism. Lennon's name was homonymic with "Lenin," and he intuited a kind of revolution. Elvis construed the Beatles as pro-drug and anarchy, which was true, though he himself used drugs, and promoted a sexual, and later, idolatrous frenzy. ("Drug" has been largely defined by who gives them out. Elvis took legal, prescribed drugs; The Beatles took illegal, proscribed drugs. The Moptops didn't recognize the Divine Right of Doctors and Kings.)

"This Time, A Personal Woodstock," by Michael T. Kaufman in the August 16 *Times* begins, "Hundreds of people who wandered over the grassy pasture where the Woodstock music festival began twenty years ago today pointed out features of the terrain as if they were revisiting a historical battlefield,"—and Woodstock *was* a battlefield. The current wars—in this country, at least—are fought at rock concerts, in movies, and by dolls.

Most deaths today are fictitious, which doesn't make them less severe. G. I. Joe kills more men than the U. S. Army, and these deaths are more tragic than real deaths, because the men who died threatened no one, being nonexistent.

We are living through an imaginary holocaust of staggering proportions. Among the movies, TV, and children's games, more imaginary people die than are born into the real world every day.

About 500 vacant buildings in New York City were covered with "occupied-look" decals (on tin plates, over windows) from 1980 to 1986, according to *Newsday* (July 13). Silhouettes of women cooking and men leaning over tables gave the impression of habitation. Everyone has thought of this idea, but largely when they were three. The fact that it was *done* suggests the Walt Disneyfication of our time —that stage sets and architecture have merged. The same people G. I. Joe kills live in these apartments.

One question social observers have is "Why was *Ghostbusters* such a success? Why did it make almost a quarter of a billion dollars?" After the filming of *Ghostbusters II*, Harold Ramis said, "It's like being a modern folk hero . . . People would hold their children up to be blessed." (*Movies*, June)

Who are these ghosts we all fear, whom we want "busted?" Perhaps the men Rambo and Dirty Harry killed are haunting us.

The review of *Comic Visions: Television Comedy and American Culture* by David Marc in the May 9 *Voice Literary Supplement* explained that Joseph P. Kennedy underwrote the original pilot of *The Dick Van Dyke Show*, which aired the summer his son campaigned for the Presidency. "Rob and Laura came to stand for Jack and Jackie, their sophistication a sharp departure from the square Eisenhower families of fifties sitcoms," with "their social ease among Jews and blacks, their relative detachment from their son's life, and Rob's familiarity with his nominal subordinates, Buddy and Sally."

Dick Van Dyke was J.F.K., we learn 29 years later, and this seems like another branch of the vast assassination theory. (One *did* feel the show emanated from the White House, at the time.)

The situation comedies rule us. Bill Cosby has presided over America for years, and Bush borrows his tone from him. We live in a videocracy.

New YABA World (April/May 1989), a children's bowling newspaper, featured a column "Bif's Adventure: Being the bowling mascot is a learning experience" alongside several photos of a human-sized bug with two antennae, a protruding tongue and a yellow bowling shirt. His memoirs read, in part: "Christmas parties and Christmas parades are very special to me. I especially enjoy parades because they give me the opportunity to spread the 'Bowling Is Fun' message to non-bowlers. I was in Christmas parades in Seaford, Del., Ottawa, Kan., and Decatur, Ala."

Bif The Bowling Bug—a kind of elevated phony—presents the antic world we force on children. For some reason, we all love lying to children. We lie to children to insure that they will lie to us. We fear they will be unhappy and will tell us, so we entertain them unsubtly and unendingly. This is similar to what we do to ourselves, and increasingly it is impossible to separate kids' culture from ours. The five best-selling films of all time (*E.T.*, *Star Wars*, *Return Of The Jedi*, *Batman*, and *Jaws*) can't be classified as adult or children films. They are children's films that have grown beyond recognition, to include death and sex and sadistic humor.

Bif The Bowling Bug has, in fact, a political role. Politicians also go to parades, wearing a suit and seeing the bright side of everything. Dan Quayle's famous utterance to the Samoans: "You all look like happy campers to me. Happy campers you are, happy campers you have been, and as far as I am concerned, happy campers you will always be," reads like an excerpt from Bif's diary.

Walter Kendrick, in the *Voice Literary Supplement* (January/February), listed what was thrown at an inferior production of *Richard III* in Sacramento, California in December, 1856: "Cabbages, carrots, pumpkins, potatoes, a wreath of vegetables, a sack of flour and one of soot, and a dead goose." In Act II, the *Sacramento Daily Union* continued, "A well directed pumpkin caused [the actor] to stagger, and with still truer aim, a potato relieved him of his cap, which was left upon the field of glory, among the cabbages." This account is somehow salutary, even healing. One of the relationships gradually lost this century is that between vegetables and art.

Today there is nothing to throw a parsnip at—it's not clear who the target is. If you throw it at the television, you're a fool, because it's *your* appliance—you bought it. (I know Aaron Kaye, the 'Pie Man,' who made a name for himself by throwing cream pies at prominent men, like Sun Myung Moon, in the mid-seventies, but even he seems to have lost touch with his enemies.) The cathartic act of pelting bad actors with bananas has gone, and now, because of that, they rule us.

In the July 23 *Parade*, Candice Bergen [daughter of the ventriloquist Edgar Bergen] told Cleveland Amory how she grew up in the shadow of Charlie McCarthy, her father's dummy: "When I was born, the papers called me his sister. And I guess there were times, as I was growing up, when I did feel as if he were my brother. After all, he had a whole room of his own right beside mine."

In later years, Candice had trouble explaining to European nobility what her father did. "I'd tell them that he had these dummies—large dolls sort of, and he'd talk to them or make them talk, or actually they'd talk to each other. 'Really?' they'd say. 'How amusing. And where does he do that?' 'On the radio,' I'd say. '*He'd talk to dolls on the radio*? How extraordinary!'"

America is the only country ever to put ventriloquists on the radio, and perhaps we have the best imagination of any nation. Because of this, the imaginary here has become quite strong. It has reached the point where bad actors are throwing potatoes at us.

"Everybody who isn't homeless go home," a black man proclaims in Tompkins Square Park (my local park) in an article by Evelyn McDonnell in the *New York Press* (June 9)—and he's right. At the end of the day we all go home, except the homeless, who go to their no-home, and there we are, a house divided that cannot stand, half indoors and half out.

'Homeless' is a beautiful word, the kind of word used in mournful ballads of the Appalachians. 'I ain't got no home in this world anymore,' Woody Guthrie sang, and we Americans are particularly a homeless race—a race that left home to come here and create a new home, but somehow keep leaving our new homes for newer homes—over to Albuquerque, north to Nevada, back to Maine, back to Chicago, again to Utah.

The nomadic Indians preceded us here, and by taking their country we have become them, in some way—precisely because we think we haven't. We are the Lakotas, in our motor-tipis, wandering our fields and deserts, scandalized by the homeless, who are nomads without dignity.

The *Upper East Side Resident* (February 3) profiles "Merchant Of The Month: Tyyni Kalervo," the eighty-eight year old owner of the Little Finland bar on Second Avenue, who was awarded President Reagan's Ellis Island Medal, an honor given to only one immigrant from each country. She left Finland at age twenty-two (in 1922) knowing no English, and found a job as a maid for $20 a week. "Things were very hard at the beginning, yes," she says. "I cried myself to sleep many nights. But what could I do? I had come to this country, and I had to stay here."

Like Tyyni, all of us Americans are thousands of miles from home, and none of us speak the language.

Entertainment is the nomadic sport. The homeless can see the same movies as they trek across the nation that we do, and every Thursday night Bill Cosby is on, wherever you are. We have made a landscape not of place but of time, with maps filled with entertainment. The way each state has a senator, each hour has a game show or soap.

"Are Our Zoos Humane?" by Bernard Gavzer (*Parade*, March 26) tells how Medundamela, a disobedient elephant at the San Diego Zoo, was beaten on the head with axehandles over a two day period in February, 1989 by five keepers, until she accepted an apple from Alan Roocroft, the chief elephant keeper. "She needed to be disciplined for her own welfare," Roocroft remarked, but Florence Lambert, a founder of the Zoo Animal Protection Society, said: "He broke her spirit."

An article in the *New Haven Advocate* described the Amistad affair, an event which "should have ended slavery," according to Professor

Slyvia Ardyn Boone of Yale, though it is unmentioned in most encyclopedias. In 1839 a Spanish slave ship, the Amistad, revolted in Cuba and ordered the sailors to return to Sierra Leone, but the crew tricked them, sailing east by day and north by night, until they reached Long Island Sound. The blacks were imprisoned there for two years, until the Supreme Court found in their favor in 1841, and they returned to Africa. The argument which won their freedom was that they were not really slaves because their spirits had not been broken. "If they had not been broken they were not property," Boone said.

As with Medundamela, the question is: Whose spirit is broken? Those who accept the apple (as Eve did) become slaves. Are there still slaves in the present day world?

When the government rules through fun, the broken spirit is one that is entertained. The revolutionary refuses to be amused.

Visiting Holland, George Bush was startled to learn he shared an ancestor with Dr. Thed N. Schelmaas, Keeper of the Records of Leiden (*Times*, July 17). "You and I are related?" he asked, as if embarrassed. We have forgotten that we're related to the Europeans, or to anyone.

I was surprised that Bob Kane was inspired by Leonardo Da Vinci's sketch of a bat-winged glider to create Batman (*New York Post*, May 28). Our culture's discontinuity with the past, too, is an illusion. We carry Mozart within us, as well as the Comanches; we are Mozart-like Comanches, wandering the West.

In the *Times* article on the twentieth anniversary of Woodstock, Michael T. Kaufman meets a couple who call themselves The Happy Campers, and explain their evolution from working in an ammunition plant to living in a truck and making jewelry. "Maybe the Woodstock ethos is in retreat, like everyone says, but I think what's left of it is pretty strong," the man says. "You know, last week, I met some people who had not touched money for two years."

Quayle blithely mentioned The Happy Campers, and somehow they stepped out of his utterance to actually exist. Perhaps the very showbiz/political forces that rule us are generating images to save us. Someday we may realize that the Ghostbusters *are* the ghosts, and we'll bust them.

ON BATHIFYING

I am a bath mystic. You can also be one. Once you have read this article, decide if bath mysticism intrigues you. Here are the details:

First, you need a bathtub. I recommend one with lion's claws for legs. Or eagle's claws. Old bathtubs are best. They have the most "bath memory." The more baths in a bathtub, the deeper and prouder its bath memory. New bathtubs are mostly inhospitable to bathing. They are composed of plastic, and often the only place to lean is a painful metal grate. Today's bathtubs are built to stand in while one showers.

America is the hardest-working industrial nation. Americans make Germans look like a nation of hobos. Inhabitants of the USA awaken early, drink a cup of coffee, work all day, then return home and mow their lawns.

In comparison, bathing is inactive. While bathing you lay in a bathtub, closing your eyes. You accomplish nothing. By the end of the bath, you're slightly older and slightly cleaner.

As I say, you need a bathtub. Or you could use a large canvas bag, filled with water.

My wife and I once bathed outdoors in a bathtub in Scotland. We heated water on a wood stove, poured it in the tub, and waited until it was cool enough to descend into. Above us, the sky grew crowded with hundreds of Scottish stars. (It was night.)

How silent and aware is the Scottish night sky!

Another necessity is soap. Soap is an infinitesimal part of bathing, but nevertheless a part. Over my years of bath mysticism, I have hazarded various choices: hippie oatmeal soap, brown Egyptian soap, the nostalgic and thrifty choice of Ivory. At the moment I use Dr. Bronner's Almond Soap, diluted nine to one. It foams, but does not sting.

Warmth is the key to bathing. True, there are cold baths—particularly in summer—but a cool bath is to a warm bath exactly as a cool soup is to a warm soup. (A cool soup is never humanely satisfying.) In fact, a bath is a kind of soup in which one's body is the main dish—the chicken in the chicken noodle soup, if you will.

It would be possible actually to bathe in soup—to be surrounded by chunks of parsley and potato. This would be healthful for the skin and pores, probably——however the sight might strike observers as mirthful.

Bathing, in fact, is extraordinarily beneficial. It relieves almost all diseases. The only disease it does not cure is a fever—and a fever is a kind of walking bath.

I don't believe we bathers are seeking the womb. Instead, I feel we are seeking a home. A bathtub is the smallest home, combining several of the the necessities of a house: a bed, a hearth, a sink. (Some may even say a toilet. For certain persons, let us admit, pee in the tub. I personally do not follow this practice, although I feel this is a question each person must decide for herself.) The only piece of a home missing is a roof.

While in the tub, I remember my dreams—but not their details. I recall the *sensations* in the dreams: the feeling that dinner is almost ready, the sense of meeting a new person I don't completely trust. These non-exact memories return to me. Being in water, a medium wherein most substances dissolve, exact truths dissolve, too. Only near-truths remain— with almost the same intensity they had in sleep. The bath world and the dream world have a similar agenda.

Even fingerprints change in a bathtub. They certainly soften.

You may allow your hand to rest on your genitals, as you bathe. I pursue the Middle Path in regards to masturbation. I neither truly masturbate, nor deliberately refrain from self-touching.

(So unvalued are baths in our culture that there is no word for "taking a bath," as there is for showering. The word "bathing" covers all types of personal cleansing. For this reason, I suggest the word "bathifying", which conveys some of the leisurely thoughtfulness of the bathtub. "Bathifying" resembles the word "edifying," meaning tending to educate or uplift. In the bulk of this essay, I will use "bathifying," and its related verb forms—"to bathify," "bathifies"—plus the noun "bathification.")

5/6

I drew a bath for myself, and Sylvia asked, "May I take your bath?"

"Yes, okay," I said. She has learned the allure of a full tub, I thought, pleased with the values I am imparting to her.

Sylvia stripped off her clothes.

One must take a bath naked (unless, of course, you wish to later hang your skirt, blouse and trousers out to dry—or throw them away!). Normally, nakedness is requisite.

The primary state, without social decoration—you remove your army helmet, your beatnik beret, your businessman's necktie, your Slovakian suspenders. The way a Buddhist monk shaves her head, you are shorn of your societal meaning. No longer a "Chaucer scholar" or "diesel mechanic" you're a big 6' 1" person with brown skin, or a girl with freckles. Like a dog without dogtags, you repose, looking down at your own intrinsic legs and upper abdomen, which you hide from your priest and landlord—and from your own mother. What is the big secret you are withholding from the scrutiny of your neighbors, and all policemen? Here it is, slightly bulging with relaxedness, looking quite the opposite of a mystery, open to your own ambivalent scrutiny.

"I am beautiful," you think, then "I am fat," and the two thoughts become confused together: "Fat am beauti-I-ful!"

5/9

I was in Manhattan two nights, and had no time to bathe. Now, back in Phoenicia, bathifying for the first time in three days, I recall with my skin and nerves the exact pleasure of warm—or even hot—water. You can forget this experience, like forgetting how it feels to be in Hebrew school.

Because this society is directed, for some reason, toward sex, smoking and food, we forget other primal satisfactions—napping, bathifying, wiggling one's head—which may be more noble, and more fun than a cheeseburger.

5/12

I bring down the rubber ducky (who sits on the rim of the tub) to experiment with sharing my tub. Immediately, the duck falls over on its side, gazing toward me with its penetrating black eyes, as if asking my help.

But I do not help. I allow this creature to float pathetically. How tedious are rubber ducks!

5/15

In the bathtub tonight, I have this sudden tactile intuition: I feel as if I am wearing a lace gown. The soft, yielding water rubs me somewhat like lace. For a man like me, who never wears a dress, a bath is the one place to feel silk-clad.

5/19

While bathifying, I began considering the concept of a miss. What is a miss? Suppose you are walking in the forest with a friend. She picks up a rock, throws it, and exclaims unhappily: "Oh! Missed!"

What did she miss? You cannot know, indeed. She chose a target, but her rock did not reach it.

There are two options, in the universe, if you throw a rock at a target: hit or miss. The target is "hit;" everything else is "miss." Mathematically, these may be noted as t (for "target") and ~t ("not t"). For the purpose of this computation, all of the world that is not the tree is united: the nation of China, Cher, all automobiles, the Pacific Ocean—all are within the category of "miss."

The inclusivity of "miss"—a near-universality—is the inverse of the exclusive "hit." How vast is "miss!" Almost as large as God! "Miss" is everything in all places, minus a single tree.

And the bathtub—in the whole world my lone tub—is my "hit" now (compared to the "miss" of the dry world outside).

5/20

Bathtubs to not exist in nature. Showers do. The word "shower", in fact, may refer to a rainstorm. Also a waterfall is a shower, of sorts. But a bathtub is a modification of a pond or lake. I noticed today that the faucet, when it's running, is just like a stream feeding a lake. But lakes are large, and ponds are also large (compared to a tub). Nature does not create a body of water the shape of a person, the same way nature does not create clothes.

5/23

In the bathtub, my last night dream returns vividly to me. I lived on Mars, in a colony. I was riding the subway home with a co-worker—a

42-year-old woman with close-cropped hair. In my seat, I was playing with small abstract figurines colored blue, yellow and red.

I held one up, and said, "This looks good with Mars in the background." (Through our subway window, we saw the dry landscape of Mars.)

My friend snickered.

5/26

My daughter Sylvia rarely bathes, but recently, red itchy welts have emerged on her back, so I am giving her baths daily. I can see she is learning the bathifying art. At first she had an anxious, "what-should-I-do?" look. But she has begun to lay back and float. (Because of her size, she can actually float in a bathtub.) And later, when she emerges, she is sparkling with limb-intelligence.

5/27

Today Sylvia complained of a pocket of cold water in her bath: "It's cold right here!"

Why don't I have pockets of cold in my bath?, I questioned. Later, when I took my day's bath, I noticed that I hunch my shoulders forward occasionally, sending small waves forward and back. I mix my tub's water, unconsciously! There is more than passivity to bathifying. A gestural stirring occurs.

5/29

Is it possible to pray in a bathtub? I pondered today while bathifying.

No, I decided. In a tub one cannot be pious. One may remember a joke one has forgotten, but one cannot pray.

(All right, maybe a *saint* can pray in a bathtub.)

6/2

Sylvia and I saw a snake in Lt. Rohmer Park, here in Phoenicia. We were walking home from her school. The snake moved towards us slowly, then must have noticed us (Saw our sandals? Heard our speech?) because she turned north, toward the stream, still moving slowly.

The entire time, she retained her rippling S shape. She was brown, with orangeish sides. And of course, she was faceless. True, she had eyes and an (invisible) mouth. But that is not a face. The snake is the most faceless animal. A stove has more of a face than a snake.

Now I am lying in the bathtub, and the water ripples—as if snakes were moving over me.

6/4

The bathtub is good for remembering names of old girlfriends. I once slept with a girl named Julie (at that time she was a girl—perhaps 19? Or 17?). She had no birth control, so I had to ejaculate outside her. Actually, she didn't care where I ejaculated.

In fact, there is a small chance she became pregnant. Somewhere a 26 year old man could be walking down a sidewalk in Florida, who is my son.

Or was her name Chris?

6/6

Until today, I never noticed that my arms float slightly in the tub. The rest of my body doesn't obviously float, but I think there is a slight upward pressure, particularly on my back.

The sense of being lifted upward is a hopeful sense—"buoyant" is a cheerful adjective, meaning "happy." Possibly the secret happiness of bathifying is its assurance that "something is lifting me up." It is a faith made tangible.

7/3

What is the role of the plug in the bathtub? I have spent several months contemplating this, while writing this journal. Without the plug (or some such stopper in the drain) there can be no bath, and thus no bathifying. But what does the plug represent, philosophically?

Today I realized: the plug is the ego. All of the world's water can merge together into one vast ocean; water does not distinguish separate entities. But a bath is separate. A bath is one tiny pool of water, alone and warm. A bath is individual, like the person inside it.

Lift the plug, and the water escapes, ultimately to mix with every other water on earth. Perhaps when we die, another plug is pulled, and the "life" within us merges with all life.

7/6

My friend Norman is staying at my house, and he takes a shower every morning. Tonight during bathification, I heard the shower drip. Lying back, I attempted to write (in my mind) the sound of the drip. I decided it was "pt." So the sound of the repeating drip is:

pt pt pt pt pt pt

Except one can hear—faintly—the drip descend, which makes a sound like "ooooo". So the whole sound is:

oooooopt ooooopt ooooopt ooooopt ooooopt ooooopt

MY MACHINES

This morning I met the man I talk to in the Astor Place subway stop. He lives there, and he's missing a tooth. Today his hair was wound around sticks.

"I heard you have a machine that writes down thoughts inside of people's minds," he said. "I heard Satan gave it to you."

"You think I'm Satan?" I asked of him.

"No, I know who Satan is," he said.

"Who?"

"My uncle is Satan."

"I have a computer," I said. "It writes down thoughts inside my mind. Then I make them into poems."

"You better be careful," he said. "If you do that kind of work, you have to see a doctor regularly."

"What kind of doctor?"

"A psychologist or a psychiatrist."

"I do see a psychologist."

"What's his name?"

"Dolores Murray."

"Dolores Murray," he repeated. I worried he might kill her.

"Is your computer a female?" he asked.

"My wife bought it."

"Then it's a female."

My friend George is in from LA this week, and he's been working on me to get a Macintosh computer. He used to try to convince me to read philosophy, now it's this. Actually, after midnight, coming back from the Second Street Bar, George told me a secret about his computer.

"I've been having trouble with my girlfriend, you know, and on the computer, I can make an image of her and have her say, 'Oh, George, you're right, I agree with everything you say.'"

In California, people want to interact with their machines. They hold a mouse in their hand, that moves the computer deeper and deeper into a world of cognition. Here in New York City, we write on our machines like typewriters. We don't want to marry them, we just want to type on them.

Towards answering machines we have much more affection. After all, answering machines have people inside them—our dearest friends. When I come home, and the small red light is blinking once for each call, I tear off my coat, and stand by the grey wooden stand, concentrated. Unfortunately, Gum, one of our cats, sits on the "record" button sometimes, and the voices are interrupted by long, awkward spells of cat-rustling and silence.

This reminds me, Violet and I made a collection of our best tapemachine messages, which is available from us for $2.50 (322 E. 11th St., #23, NYC 10003). They tell the story of our marriage and honeymoon. Perhaps in the future literature will entirely be replaced by answering machine messages. Even old books could be rewritten. *The Odyssey*, for example, could be expressed as a series of long distance phonecalls to Penelope.

The radio is my other love. Radio has lots of people inside it, speaking Yiddish, Spanish, Finnish, and other languages. The radio is a friend, but a false friend. The man on the radio, who seems to know you so well, cares nothing for you. If you moved to China, he would speak on. One day this thought came to me, mixed with fear, and I ceased listening to Howard Stern every morning.

The telephone is a reliable person, because it's one person at a time. The only problem is sometimes the guy on the other end is doing his income taxes or watching Championship Wrestling, and after you explain your whole theory on Harry Truman says, "Uh huh . . . what?"

I love all machines that have people inside. My computer only has me inside, so I love it less, but I need it, to explain what I'm thinking to other Americans.

If you have a small number of thoughts, you can buy a notebook, but if you think a lot of thoughts, you need a computer to put them on a big virtual roll, like paper towels.

The machines with people in them are the haloed ones. The other machines don't concern me, such as our can-opener, which we use to feed our cats. It has a rather threatening shape, as if you could perform a gall bladder operation with it.

One of the moving facts about tenement life is that other people's possessions are also yours. For example, the pinwheel. Our bathtub is in the kitchen, and you can't help looking out the window when you're inside. Across the courtyard, next to blue drapes with big white stars, was a silver pinwheel, leaning from the window. It often turned; that must be a windy channel. The pinwheel spun and light shot out of it in silver slivers. It spun like a ballerina, and though ballerinas bore me, this pinwheel did not. In a bathtub, summer or winter, it is a triumph to see anything spin. We never would've bought a pinwheel—it seems rather a luxury—but we had one for free, and it's the greatest machine: one that moves light, and can outlast its owner.

In Tibet they have prayer wheels; they recognize there is something solemn about spinning. In America nearly no one spins (except on the Alpine Whirl, at Six Flags Over Georgia).

As you can tell from all this past tense, the pinwheel has vanished. Violet wrote a poem for it, and read it in Tompkins Square Park yesterday. We think of it when we bathe, with regret. The pinwheel proved there are things we loved at age two that we still do.

THE BAD POETRY SEMINAR

There is a Bad Poetry Explosion, and you can
    be part of it.
Consider: right now there are creative writing
    classes in over 41,378 schools.
    And creative writing degrees are offered by
    1,119 colleges. More bad poetry
    is being written now than at any time in history.
Actually, I made up those figures. But that's
    part of the problem. One of the reasons
    no one writes good poetry anymore is that
    poets don't do painstaking research, the way
    they used to.
When Longfellow wrote "The Village Smithy", for
    example, he interviewed 19 village smithies,
    and spent two weeks living and working with a
    smithy in Lowell, Massachusetts, pretending to be
    his apprentice, though Longfellow was a 51 year
    old university professor at the time. Who's willing to
    do that now?
Actually I made that up, too. But we're not here to talk
    about me. We're here to talk about you, and your
    future as a bad poet.

But first, let us examine the philosophy of Bad Poetry.
Here it is:

1) All the great poems have been written.
    (When was the last time you remember a great poem
    being written?
    Has a great poem been written in your lifetime?
    No.
    This is proof that all the great poems have been written.)

2) "Most of the "good" poems have been written.

(If it's impossible to write a Great Poem, it must be very hard
    to write a Good Poem. That's just logical.
Think of all the people you know. How many of them have written
    a good poem?
And it's getting harder.
This is because the world is getting more unpoetic.
    How can you write a good poem about digital clocks, or
    about *Forrest Gump*? The only way to write a good
    poem is to stand by a stream and pretend you're still in
    the 19th Century. And most of those poems come out
    awful.)

3) The number of bad poems that can be written are
    infinite (or "nearly" infinite).
So let's get to work and write bad poetry.

THE HISTORY OF BAD POETRY

First let us consider the history of bad
    poetry.
Luckily, this history is not so long.
Originally, all poems were good.
For example, all the Icelandic epics are
    good. (*You* may not like them, but
    trust me, they're good.)
The *Vedas*, Homer, *Gilgamesh*, *The Bible*,
    The Egyptian Book Of The Dead are all
    good.

(It's *possible*, of course, that a lot of
    awful Icelandic epics were written and
    later forgotten, because they were so
    tedious, but I doubt it.
    Do you know how Sappho's poems
    survived? Because they were used
    to wrap mummies with, in Egypt.

That's why they exist in fragments,
because they were torn into *strips*,
to wrap the mummies with. My point
is that the fucking *mummies* were
wrapped in great poetry! Why? There
wasn't any bad poetry yet.)

Bad poetry was invented in 1810, in Dovershire,
        England, by Reginald Sporson,
        a curate and minor rugby coach.
        The first bad poem was "The Dawn Upon The
        Lily," which consisted of two short stanzas,
        the second far worse than the first.
        Sporson went on to write for 35 years,
        and birthed the first wave of bad poetry.
        By 1847, there were 119 bad poets
        writing in Great Britain.
        Bad poetry quickly emigrated to America,
        France, Portugal, Spain,
        Argentina, Norway, Nigeria, Turkey,
        Canada, Lebanon, Bolivia, Ghana and Mexico,
        in that order. The last place bad poetry reached was
        China (in 1894).

Bad poetry has a simple genesis: people
        who are not poets write poems. Before 1810,
        it never occurred to anyone who wasn't a poet
        to write a poem. People believed in the "Muse",
        a mysterious force that overtook the conscious mind,
        and forced it to write poetry. Reginald Sporson denied the
        existence of the Muse, and his theory has eventually taken hold:
        now *no one* (outside of Western Pakistan) believes in the Muse.
        Everyone thinks they can be a poet. That's why there is more
        bad poetry than ever before.
So join with us! Fuck the Muse! Every
        man a poetess! Every woman a poet!*

* Notice the non-sexist language.

Let us begin.

A Course Of Study

First, before we actually *write* bad poems, let us
engage in some study. How can we truly be
bad poets if we don't understand bad poetry, from the
inside out?

Luckily, I recently found a book in the garbage, *Poems For Memorizing: Grades One To Nine* (Houghton Mifflin, Boston, 1916), which is a treasure trove of bad poems.

For example:

October's Bright Blue Weather

O suns and skies and clouds of June,
  And flowers of June together,
Ye cannot rival for one hour
  October's bright blue weather.

When loud the bumble-bee makes haste,
  Belated, thriftless vagrant,
And golden-rod is dying fast,
  And lanes with grapes are fragrant;

When gentians roll their fringes tight
  To save them for the morning,
And chestnuts fall from satin burrs
  Without a sound of warning;

When on the ground red apples lie
  In piles like jewels shining,

And redder still on old stone walls
 Are leaves of woodbine twining;

When all the lovely wayside things
 Their white-winged seeds are sowing,
And in the fields, still green and fair,
 Late aftermaths are growing;

When springs run low, and on the brooks,
 In idle golden freighting,
Bright leaves sink noiseless in the hush
 Of woods for winter waiting;

When comrades seek sweet country haunts,
 By twos and twos together,
And count like misers hour by hour
 October's bright blue weather.

O suns and skies and flowers of June,
 Count all your boasts together,
Love loveth best of all the year
 October's bright blue weather.

©Helen Hunt Jackson

Notes to *October's Bright Blue Weather*

Let's begin with the title. What a wonderful, long collection of ugly sounds! The "b"s all bump into each other, and bumble along inexorably to the final word "weather," perhaps the most uninteresting word in the English language.

If the poem were called "October's Bright Blue Abortion" or even "October's Bright Blue Helicopter" you would expect a surprise, but a certain hopelessness sets in the moment one reads the word "weather."

Stanza 1

You expect her to move from June to some metaphor. What will she compare it to? What can "the suns and skies and clouds of June" rival? Then it hits you. Oh no! We're back to October's bright blue weather! The whole first stanza, in which the poet can charm you, dazzle you and invite you into her poem, is wasted on bringing us back to that awful title.

Then a horrible thought strikes - how many more times will she end stanzas with "October's bright blue weather"?

Most likely, one reasons, the poem will *end* with this dreary phrase.

Stanza 2

Here is a pretty tedious list of plant and insect activity. It's true that the line "Belated, thriftless vagrant", even if it doesn't mean anything, threatens to lift the poem to an eccentric, lyrical plane, but then the awful, literal rhyme "fragrant" for "vagrant" (they're almost the same *word*) pulls the poem back to mediocrity.

Stanza 3

Who knows what gentians rolling their fringes tight means? Let's hope that in 1916 everyone was aware of this phenomenon. You can see that the image of the gentians rolling their fringes tight and saving them for the next day really captivates Helen Hunt. (Though why *would* one save fringes for the next day? Isn't this one of those poetic metaphors that stupefies the mind, on examination?) And she is so desperate for her obligatory stupid rhyme, that she forgets that chestnuts do generally give a little sound of warning before they fall.

Stanza 4

Now she is even more desperate.
Line 1: Poetic inversion is always a sign of desperation.
(Poetic inversion means that instead of saying:

> When red apples lie on the ground

you say:

> When on the ground red apples lie.)

And where *are* we? Where is this poem located? One minute we're admiring apples in an orchard, the next we're contemplating "old stone walls." Are these *ruins?* Crumbling pasture walls? An Ivy League laboratory?

Stanza 5
Line 1: Why use the word "things"? It's unspecific, it's dull, it's not even a rhyme. Does she honestly think it's cute to say "lovely wayside things"? If so, she is sicker than I thought.
Line 2: You mean *every* "lovely wayside thing" has white-winged seeds? Or does "lovely wayside thing" refer to a specific species? Is there a particular plant that just happens to be named "thing"?
Line 4: Here is one of those great lines that only bad poets can write. "Late aftermaths are growing." That's priceless. (I am serious.) "Late aftermaths are growing." It's profound.

Stanza 6
This is a particularly worthless stanza, except for the awkward felicity of "idle golden freighting," and the way the meter goes to shit in the 3rd line.

Stanza 7
Line 1: Suddenly, there are *comrades* in the poem. And what *are* comrades? Drinking buddies? Hunters? Gay lovers? Revolutionary Marxists? Out of nowhere, the poem has *protagonists*, who presumably live in the city, and wish to visit the country.
Line 2: Oh, I see, she's comparing them to the animals in Noah's ark.
Line 3: I will ignore that crack about "misers."
Line 4: It is really unfair to *also* end the penultimate stanza "October's bright blue weather."

Stanza 8
I told you the poem would end "October's bright blue weather."

Writing Our Own Poems

Now let's try writing our own poems. Here are some suggested topics:
  Dogs And Their Lovely Barking Sounds
  Why I Enjoy Drinking Tea
  God: My Hope And Salvation
  The Many Uses Of Leather

Final Benediction

This is the Bad Poetry Generation!
        Let it rip!
        Let its mediocrity
        offend the librarians!
        Let its witless profanity
        embarrass the churchgoing!
        Let its saccharine sentiment
        nauseate the aesthetes!
        Let its sheer volume frighten
        everyone!

With our Sword of Bad Poetry we will rend the
        chains of earth!
With our mighty Bad Poem Cannon, we
        will blow a hole in history!
With our legions of Bad
        Poets, we will
        outnumber the Future!

Ending section:

Please send us a bad poem of your choice. Below are the requirements:
1) Length: It may be any length.
2) Topic: It may be on any topic.
3) Style: It may be in any style.

4) Language: It may be in any language.

5) Symbolism: It may use symbolism, or not. It's up to you.

6) Religion: It may refer to any religion.

7) Setting: It may be set in any nation or state
or on the sea, or undersea, or in space. Or on
other planets.

8) Assonance: You may use assonance or not, as you
choose.

9) Time of Writing: It may be written very slowly
or very quickly.

10) Person: It may be in the first, second
or third person. Or any other
person.

11) Misspelling: It may contain misspelling,
or not.

12) Margins: You may choose any
margins you like.

13) Emotions: The poem may contain
any emotions.

14) Stupidity: The poem can be very
stupid.

15) Good poems: Good poems are forbidden.
We will *not* read them!

MAKING BAD POETRY WORSE

We have succeeded in writing bad poetry, but we must not rest on our laurels. We must make our poetry worse.

But how can I do it?, I hear you ask. How can I degrade
my poetry even further?

Here are some hints, from a Bad Poetry Master:

1) Write extremely short poems. Almost every extremely short poem is awful. I have made a career establishing this fact.

For example:

A Food That I Enjoy

    Beans.

Ice Cream

    When I eat ice cream
    I feel awful.

Under The Ground

    Worms.

Who Reads The Paper?

    Old men.

Tuesday

    Tuesday is the
    dumbest day of the week.

2) Another similar method is to write haiku. Just about every haiku in English is a waste of time.
    For example:

        A butterfly has
        alighted on my red hat
        so I hold my breath.

    A June breeze ruffles
    the oak tree's leaves, as a thrush
    chatters, in another tree.

        The cat rubs against
        my leg, and says, "Arrnnn", but looks
        only at the floor.

3) Another plan for bad poetry: lists of anything.

In This Room

a blue bottle
a clear bottle

a chair with a white seat
a ladder
a stove
drums
6 plastic crates

4) Another idea for bad poetry is to just take the vowels out of
a poem:

 f sh ld d , th nk nly th s f m :
  Th t th r 's s m c rn r f f r gn f ld
 Th t s f r v r ngl nd. Th r sh ll b
  n th t r ch rth r ch r d st c nc l d;
 d st wh m ngl nd b r , sh p d, m d w r ,
  G v , nc , h r fl w rs t l v , h r w ys t r m,
 b dy f ngl nd's, br th ng ngl sh r,
  W sh d b th r v rs, bl st b s ns of h m .

 nd th nk, th s h rt, ll v l sh d w y,
  p ls n th t rn l m nd, n l ss
   G v s s m wh r b ck th th ghts b ngl nd g v n;
 H r s ghts nd s nds; dr ms h ppy s h r d y;
  nd l ght r, l rnt f fr nds; nd g ntl n ss,
   n h rts f p c , nd r n ngl sh h v n.*

* This was "The Soldier" by Rupert Brooke:

If I should die, think only this of me:
  That there's some corner of a foreign field
That is for ever England. There shall be
  In that rich earth a richer dust concealed;
A dust whom England bore, shaped, made aware,
  Gave, once, her flowers to love, her ways to roam,
A body of England's, breathing English air,
  Washed by the rivers, blest by suns of home.
And think, this heart, all evil shed away,

A pulse in the eternal mind, no less
  Gives somewhere back the thoughts by England given;
Her sights and sounds; dreams happy as her day;
  And laughter, learnt of friends; and gentleness,
    In hearts of peace, under an English heaven.

5) Poetry with only numbers is usually quite bad. For example:

Agony

```
4  0  0  7  0  9  0  2
1  8
1  8  6  0  4
4  9  2  1  1
8  0  7  1  2
1  1  2  4  9
9  0  6  7    0
8  1  9     4  1  2
1  1  0  8  0  9  0  7
6  4  3  3  3  0  8
1  2  1  4  7  7  6
7  0  8  0  3  0  4
1  4  7  1  8
6  2  1    0  4
1  1  6    7  1  2
```

6) One easy way to write a bad poem is to imitate Allen Ginsberg. Anyone who imitates Ginsberg is doomed to failure:

Mosquito

A Mosquito buzzed around me
as I bathed in tenement bathtub
June 3, 1964 A.D.,
looking down at soft white flesh and curling
pubic tendrils, gentle creature of

bathtub woe. I addressed the Mosquito:
"O insect of tickling
proboscis, you choose to extract my blood
as CIA extracts blood
of Laos Iran Vietnam Argentina
and I in innocent Eve-in-Garden
nakedness may only protest in human
words, as 3rd World peasants do daily!"

7) The last good epic was written by John Milton in 1613 (*Paradise Lost*). Since then, all epics have been awful. So a sure-fire way to write a bad poem is to write an epic. One virtue of this method is that you have a *lot* of bad poem:

from *Beltrune*

Beltrune The Warrior marched forth
into Tril, his steed beneath him, as the
Sun rose mightily in the Eastern Hills.
"Onword, Smor!" called Beltrune to his charger.
From the turrets of Tril, he was recognized
by the lone sentry, Abbator. "Beltrune, thou
has returned!" Abbator shouted. "It hath
been 4 years, I reckon, since last we
hath beheld thee!" "Aye," Beltrune nodded,
lifting the helmet from his large and
mane-like head, "4 years have crossed the
yonder horizon, since I mustered forth from
this castle, and began my latest
journey, to Thom." "Much hast thou
seen, I expect," Abbator mused, beholding
with glad eyes the long-awaited sight of the
Warrior Beltrune approaching the walled door of
Tril. "Indeed, much hath I seen," Beltrune replied,
his eyes filled with the light of dawn's glow.
"Perhaps I will tell thee some of it. Do you
care to hear?"

And so on.

8) Here is a new idea that came to me. If you write 2 poems at once, they will be twice as bad as 2 poems written separately. I wrote the following 2 poems as examples, in the following manner. First I wrote the titles:

> *The Firefly*   *Loneliness*

Then I wrote the first lines:

> *The Firefly*   *Loneliness*
> As   When

Then I wrote the second lines:

> *The Firefly*   *Loneliness*
> As   When
> the firefly   I am lonely

Then I wrote the third lines:

> *The Firefly*   *Loneliness*
> As   When
> the firefly   I am lonely
> sails through the night   my world

Then I wrote the fourth lines:

> *The Firefly*   *Loneliness*
> As   When
> the firefly   I am lonely
> sails through the night   my world
> no one knows   becomes

Then I wrote the fifth lines:

The Firefly	*Loneliness*
As	When
the firefly	I am lonely
sails through the night	my world
no one knows	becomes
it is there	like a grey

Then I wrote the sixth lines:

The Firefly	*Loneliness*
As	When
the firefly	I am lonely
sails through the night	my world
no one knows	becomes
it is there	like a grey
until	blanket

Then I wrote the seventh lines:

The Firefly	*Loneliness*
As	When
the firefly	I am lonely
sails through the night	my world
no one knows	becomes
it is there	like a grey
until	blanket
one sudden	covering

Then I wrote the eighth lines:

The Firefly	*Loneliness*
As	When
the firefly	I am lonely
sails through the night	my world
no one knows	becomes
it is there	like a grey

until
one sudden
illuminated

blanket
covering
everything.

Then I wrote one ninth line:

The Firefly
As
the firefly
sails through the night
no one knows
it is there
until
one sudden
illuminated
moment.

Loneliness
When
I am lonely
my world
becomes
like a grey
blanket
covering
everything.

When I showed these poems to my wife, she asked, "Did you write these?" They were so much worse than my ordinary bad poems, she didn't recognize them!

9) Since that worked so well, I decided to try writing a poem backwards, from the last line to the first.

First I wrote:

slowly.

Then I wrote:

slowly.
I fell

Then I wrote:

slowly.
I fell
the mountain.

Then I wrote:

> slowly.
> I fell
> the mountain.
> atop

Then I wrote:

> slowly.
> I fell
> the mountain.
> atop
> I stood

Then I wrote:

> slowly.
> I fell
> the mountain.
> atop
> I stood
> the vast panorama

Then I wrote:

> slowly.
> I fell
> the mountain.
> atop
> I stood
> the vast panorama
> viewing

Then I wrote:

> slowly.
> I fell
> the mountain.
> atop
> I stood
> the vast panorama
> viewing
> In ecstasy.

Then I wrote:

> slowly.
> I fell
> the mountain.
> atop
> I stood
> the vast panorama
> viewing
> In ecstasy
> It was autumn.

Then I wrote:

> slowly.
> I fell
> the mountain.
> atop
> I stood
> the vast panorama
> viewing
> In ecstasy
> It was autumn.
> with my mother.

Then I wrote:

> slowly.
> I fell
> the mountain.
> atop
> I stood
> the vast panorama
> viewing
> In ecstasy
> It was autumn.
> with my mother.
> alone

Then I wrote:

> slowly.
> I fell
> the mountain.
> atop
> I stood
> the vast panorama
> viewing
> In ecstasy
> It was autumn.
> with my mother.
> alone
> a mountain

Then I wrote:	Then I gave it a title:	Let's view it right side up:
slowly.	slowly.	*A Story*
I fell	I fell	
the mountain.	the mountain.	I climbed
atop	atop	a mountain
I stood	I stood	alone
the vast panorama	the vast panorama	with my mother.
viewing	viewing	It was autumn.
In ecstasy	In ecstasy	In ecstasy
It was autumn.	It was autumn.	viewing
with my mother.	with my mother.	the vast panorama
alone	alone	I stood
a mountain	a mountain	atop
I climbed	I climbed	the mountain.
	A Story	I fell
		slowly.

10) Another sure method to worsen your poetry is to talk about it constantly. Particularly use the phrase "the poem I'm working on right now . . ." As you bore the person you're speaking to, that boredom will seep into your poem. There is a Law Of Discussion in poetry:

How often you discuss your poetry X 6.419 = How bad your poem is*

*According to Cooper's Bad Poetry Index

12) Here is a final idea: rewrite good poems into bad poems. I started with this poem by Edna St. Vincent Millay:

God's World
O World I cannot hold thee close enough!
Thy winds, thy wide grey skies!
Thy mists that roll and rise!

Thy woods, this autumn day, that ache and sag
And all but cry with color! That gaunt crag
To crush! To lift the lean of that black bluff!
World, World, I cannot get thee close enough!

Long have I known a glory in it all,
 But never knew I this;
 Here such a passion is
As stretcheth me apart, Lord, I do fear
Thou'st made the world too beautiful this year;
My soul is all but out of me, let fall
No burning leaf; prithee, let no bird call.

I transformed it, thus:

This World

1 World, I can't get enough of you!
 Your overcast, 40% chance-of-rain skies,
 Your lovely smog that turns the sunsets red,
Your shopping malls, this autumn day, with their sales,
5   and exciting escalators!
World, world, I can't get enough of you!

I've known a long time that the world is great
 But I never felt such a thrill as I feel today.
 This world is too cool to believe.
10 I'm practically having an out-of-body experience
Just putting another video in my VCR!

Notes

Line 1 I'm trying to use the TV-ese phrase that most
closely translates Edna's thought.

Line 2 As a result of listening to 40,000 forecasts in our
lives, we now look at the sky and *see* the percent chance of rain.

Line 3 No one talks about "mist" anymore. Mist is obsolete.

Line 4 My research shows that a shopping mall now stands on the spot where Edna St. Vincent Millay's woods once stood.

Line 7 I continue approaching this poem as if it were being narrated by a guest on the Jay Leno Show.

Line 10 It is interesting how scientific the world has become since 1904. Not only has the sky become scientific, but mystical transport now has a psychological term. This is one of the reasons all contemporary poetry sucks.

Line 11 No one really listens to birds anymore. Videotapes have replaced birds.

~Proverbs~

Every cross means the same thing.

•

Disappointment steadies the hand.

•

Geishas can't be impeached.

•

God goes to sleep with the rich and
wakes with the poor.

•

Defeat is gradual.

•

The French don't form posses.

•

Breathing makes one beautiful.

•

Toilets never meet.

•

With true prayer comes motion sickness.

•

Dogs are wolves without ideals.

•

Wit is the last virtue to go.

•

Even science has hymns.

•

A secret weapon cannot be used.

•

Peanut butter eats ants.

•

Lock the door so your furniture won't escape.

Ten can walk as fast as one.

•

Alphabet soup is the greatest teacher.

•

Even a snake can wear spats.

•

Life slowly removes one's appetite.

•

A seed escapes by standing still.

•

Man is the only animal that fears children.

•

Two heads are bigger than one.

•

The Queen was once a teenager.

•

Everyone knows where you part your hair.

•

Half a clock doesn't tell half the time.

•

All abortions are brothers.

•

A bottle sinks without a cork.

•

Flatulence can replace conversation.

•

Elephants go through mosquito nets.

•

Cardinals can't show boredom.

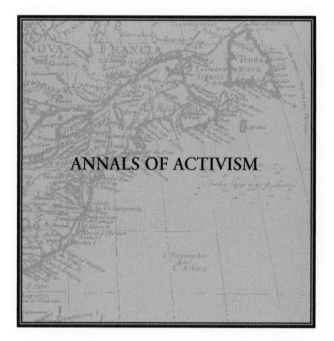

ANNALS OF ACTIVISM

A VISIT TO WASHINGTON

"They called off the inauguration. There's no parade," my mother told me Sunday night. She'd been watching TV.

"What about the protest?" I asked.

"They didn't say."

I called the All-Peoples Congress; there was a recording. "Come protest the inauguration of President Reagan," said a voice with a Queens accent. "Call the office for further details." But that *was* the office!

I sat bolt upright at 4:30 A.M. Too bad. I was hoping to oversleep. I put on two pairs of long underwear, two pairs of socks and drank a cup of sage tea. The moment I stopped outside the tea froze to my moustache.

Dyckman Street looked like a press conference for George McGovern. One other tank-like man steered toward the subway.

The A came right away. Something wanted me in Washington.

Ahead of me, a woman tapped a cane down 21st Street. I recognized her from a Union Carbide demonstration.

"Do you need some help?"

"Sure," she said. "Are we late? I didn't want to take off my gloves to find out the time."

"We're just right. You can hear the busses, I guess."

"Yes."

Inside the lobby of 19 West 21st St., ten people shivered and conversed. A woman in a wheelchair greeted the blind woman gaily: "They cancelled the parade, so *we're* going to march down Pennsylvania Avenue!"

We loaded onto the buses and drove through a city of cold, where the only light came from boutique windows and "Don't Walk" signs.

A man in a white sweater reclined in Tiffany's Restaurant and I wondered how his life had brought him there.

The remainder of the trip was woods, snow and sleep, until the bus stopped and two Hunter College women in the back started singing "Walking In A Winter Wonderland." We'd reached our rest area.

Life in America is strange. You start out to protest the President and end up in a fast food restaurant where machines try to sell you little plastic statues of dogs that smoke cigarettes. If only you could protest *that*.

Then we drove off to demonstrate against a parade that didn't exist.

It struck me last fall there would have been little reaction if they'd cancelled the election. The polls had all agreed, after all. (And the polls had been right.) Now they'd cancelled the Inauguration, and no one said a word. Of course, it's a different thing.

Still, I wish it didn't remind me of 1984. I want to be rid of that year. I was so happy when it was over, and now the movie is out. With a dead man as the star.

I took out my paper and crayon and made a sign: "WHO FREEZES TO DEATH IN U.S.A.?"

The narrow brick buildings of Washington appeared in the window. Then the drugstores of downtown. Then the empty reviewing stands of Pennsylvania Avenue. Then we were out there ourselves, in the 2°F.

"We're here to greet the chief," a black woman smiled.

Seventy of us walked in a circle and shouted to no one: "Money for jobs, not for war! U.S. out of El Salvador!"

A row of police cars watched from across the street.

And the wheelchair woman's laugh, as she smoked a cigarette— more precious than pearls!

Then the rest of the demonstrators appeared down the avenue, like the Cavalry, yellow banners streaming, chanting in an African rhythm:

> We're gonna
> beat BACK
> the Reagan ATTACK
>
> We're gonna
> beat beat BACK
> the Reagan
> ATTACK.

And we filled the empty $1 million reviewing stands, 700 of us, stamping our feet and waving our flags in the cold.

"Someone asked me why we're here if they cancelled the inauguration," a woman shouted into a megaphone. "And I told him they didn't cancel unemployment, they didn't cancel budget cuts, they didn't cancel support for the apartheid regime in South Africa, they didn't cancel plans to invade Nicaragua. We've got to show more determination than they do. That's why we're here and they're not!"

We applauded with our feet; the bleachers shook.

That night I watched the TV news. They showed the reviewing stands, empty. We had become unpersons at an undemonstration. We had been written out of history.

And two people had frozen to death in New York City.

MY CAMPAIGN DIARY

Today the first article on my presidential campaign came out in the *New York Press*, a local free newspaper:

> Sparrow, the East Village poet and wiseacre, has announced his candidacy for president and has been advertising for a vice presidential running mate. He promises he'd be "a president with balls, and even better, a president with a *dick*."
>
> To apply for the v.p. slot (include photo) write to 322 E. 11th st., Apt. 23, NYC 10003.

It was particularly gratifying in its resemblance to a personal ad.

THE PRESIDENCY

Benjamin Harrison said,
"The presidency tastes
like shrimp; a delicate
gray taste."

Ulysses Grant said,
"The presidency is like
working in a laundry;
it's hot and everyone swears."

While John Quincy Adams
compared it to an elderly woman:
"For me, it was one
long feebleness."

My campaign manager, Hal Sirowitz, and I campaigned yesterday, for the first time, at St. Mark's Place and Second Avenue—the center of the East Village. We brought along a questionnaire, to gauge the electorate:

1) Why do you think Sparrow is the best candidate for president?
2) Why is Sparrow so virtuous?
3) Do you like doing the dishes?

Immediately, two homeless men asked if I'd let them sell things on the street if I were president. Hal said yes.

"Well," I added, "I don't like people selling stolen property. And sometimes peddlers block the sidewalk."

God, I thought, *I'm starting to sound like a politician.*

We administered our questionnaire to them. To the third question, the homeless men gave touching answers. "Yes, if I get something to eat," the first one said. "But if I'm hungry, no, I don't like to do dishes."

The second one said simply (with a mysterious smile), "Yes, I love it. It does something to my hands."

The dishwashing question elicited many domestic confessions. A fortyish man named Ed said, "I never do them, except on pain of divorce," but it turned out he *was* getting a divorce.

"Because of the dishes?" I asked.

"That and several hundred other things."

A musician covered with tattoos said, "No, I hate doing them. That's why I'm married ten and a half years."

A graying man with a beard admitted, "It's the primary cause of marital difficulties in my home. We never argue about money and sex. We argue only about dishes."

I received many flattering comments in answer to the first question ("Why do you think Sparrow is the best candidate for president?"):

"He's cool enough to be standing on a street corner."

"He's *real.*"

"He's not associated with the CIA."

The answers to the second question ("Why is Sparrow so virtuous?") were a bit more vague:

"His haircut."

"He was brought up well."

"I have no idea."

Mostly I tried to hand out small books of my poems, while Hal shouted, "Here he is! A living presidential candidate! You don't have to turn on the television set to see him! You can save energy!"

We met a Dan Rather Conspiracy Theorist, who believes Rather's famous interview with George Bush during the 1988 campaign—where Bush stood up manfully to him—had been rehearsed.

•

Presidents do not eat well. They eat at banquets, where the brussels sprouts arrive deflated, in inauspicious white sauce. (This is because the best chefs cannot pass the loyalty test—they have all had some Communist dalliance—so the White House must hire mediocre, patriotic cooks.)

The President's dogs eat well, though.

Presidents also dress poorly. Come to think of it, their clothing, too, lacks piquancy. As one can't imagine a president eating curry, one can't picture him in a flowered vest.

The White House itself is dowdy, like a big antique shop. Every First Lady—or every *other* First Lady—attempts to redecorate it, but it remains Early American Ugly, to use a phrase of my parents.

Friends, too, are lacking in the White House. A president never has a best friend. (Nixon *thought* he had a best friend.) Presidents have advisors, who are smart but cruel—the sort of people who managed Elvis.

Also, for some reason, presidents are forbidden to wear hats. Lincoln did, but he was the tallest president and wore the tallest hat, so he was an exception. JFK wore a hat *once,* but after his inauguration went hatless. Along with friends, spicy food, and silly clothes, one loses, as chief executive, the right to wear a hat.

One might compile a portrait of the anti-president: she is a black woman in a floppy hat, eating lamb curry among numerous friends in a small but tastefully decorated house.

This we have denied ourselves in the presidency. Let us cough in shame.

•

As I write this, my baby is being born. My wife is in the first stage of labor; at the moment, yawning on the toilet.

This baby (as yet unnamed) is the animus of my campaign. This presidential race is my rehearsal for being a father.

POEM

The baby my wife had yesterday, Sylvia Mae,
 is suckling at her breast, as it rains,
on a Friday.
Sylvia is already at work—she
must pee on all of our feather pillows
and challenge us to remember,
if we ever knew, how to
clean a feather pillow. And she shits
deep black shits she has saved since the
Persian Gulf War, inside Violet's womb.
Oh, Sylvia, I am still running for president,
don't fear; I will fashion a world for you
where dogs wander humorously into rooms, and are
invited into every conversation,
where the opera is finally conducted honestly
— no diva upstages another —
and newspapers have short
stories, as they did in 1961,
stories which help one understand the life of
Palestinians and the beauty of Islam.
Sylvia, together we will make a world where silence
is loved, where doormen need not cringe,
where something greater than a rainbow comes —
something with more than seven colors.

•

Hal and I went campaigning again. Soon after we reached our corner, Havok stopped by. Havok is a young man who, after knowing me thirty seconds, looked me in the eye and said with a wild smile, "You can do it. You can really be president." He asked how one gets on the ballot.

"It's real hard," Hal said. "You have to get thousands of signatures, and they have to be checked out by the Board of Elections, because everyone has to be a registered voter."

"I can do it," he said. "I go to a lot of parties. I can get everyone to sign."

He was the first to sign our petition:

> We, the undersigned, support replacing the
> stripes on the American flag with sine waves,
> as well as lowering the price of milk and
> unbuttoning the vice-president's shirt.

He wrote, under Comments, "You have my unconditional support."

"Do you mind if I campaign for you?" Havok asked.

"No. Go ahead."

"This man is the next president of the United States!" he shouted to passers-by. "He will be the first honest president!"

"How do you know I'm honest?" I asked.

"I can tell by looking at you," he said. "By your beard."

After a while he said, "I have to go and study." I didn't have the nerve to ask what he studied. "But get me those petitions and I'll fill them out," he said, sincerely.

He paused a moment. "When you become president, can I have a position in your administration?" he asked.

"Sure. A very high position."

I began to worry when his giddy smile returned.

"Are you a good person?" I asked him.

"Of course. Sure," he said. And left.

Soon after, a policeman told us to leave the corner. "You can only stand on a street corner ten minutes," he explained. "Otherwise, it's loitering."

"But the first amendment gives us freedom of assembly," I pointed out.

"Yeah, but after ten minutes you have to move to a new corner."

This is the New World Order Constitution, I suppose.

We moved to the opposite corner, next to a Gap clothing store, where we met an artist and her boyfriend. "I got your leaflet last week and I really liked it," she said. "I showed it to all my friends."

They read our petition. The boyfriend disagreed with the part

about unbuttoning the vice-president's shirt. "What if he doesn't
to unbutton his shirt?" he said.

"We're not forcing him to do it," I pointed out. "We just *support* it."

"Maybe he'd be able to breathe more freely," his girlfriend suggested.

"He does seem awfully buttoned-up," I agreed.

Finally, the boyfriend found a way to endorse the petition. "I'll
write that they should *add* buttons to the vice-president's shirt, so that
he can unbutton them and still have the same number of buttons he
started with." He wrote "ADD BUTTONS TO VICE PRES. SHIRT"
next to his signature.

By then, we had spent ten minutes on the Gap corner, and could
return to our original corner.

"I refuse to be intimidated by anyone, except the police!" I shouted as we returned. The new policeman on the corner smiled.

•

After our outing, Hal and I retired to San Loco, the city's cheapest taco
stand, to discuss strategy.

Hal mentioned that he's planning to vote for me for president.

"Really?" I said.

"Well, I figure it would be hypocritical for me to campaign for you
and not vote for you."

"No, I just say I'm *running*. I think people should vote for the
Democrat, to defeat Bush."

Hal agreed that in a close election he would vote for the Democrat.

I wonder if I'm the first presidential candidate who doesn't want
anyone to vote for him.

It's discouraging to think that the Age of Great Presidents is over.
The national memorials are for the Ancient Ones: the Washington
Monument, the Lincoln Memorial, the Jefferson Memorial.

A Harding Memorial sounds ridiculous, though not a Harding
Memorial High School. Recently dead presidents become high
schools—where they are vaguely resented—rather than dollar bills, for
which all men yearn.

The best they can do is to become a four-cent stamp.

No matter how great I am as prez, I'll never have a shrine, or a five dollar bill. Alexander Hamilton's on a major bill and he wasn't even president! Not only that, but he died in a *duel!*

•

We took a survey—our first scientific study of the American people. Here are the results:

1) I support the policies of George Bush.
Yes: 0%   No: 86%   Maybe: 14%
2) I often eat clams:
Yes: 28%   No: 58%   Sometimes: 14%
3) I support Sparrow for President.
Yes: 38%   Hell No: 12%   Maybe: 50%
4) I live near trees
Yes: 63%   No: 25%   Maybe: 12%
5) More people should listen to Tony Bennett.
Yes: 0%   No: 28%   Maybe: 58%   Why Not: 14%

This was a particularly valid survey because it included people from Atlanta and Yellow Springs, Ohio. (There was a sample of eight.)

"I refuse to take campaign contributions, no matter how small!" I shouted.

•

There's a man in prison I've corresponded with since 1978. He's doing a seventeen-year sentence in Virginia for murder.

In the last six months, he's been allowed to make phone calls. Yesterday, he told me he's promoting my presidential campaign among the prisoners of Virginia. "You're gonna have prisoners all over voting for you," he said.

The thought of a wave of prisoners supporting my candidacy filled me with hope.

"What is your program?" he asked, as an afterthought.

"I don't really know. It's all in my poems," I said.

"You're a really special person," he said.

•

I feel, deep down, that if I write the best poems, I will become president.

ATLAS

Atlas held up the world, in ancient times,
and on this continent, a turtle was
believed to carry the earth. Now we know
the earth stands unsupported in infinity.
Why believe, then, that a president is
needed to support our nation?
We fear this final break with history.
Julius Caesar, Charlemagne,
Chief Sitting Bull—we need a *name*
to place our nation under. Someone must
sign the checks, we believe. And that will
be me. I will sign the checks,
I will pretend to support America, though America
floats in a universe of emptiness.
I will be the phony Atlas whose
rippling muscles convince children they
are safe. A president
is like Santa Claus—past a certain
age one no longer believes in him, then
suddenly, one becomes him.

•

Yesterday, Bush collapsed in his own vomit at a banquet in Tokyo, while begging for economic support.

•

No one realizes that America's decline can be a boon. A civilization's autumn can have the same virtues as retirement. It's a time to relearn chess, to listen to Dixieland jazz. I'd be the perfect president of a declining America, as I've been in retirement since 1973, when I flunked out of Cornell.

I fill each day with an array of personal whims. I stock the bird feeder, visit lobbies of famous hotels, read *New Yorkers* I find in the garbage, call my friend Sheila.

I spend three dollars a day, and my life is plentiful.

I can teach this to America.

•

All this talk of the United States increasing its productivity is wrong. We should do less, not more. Our goal should be to have enough time to make birthday cards for each other.

Bush, with his relentless quest for the Win, is the worst possible leader for us.

We need someone like me, who has developed the art of losing.

Of course, I'll lose this election, too.

•

I told Hal about the disturbing op-ed piece I read in *The New York Times* yesterday. A television producer received a summons because she'd thrown a letter into a public wastebasket. (In small print on every NYC wastebasket is a sign: NO HOUSEHOLD OR BUSINESS TRASH.) She had been walking down the street, reading her mail, and dropped the envelope in the trash.

A public organization—the Sanitation Police—sifts through trash cans and issues summonses for 45 dollars to names they find on envelopes. "We must oppose this practice!" I told Hal. "We'll make it part of our campaign!"

•

Then we went out, with two posters—OUR PRESIDENT IS VOMITING IN ASIA and AMERICANS NEED AMERICAN VOMIT—and a petition:

> We, the undersigned, feel our president is vomiting in Asia when he should be vomiting on the American people. Bring the president's vomit home! And we support Sparrow for prez!

On St. Mark's Place, a woman with long gray hair signed her name "Jo Mama" and told us, "You should call CBS News. You could be famous."

"Really? It doesn't seem like a good enough idea," I said.

"It is. You just need larger signs."

She herself had been briefly famous, in 1967—having appeared on the cover of *Look* magazine and on "What's My Line?"— for being a body painter at the Electric Circus, the first hippie nightclub in New York.

"I liked it," she said, of fame. "I had a lot of fun with it."

Just then, she called to a passing friend, "Hey, Mark, come sign this petition!"

He was a tall, unshaven man, reading *History And Utopia.*

I explained that I was running for president, and read him the petition.

"I don't want the president vomiting on me!" he replied. "Is that your whole platform?"

"No, I have another plank. I'm against the Sanitation Police." I explained the op-ed piece in the *Times.*

"So, you're kind of a libertarian?" he inferred.

"Wait!" I said. "I have another issue. Do you realize September, October, November, and December are all misnamed? September isn't the seventh month, October isn't the eighth month, November isn't the ninth month, and December isn't the tenth month!"

"But isn't there a kind of poetic license?…" he suggested.

"And July and August are named for two fascists, Julius and Augustus! And do you know what April means?"

"No," he said.

"It means 'next.' It's the next month after March! All our months are named for emperors, worthless Roman gods, inaccurate numbers, or the word 'next'! The French Revolution tried to change the names of the months!"

"And look what happened to them!" he said.

"They didn't go far enough!" I rebutted.

"That's right," Hal agreed.

Still, he wouldn't sign.

After he left, Jo Mama told us, "That man writes the ethics column for *E—— Magazine.*" (I am forbidden to mention that name here.)

Hal and I continued to shout.

"There's a balance-of-vomit deficit!" I explained. "We're throwing up on the Japanese, but they're not throwing up on us!"

We filled our petition (eight names), and left.

•

When Violet and I were married, my friend Claude gave us a bird feeder. I put it on the fire escape, and birds come daily. First, a family of finches came, but the sparrows drove them out, and now it's a spa for sparrows, with an occasional mourning dove.

For fifty cents a week, I support scores of birds. I am their Welfare State.

I protect them from an aggressor, too—our cat, Gum, who crouches by the window, hoping to eat them. I am their Department of Defense.

As I contemplate my nation—I, the president of sparrows—I confess I dislike my people. I find sparrows boring and nervous. They seem motivated entirely by gluttony and the worst kind of hustling sociality. The noble mourning doves, on the other hand, sit quietly on the railing, as if they read Shakespeare.

So I am no better than my political enemies. I'm a lover of the elite, a despiser of the Common Bird.

What I hate most about sparrows, of course, is that I share their name.

FISTS

My infant, Sylvia, is
learning to raise her fist,
thrust it toward the
light, and smile.
Thus we must all do.
We must raise our fists,
thrust them toward the light,
stare at them, and smile.
We must feel, as a nation,
there is power in our hands.

In a fist one may
hold a dime, or a note with the
words "I love you, Violet" —
but a fist can't hold a novel.

If we could see our fists, and
others', upraised, in the light,
we might
lose our fear. A fist can't
hold a gun. A fist can hold a
candy, or a slice of tangerine.

I am the first presidential
contender to raise his fist,
smile, and like Sylvia,
place it in my mouth.

STAND UP TO NATURE: A RALLY

Allow me to begin by reading a small article from the Saturday, June 5, 1994 *New York Times*, "Marlin Pulls Man in Sea":

> MOREHEAD CITY, N.C.., June 17 (AP)—A crewman on a sport fishing boat was missing today after being pulled overboard into the Atlantic Ocean while trying to haul in a blue marlin during a fishing tournament. Coast Guard and Navy ships searched through the night for Chris Bowie, 41, of Ocean City, Md., who went overboard about 11 A.M. on Thursday 60 miles off the coast. He was not wearing a life jacket. Blue marlin, which can weigh more than 1,000 pounds and reach 14 feet, are known as ferocious fighters.

Normally one reads a story like this and shrugs. "So what? The guy must've been stupid," one thinks. "What kind of idiot goes marlin fishing to begin with?" Or one is momentarily diverted by the image of a man skimming though the waters off North Carolina shouting: "Whoa! Let me off! I can't swim!"—but this is no joke. This is a deadly form of waterskiing, the last waterski ride Chris Bowie will ever take, and I'm afraid we will not find his body until two years from now, when, swollen with the gases of decay, his bloated corpse bobs up into the sunlight of a September day near Cape Hatteras.

Do you know how many people drown a year throughout the world? Over 41,000! Do you know how many die in quicksand? At least 48. Do you know how many die in typhoons? At least two million. Do you know how many die in earthquakes? Up to six million.

You can check these figures yourself. I'm sure you'll find different ones. The point is that 50,000 people perish a year on the roads of America, and an organization of angry women, Mothers Against Drunk Driving, has mobilized against this—while throughout the world, over sixty-one million people a year are murdered by Nature, and no one says a word. How about Mothers Against Drunk Nature?* Nature is out of control, drunk with destruction, and no one speaks.

Until now. Today, for the first time in history, a group of concerned humans has come together to stop Nature in its tracks.

Do we accept Nature's abuse?

I say no.

Will we allow ourselves be pulled out to sea by marlins?

I say no.

Are we spineless Nature-victims?

I say no.

Will we accept quicksand and volcanoes as some inevitable punishment for our misdeeds?

I say no.

Allow me a brief moment of Marxist analysis. I agree that humanity has been cruel to nature, that acid rain, the ozone hole, and nuclear waste are evils. And I believe someone should suffer for these evils. But who perpetrated these disasters? Not me, not you. We have no beef against the earth. I haven't eaten a chicken since 1971! If Nature wants retribution for humanity's evils, let it create tornadoes in the board room at Exxon! Let a volcano sprout up in the office of the CEO of Dow Chemical! They are the ones who deserve punishment. But this bullshit of pulling some North Carolinian fisherman out to sea because Con Edison spews monosulfate hydroxylate has to end.

Nature, stop blaming the victims!

If you must kill, have better aim!

Nature, murder is not funny!

Nature, stop the shit!

Nature, firebomb Exxon, not us!

Introductions:

And now I give you one of Nature's most implacable foes, Jessica Chalmers.

I give you a man who hates Nature so passionately he often feeds the squirrels in Union Square Park, then insults them: Jim Nachlin.

And now, someone who thinks even sunsets are ugly: Yuko Otomo.

They say Nature abhors a vacuum; I give you Lawrence Fishberg and James Braly.

And now, someone who hates even human nature: Susan Scutti.

Here is a poet who can commonly be seen shouting to the birds outside his window, "Shut up!": Steve Dalachinsky.

Now I present someone so unnatural she doesn't even shit: Marcella Harb.

Here is a poet who hates Nature so intensely that he has visited Mt. Rushmore 16 times: Alfred Vitale.

I give you someone who refuses even to watch Nature shows on TV: Joe Maynard.

Here is someone who is allergic to every plant in the Catskills: Brendan Lorber.

Here is someone who believes Nature should be utterly abolished (I must caution you that this is the extreme wing of our movement): Jim Feast.

[At the end]
Let me end with a small anecdote. As I began to organize this event, I

called a friend of mine. In order to protect her identity, I will call her Kate Hunter.

"I'm demonstrating against Nature," I said.

"Aren't you afraid?" she replied. "What if Nature takes revenge?" You know, a lot of people think this way. But the fine, brave people who read here tonight, and the finer, braver people who dared the elements to come here tonight do not agree.

You see a wrong and you right it. You see an injustice and you rush to ameliorate it. And for that I must humbly applaud you.
[Speaker applauds.]

* The acronym is MADN.

[This rally was held at Gallery 12, 141 Avenue B on June 6, 1994.]

A LETTER TO THE PRESIDENT

Mr. Clinton,

You're not aware of this, but you and I both ran for President last year. In fact I ran longer than you did. When I entered the race, only Paul Tsongas was running. George Bush wasn't even running.

I campaigned fifteen months; you campaigned thirteen months. You received forty-five million votes; I received none. Obviously, you were a more effective campaigner than I.

You articulated a clear message to America: you would create jobs, fight crime, cut the military, etc. The few promises I made were surreal: I would rename the months, take dead men off of postage stamps, make subways quieter. Mostly I stood on street corners and shouted whatever came into my mind: "I refuse to be a lawn ornament!", for example.

And I made my own hours. While you spent fifteen hour days stumping, I spent an hour every other week.

Also, I didn't *want* to win. One morning I sat up suddenly in bed, struck with the terror that I might be elected.

Now that the campaign's over, I have returned to more private concerns. I fixed my bookshelf, which had been sloping for the last year and a half, by placing an empty jar of Hellmann's Mayonnaise on the bottom shelf. I bought a new fixture for the bathroom light, so I can pull a string, rather than have to stand on the toilet and screw the lightbulb in.

I must admit I get a twinge when I read an interview with Havel, the avant-garde playwright who become President of Czechoslovakia. "A poet *can* be President," I think.

"I would have been a great Prez. I would have baked donuts, and handed them out on the street. I would have sung my entire State of the Union message, dressed as a Viking. I would have visited morgues and shaken hands with the dead."

Lincoln, our one magnificent president, had an artist's mind. He was also the funniest President.

"No matter how much cats fight, there always seem to be plenty of kittens," he said.

George Bush, our most inartistic President, made the whole nation tone-deaf. Under his Presidency, popular music got worse than it's been for centuries.

At least *you* play the saxophone, which is a first in history. The problem is the *way* you play it. Probably the greatest service you could do for America is to practice the saxophone.

You and I met once. Perhaps you don't remember. You were walking down 86th Street, shaking hands with multitudes of people, on your way to buy a book at the Barnes & Noble bookstore. This was a photo opportunity, part of the New York Primary. I shook your hand, then watched you shake other people's hands. I looked into your eyes, so close to mine, and tried to think of something to say.

I considered telling you, "I'm running for President, too!", but I imagined your condescending response—"Good luck!"—and couldn't bear it.

Later, while you were inside the store, I gave fliers to two of your assistants; perhaps you remember them. They contained this poem:

AIDS
AIDS, AIDS, AIDS, AIDS, AIDS, AIDS, AIDS,
Who shall cure thee? I shall cure thee. When
I am President of the United States of America,
I shall erect a laboratory in the basement of the
White House, and, wearing a white coat, I shall raise
Beakers to the light, filled with
Blood, and expose them to gamma rays, all night.
As dawn climbs manfully over the
City of Washington, I'll throw myself into a cot,
My hair in disarray, and sleep.
Each night I shall labor thus, and each day I shall
Return to the humdrum life of President. Then,
In my third year, as I am
Delivering my State of the Union message,
The answer will come. I
Will thrust down my speech

And run from the Halls of Congress, in the middle
Of a sentence. The next day, a stunned nation will see
Me, on nationwide TV, unshaven, circles under my
Eyes, holding a test tube. "Eureka!" I will shout,
AIDS will end, and men and women that night
Will have loud, groaning sex, all over America.

You seemed swamped and lost, on 86th Street. The look on your face was almost one of addiction. You seemed to be asking yourself: "Why do I enjoy shaking hands so much?"

The American system chooses the candidate who most wants to be President. The Parliamentary system elects the most qualified candidate; the American system elects the most ambitious one.

Now that you have succeeded in your goal, you must feel awful. (Your public statements give a hint of this.) Instead of receiving a prize, you have won the most back-breaking job on earth.

It's exactly like chasing a woman. Once you get her, you must live with her, which is more difficult than driving a taxi.

Last Wednesday I walked out of my building to see a crowd of people across the street, looking up. I asked a guy in a black leather jacket what was happening.

"There's a man on the roof," he said. "You can see him." He pointed.

A man was standing on the edge of the roof in a green Army jacket. His back was to us, and his shoulders were hunched. I couldn't tell if he was black or white. Only the tips of his toes were on the roof; the majority of his feet were suspended in midair. He looked impossible, like a cartoon character.

It gave me a strange comfort that he was on my neighbor's roof, not mine.

After a few minutes, police pushed the crowd away. "If he sees a lot of people, he might jump," they said.

We dispersed. I was struck by the look of concern on people's faces. In one famous incident in the sixties, a crowd chanted for a man to jump. No one here wanted the man to die.

The rest of the day, the picture of the man on the roof wouldn't leave my mind. America is on top of a roof, I began to think. A nation can die, even if all its inhabitants don't perish. Babylon is gone; ancient Rome is no more. A nation dies, then another nation pours into it, and people say it was conquered. America may become like ancient Israel. Its inhabitants may wander the earth for centuries, wishing for a home.

Mr. Clinton, you are famous as a nonstop talker, but you actually prefer to listen. This is revealed in your choice of a wife, and a Vice-President. Even your sax playing is more a tribute to men you've listened to than to your own talents.

You are young (for a President), smart (for a President) and brave. It is a miracle you were elected, a miracle you largely engineered yourself. If reform can save American capitalism, you can do it.

I wish you luck, for the sake of myself, my baby, and the millions who are under the heel of this nation.

Love,
Sparrow

P.S. Last Wednesday night, I came home and a cop was in front of my house, flirting with a blonde.

"Did the man jump?" I asked.

"No, he didn't," the cop said.

"That's good news," I said.

"Yeah, it *is*," the cop said, as if that hadn't occurred to him.

MEET THE BEATS

I went to the Beat Exhibit at the Whitney to protest it. My friends, The Unbearables, had called a protest on the second day of the exhibition—the first free night. (The Unbearables are a group of writers who give long, democratic readings and protest Wrongs. So far we have protested the poetry in *The New Yorker*, the Kerouac Conference at N.Y.U., and this.)

I wasn't sure what to protest *about* "Beat Culture And The New America: 1950-1965" until I ran into Mike Tyler at the Nuyorican Cafe.

"Did you see the ad in *Paper*?" he asked. "AT&T is sponsoring that exhibit."

I went to my local Gujarati newsstand, and there was the ad in *Paper*, showing a collage of the Beats, the famous bell logo, and announcing: "Communication. Whether it's poetry, jazz, or your Grandmother calling you for Christmas, we're involved. AT&T." Or something like that.

So I wrote this flier, and mimeographed it at the St. Marks Church:

> We would like to thank AT&T for generously supporting the Beat exhibit. This demonstration, against the exhibit, is brought to you by Pepsi, the drink that *demonstrates* its taste again and again. Give the gift of life. Give Pepsi.

Then I wrote a second flier, explaining my first flier:

> I envision a Future where not only cultural rebels are underwritten by corporations, but the rebels *against* the rebels are similarly sponsored. Thus, rivalries between Schools of Art are actually advertising wars.

We gathered outside the Whitney at 6:00 on a Thursday, and began handing out pamphlets, shouting inflammatory slogans ("The Revolution will begin on E. 75th St.!" I prophesied), and confounding the populace, who could not decide if we were somehow part of the exhibit.

At 8:00 the flow of visitors slowed, so we went inside. Immediately I was depressed. "Beat Culture And The New America:1950-1965" was so *quiet.* It reminded me of the Asian Peoples exhibit at The Museum Of Natural History, where you see, within glass, wooden Siberian tribesmen ladling out stew and curing venison—except *this* exhibit had wooden bohemians and artists: Poets Under Glass.

And the artifacts! This was an art museum, so the curators had to produce art to illustrate Beatdom (although "Beat" was never, to my knowledge, an art movement) and they poured on paintings—canvases by Kerouac, Burroughs, Julian Beck (of the Living Theatre) and even *worse* paintings—particularly on the left side of the exhibit, entitled "San Francisco." (Michael McClure's art was both bad and giant.) On the right side, "New York," they exhibited Art (Jackson Pollock, Franz Kline, Larry Rivers) by non-Beats.

It became painfully obvious that the curators had collected the Beat material, shouted: "Oh no! We're doomed! This stuff is awful!" and thrown in three walls of great abstractionists (which no museum-goer, as far as I could tell, looked at).

So what *were* the Beats? Clearly, a bunch of hopped-up guys (and about three gals) who painted awkward paintings, wrote immense novels on speed (we see the Sacred Scroll of *On The Road*—with no paragraphing—written in three days on Benzedrine) and gave intense poetry readings in tenements on E. 3rd St. For it is in their photos that the Beats truly live. The fatalistic French charm with which they smoked, leaning against walls, in the photographs of Allen Ginsberg, excites a painful nostalgia. Life was a Mystery then, which the Beats knew they could intuit, with enough drugs, coffee and sleeplessness. Their artifacts were largely inane, but their passion for them was holy and pure. (My God, I'm *writing* like a Beat!)

Then I put on headphones to hear The Music That Inspired Them (Miles Davis' "Round Midnight") and thought, "This is the *real* art— cool, gracious music, like water washing a mountain."

A CONCISE HISTORY OF SUCCESSFUL
ANARCHIST REVOLUTIONS

INTRODUCTION

This book attempts to fill a void: the lack of concise histories of successful anarchist revolutions. While not intended purely as a workbook, I hope it will be of value to the contemporary revolutionist, as well as to the armchair scholar, and the general reader.

Sparrow

A Lesbian Revolution

In May of 1911, two Ceylonese women fell in love. This was highly unusual at the time, and neither appears to have considered herself a lesbian. Both were young widows forced into labor to support themselves at a sugar plantation in the center of the island, near Dagur. Their names were Chandra Devi and Susmita das Abil. Both were Tamils, and both were beautiful, by contemporary accounts.

One night, during a rainstorm, they slept together in a warehouse. After a passionate night, they became inseparable. As they nurtured their forbidden alliance, an ambition arose in them—to celebrate their love with a great deed.

On June 14, they rode to Colombo (the capital), and took over the main newspaper, *The Colombo Star*, at gunpoint. They printed a special edition of the paper announcing that a revolution had occurred, and that the British no longer ruled Ceylon.

The response in Colombo was swift and brutal. By the afternoon of June 15, their words had come true. The governor of Ceylon, Sir Hedwilde Brook, had been delivered to their headquarters at the *Star*, and decapitated.

The brief rule of Chandra and Susmita was marked by whimsy. Babies were given full status as citizens, and in some cases two year olds held political office. Singing was encouraged almost to the point of mania, and it is said that in Colombo during those three months, one never heard silence. Chandra and Susmita often walked through the streets on stilts, to cheering crowds.

The British returned on September 15 and captured the lesbian governors. They were imprisoned for fourteen years, and then hanged.

ZHWA TAN

On May 4, 1921, Lee Chung Hwa had a vision on a road outside Taipei. Buddha spoke to him, explaining that devotion and prayer were the keys to personal progress, and to receive further instruction only from the Spirit Light, an inner prompting that comes after long silence.

Lee Chung Hwa immediately began to promote this doctrine. (Up to this time, he had been an illiterate peddler.) He learned to write, and produced small religious tracts which he distributed for free. He lived on donations, and christened his doctrine the Spirit Way (Zhwa Tan).

His ideas were new to Taiwan, and occasioned great upheaval. As adherents arose, they were faced with a religious dilemma; should they accept instruction from non-spiritual sources—i.e. their foremen and bosses? The resulting religious frustration led to a vast civil disobedience, in which thousands of workers refused even to speak to their supervisors. (In many cases the bosses also converted to Zhwa Tan.) Workers abandoned their plantations and stores, and developed cooperatives.

Lee Chung Hwa appeared startled by these developments, as he had envisioned his philosophy as purely religious. Nevertheless, he supported the changes he had inspired.

For ten years, virtually all of Taiwan was governed by Zhwa Tan. Then, in the early thirties, Methodist missionaries arrived and quickly discredited the philosophy.

A FISHING ACCIDENT

On March 24, 1934, three prominent Brazilian industrialists went fishing in the interior of Brazil. In an accident, all three drowned in the Orinoco River.

Due to the particularities of Brazilian law, their companies now belonged to no one. In all three cases, a similar process occurred: the head supervisor took over the factory and was murdered by a group of workers. From then on, a congress of employees assumed control of the plants, and ran them in a democratic method.

Workers had such influence that they actually changed the formula for steel at the Coracona Steel Plant, resulting in one of the strongest steels in the world.

Other laborers of Sao Paulo, admiring the higher wages and greater happiness at these three plants, rose up and killed the owners of their plants, or drove them off. By 1939, forty percent of the factories of Sao Paolo were run by workers.

The process of reownership was gradual. Usually, a "management firm" would contract to handle some of the administrative duties, such as payroll, and would slowly assume control of the factory. In some cases, workers sold the factories outright to investors, and split the profits.

Today, there is only one employee-owned factory in Sao Paolo: a lace manufacturer, whose workers are legendary for their stubbornness.

A Broken Bicycle

On Feb. 2, 1905, Sevilla Quartzo stopped to repair his bicycle on a boulevard in Barcelona. (His front tire had a flat.) While he worked on the bike, two other men stopped to fix their bicycles. They began to talk. At first, they spoke about bicycles, and their repair. Later they spoke about their wives. Lastly, they spoke about the government. By coincidence, all three agreed on the political crisis facing Spain. At that time, Carlos IV, a weak, Italian-speaking monarch, held sway over the country.

The three men grew angrier, as they spoke. Finally, they were so angry, they drove their bicycles (now repaired), to the nearest bar—El Grande Cocorico, on Selphira Boulevard. They spoke to the men in the bar, who joined in their fury, and marched into the street. From there, they proceeded to another bar, and from there to a third, until a huge mob had gathered.

It happened that King Carlos was visiting Barcelona at the time, for the yearly flower show, where the mob found him, and put him to death.

For the next six weeks, there was no government in Spain. The theatre blossomed, as numerous plays were written on the regicide, and the kingless future. Two of the plays, *El Seguaro Con Sciencia (The Cactus of Science)* and *No Violinas (No Violins)* are still performed. Also during this period, a new game, hoop-hockey, became a national passion, among both children and adults. It involved rolling a hoop into a goal, using a fork as a goad.

Besides this, little marked the interregnum—no strikes, violence, or agitation—until King Philippe was installed March 21, in Madrid. Thus, this period in Spanish history has been largely forgotten.

A Pair Of Tight Shoes

On May 6, 1909, in Turela, Bolivia, Jason Vasquez tried to return a pair of shoes that were too tight. The salesman refused to accept them. (Jason had already worn the shoes for three weeks.) Jason attempted to strangle the salesman, and the salesman punched him in the jaw. At this point, a passing regiment of soldiers burst in and shot Vasquez. A riot ensued, which ultimately toppled the government. (The sovereign, Jorge IV, seeing his palace surrounded by an angry mob of 200,000, escaped, disguised as a butler.)

Emperor Maximillian II, who claimed to be descended from Napoleon, then assumed control of the nation. He ruled for eleven days, until he was revealed to be a woman dressed as a man. At this point, she was deposed, and a group of labor unions took over the government. After a brief discussion, it was decided that a rotating method of government would be attempted. The government would be communist, anarchist, Fourierist, Adamist and Turreroist each for three month periods, after which the nation would vote on their preferred form of government. (Adamist referred to a system based on the Garden of Eden, and Turrero was a Bolivian social philosopher of the nineteenth century.)

The Turreroist method won, and prevailed for seventeen years. This method involved a complex lottery sustem, in which most of the population switched jobs every six months. Teachers, streetsweepers, farmers, and engineers all changed places. There was even a randomly-chosen monarch.

A bloody counterrevolution—ironically led by Jason Vasquez's son—ended this era.

An Eskimo Revolt

One does not associate Eskimos with revolutions, yet there is one documented Eskimo revolution, in June of 1893. Missionaries living with the Tuliak Eskimos near Ft. Melwood, Alaska recorded the rule of a tyrannical chieftain, Skar Ilyuk, whose abuses included exposing the infants of his rivals to blizzards, and taking over ownership of all the tribe's dogs. Discontent in the tribe grew, until June 15, when all the males in the tribe prostrated themselves before him, begging him to resign the post of Chief—an unprecedented act.

If he refused, they said, they would commit suicide one by one. The chief refused. One young man killed himself, with a Smith & Wesson revolver, and a second was preparing to, when the chief stepped down.

He was immediately accepted back into the tribe, and lived the rest of his life as a devout Christian.

A Revolution Led By Dogs

It is hard to believe that dogs once conducted a revolution, yet this has been recorded in the history of Denmark.

Medieval Denmark, unlike the rest of Europe, was administered rather equably. Though there was a nominal feudal hierarchy, peasants essentially owned their land, and were free to create associations to compensate them for crop losses, thus assuring a high standard of living. In 1384, the third King Ethelred arose, who abolished these associations, reducing farmers to the level of serfs. The Church backed him in his efforts, and the pious populace could not bring itself to oppose Holy Writ.

For six long years, the masses suffered, until Jan. 19, 1390, when a pack of dogs gathered in Copenhagen. The lead dog, Frij, was the loyal pet of a freethinking barber named Heinrich Zeeler. The dogs converged on the royal castle, overpowered the guards, and burst into the King's chamber. In minutes, they devoured Ethelred entirely, except for his brain, which is still preserved in the Danish Museum of Science.

Ethelred's 19 year old son, Cedric, became king, and rescinded all his father's policies.

THE REVOLUTION BEGUN BY A MACHINE

On the morning of September 11, 1906, the Major Mill in Kingsbridge, Oregon was all tension. A man had died that morning, mangled by a huge press, and the workers were threatening a walkout, unless safety was improved. At the last minute, the owner's brother-in-law, Raye Henry, a local lawyer, had convinced them to return to work, but when they took their places at the machines and the switch was thrown, nothing happened. The machines themselves went on strike, as it were, and the workers quickly joined them. (To this day it has never been discovered why the mill machinery failed.) The workers nearly lynched Raye Henry, and finally did lynch the boss, Joyce L. Rand.

They spilled out into the street, and summarily took over the city and county administration.

The next Monday, the mill resumed operation—the machines worked perfectly—and a new section of the factory began inventing garments. Over the next sixty-two years, an enormous variety of accessories were created there—the modern bandana, the clip-on bowtie, lace collars—as well as experimental items which faded into obscurity: shoes with attached socks, "cucumber hats," button-up sleeves, etc.

Workers also took over several local factories, which became similarly inventive. A bottling plant created soda bottles which doubled as binoculars, and a lumberyard began perfuming sawdust.

This experiment continued until 1962, when the recession drove most of the factories—still worker-owned—out of business. Only the lumberyard remains, which recently began marketing skis for dogs.

AUTUMN NOW

[*Written a month after September 11, 2001.*]

I was born in the autumn—born into a regretful season. The days before and after my birthday are ones of lonesome walking, over susurrant leaves, days in which one recalls the cadences of Ecclesiastes:

> All things are wearisome;
>   more than one can express;
> the eye is not satisfied with
>   seeing,
> or the ear filled with hearing.

Viewing thousands of abandoning leaves, one senses the futility of a worldly career. One publishes an article in a newspaper, for example—perhaps to full acclaim. Two days later the same newspaper billows down an avenue, pushed by the October wind.

So strong is the October wind, it blows all accomplishments—all diplomas, money, press releases—before it. And in this wind is the first taste of winter's grueling breath.

But this fall is different, for me. Walking in Phoenicia Park, toward the rising Tremper Mountain, now beginning to show its varied color, I am not melancholy. The recent horrors in Manhattan and at the Pentagon change the tone of this autumn to reassurance. Stepping over deep red maple leaves, I observe: *This is not blood.* Here are a thousand deaths I need not mourn. The leaves did not leap from a burning tower; they simply fell, as gravity tugged. The earth is designed with four seasons—at least in the higher latitudes—one of birth, one of florescence, one of harvest, one of contemplation. Despite war, and acts of ruthlessness, Nature preserves her subtle intent.

There are years one resents Nature's inevitable plan, and there are years one is thankful for this same inevitability. I would rather be helpless before autumn than before soldiers and grim battle.

ON FAHRENHEIT 9/11

Because I own no television set, I have never watched George W. Bush in motion. I only see him stand still in newspaper photos. Much of my fascination with *Fahrenheit 9/11* was in studying this George. Here is what I discovered:

George W. Bush is serious about golf, but finds war slightly humorous.

He has that extreme jokiness of a man who grew up with a famous father. Though the world saw his dad as "The Commander of the CIA," George W. knew him as a person who slowly put on his brown socks. Because of this, young George can't believe anyone is strong or valuable.

W. is (and I don't usually speak in fifties slang) "one strange cat."

Why do I find myself using hiptalk when I mention him? Perhaps due to the aura of drugs that surrounds him. George W. actually *seems* high, most of the time.

I believe that he took cocaine, marijuana, a great deal of Jack Daniels (but very little vodka)—and now, after seeing his movie, I am convinced that he actually "tripped" (i.e. ate LSD).

George W. says: "I am a war president" the way he might say, "I am a Diet Coke president." His whole manner suggests the thought: "Everything is a game! Nothing is real."

But Michael Moore, this large, overweight, mournful figure, stands in opposition to Bush. Moore says*: "You are wrong; the world *is* real. You kill the sons of loving mothers; soldiers lose their legs."

How did the Right become so insouciant, and the Left so grim? It's like the sixties played backwards.

Moore is the disapproving parent of glib George W.

•

Fahrenheit 9/11 has a remarkable analysis. On one level, it is a Marxist movie. Why do poor soldiers enlist and fight? Because they lack money. They bet their lives against a possible college education. And why do the rich plan wars? Because the countries they invade have oil.

But the movie avoids "vulgar Marxism." Not everything is purely

economic. Politics exists, too. The Ruling Class manifests in the pup-
pet-like figure of George W. Bush—yet his personality affects our life.
Within this personality lies some vast brutality.

Do you remember that Death Metal song the American soldiers
play in the film as they roll into war in Iraq?:

> Burn, motherfucker!
> Let the motherfucker burn!

For three days that song remained in my mind after seeing *Fahrenheit
9/11*. I feared I would begin killing innocent citizens of my town
(Phoenicia, NY). I felt the seduction of anger and murder.

(It is interesting that this song derives from "Disco Inferno" by The
Trammps [from the *Saturday Night Fever* album]—one of my true
favorite songs:

> Burn, baby, burn!
> Disco Inferno!)

Most deft is Moore's presentation of American soldiers—victims of
poverty and destroyed neighborhoods, yet themselves exploiters of our
Colonies. Moore doesn't blame them, but doesn't deny their deeds. He
has "squared the circle" of American anti-war critique.

•

I couldn't believe that George W. is a Christian, after this movie. He
functions in this fluid, existential circle of action. George is constantly
moving—both toward you and away from you, at the same time. And
his strangely expressive face! A kind of threat, or jest, always plays there.

•

Movies are mysterious—the way they move through the populace, like
an illness. Thousands of people line up for them; they tell their friends:
"You must see this film!" Then, after two months, the movie departs,
barely remembered. People are now "immune" to the film, the way
they are to measles after an epidemic.

This happened to *Fahrenheit 9/11*, of course. I loved the (apoc-
ryphal?) stories of Republicans "converted" by the film.

If Bush loses in November (which seems impossible—like Bismarck quitting), Moore will be a public saint. As he should be. (Though perhaps, in person, he is egoistic.) Because Michael Moore is the bravest man in the United States. You *know* Dick Cheney has four different diagrams on his desk arranging Moore's death as an "apparent suicide."

Part of the reason eleven million people saw the film was to watch this ballsy king-slayer, Moore.

*I mean "says" metaphorically.

MY POLITICS

My personal life is particularly political. In fact, now that I ponder this subject, I was one of the first personal-as-political activists (or is the term "inactivist"?). Here are a series of my achievements:

1. I have not watched television in 28 years.

2. I have not eaten meat for 29 years.

3. I have meditated every day for 26 years.

4. I have worked a 40 hour week for a total of 9 1/2 months. (The rest of my working life—27 years—I have worked part time.)

5. Never have I lived alone. I have always had a roommate, or a wife.

6. The most money I have made in a year is $11,806.

Also I have run for President three times—the first time in 1992, with the Pajama Party (which I pioneered)—when I became the first candidate in history to oppose the law that all people pictured on stamps must be deceased. DEAD MEN OFF OUR STAMPS was my rallying cry. In 1996, I ran for the Republican nomination (vs. Bob Dole) as a Marxist, citing Abe Lincoln's quote, "Inasmuch as most good things are produced by labor, it follows that all such things of right belong to those whose labor has produced them." During this election I guaranteed a Jubilee Year in which all debts would be forgiven and all slaves freed. (And in a novelistic twist of fate, the Pope later declared the year 2000 a Jubilee Year.) Currently I am running on the Ear Of Corn Party, whose name derives from an exhilarating letter to *The New York Times* from Nancy A. Ransom, who wrote: "In the summer of 1952, when my husband and I lived in Princeton, N.J., a friend told us that corn grows so fast you can hear it. So one night we all went out to a corn field and lay down under the stars, listening to the ears of corn pop and crackle as they grew."

But these are just my most visible accomplishments. Please, accompany me on a day-by-day account of my personal political life:

6/17

I speak to Julie on the phone. She has two cats, so the conversation turns to fleas. "We have had severe infestations," she says. "I go through their fur two or three times a day, looking very carefully for fleas."

This inspires my sadistic curiosity.

"How do you kill the fleas? Do you drown them in kerosene?" I ask.

"I just put them in water. Soapy water or water."

There is a thoughtful pause in the conversation.

"Actually, I like fleas," Julie reflects. "I'm sorry I have to kill them. I admire their tenacity, their talent for survival. And they can leap really far!"

"Good," I reply. "I am happy you respect fleas."

You see, that was politics. To express love for the forgotten and the hated—particularly fleas, who have no voice in the outer world—is political.

6/19

My mother-in-law gave us curtains of a heavy olive-covered fabric decorated with flowers—almost a camouflage coloration. These curtains shut out the light so well that even in morning the room is dim—you cannot distinguish the pants hanging in the closet.

Nevertheless, at these moments, I never turn on the light; I move to the window and pull open the curtain. Why waste the earth's riches, in the shape of electricity (generated by nuclear plutonium or coal) when the purest sunlight is available, for scant exertion?

6/23

When I walk down a street, or road, and I need to spit (I have become quite a spitter in the last 6 years), I will pause and consider: where can I best bestow my spit? What flower, or tree, is desperate for water, and whatever nourishment spit can provide?

Suppose I see a yellowing four inch high plant with spoon-shaped double leaves, and a thick brownish stem. I will attempt to guess this creature's mental mood. Is she (or he) thirsting? If I suppose she is, I give her my small feast of saliva.

6/24

Several people have ordered copies of my poetry book. Here is my ritual for mailing books: I search through a pile of used manila envelopes, find an untorn one, head to my pile of scrap paper, choose a page, write the address, cut the paper so that it covers the former address, and glue it on. Although I have little time for this process today (the post office closes in fifteen minutes) I hurry and do this work. Why?

Not only because trees are sacrificed to our urge to create envelopes. Also because in this modern twenty-first century, there are so few eccentric public gestures. A manila envelope with an address pasted over an old address projects a kind of enigma, and personal craft, that is particularly rare now.

6/25

On the stone wall of a toilet stall (at the college in New Paltz) a man has scratched DEATH TO followed by the ugliest word in the American language, a word used to justify slavery and vigilante murder.

Nowadays I carry a felt tip pen, so I quickly crossed out this word, and deliberated. Should I write

DEATH TO
WHITES

DEATH TO
IDIOTS

DEATH TO
ARYANS

or

DEATH TO
RACISTS?

Finally, I settled on DEATH TO BIGOTRY, proud that I had chosen to kill an abstract wrong rather than a group of humans. (Even DEATH TO RACISTS implies that education is useless.)

6/17

When we moved into a new apartment, a certain relative gave us plastic plates. They are off-white, flat, with a little rim. In the manner of plastic plates, they have no ornamentation. There's something even aestheticly clever about them. Yet I do not use them.

I make the small effort to use a china plate—one that we were left by Violet's grandmother, with roses and sprigs of ferns pictured. There is a tradition of plates going back centuries, and plastic breaks that tradition. Touching plastic to your sandwich is like gargling with contact lens fluid. It introduces that alien technological presence, that sense of self-disrespect that is so modern.

Why don't I discard the plastic plates? Do you know the joke about the Jew on the desert island? He builds two synagogues. When he's rescued, the captain asks him: "Why did you build two synagogues?"

He points to the first one. "This one I go to every week," he says. Then he points to the second: "And this one I wouldn't set *foot* in!"

The plastic plates serve this purpose for me. They are a spiritual temptation, which I resist. And they may be useful someday, if we have a lot of guests.

6/26

New York City
I was on my way to my friend Susan's birthday party in Hudson River

Park, when I walked by the Albanian consulate on East 79th Street. A stack of books and typewritten pages stood beside two garbage cans. I sorted through this pile, which was entirely in Albanian. I found a thin text on biology, *Materialet e Mbushjes Ne Terapine Stomatologile.* "This will be a divine gift for Susan!" I presumed.

Most Americans don't know that the right gift will arrive, by surprise, if you choose not to buy anything. (Susan has been to 45 countries, and was leaving the next day for Thailand, Indonesia, and Nepal.)

See how genuinely beauteous the first sentence of this Albanian book is:

> Materialet e mbushjeve teperkohshme per-
> doren per mulimin apo mbushjen e zgavrave
> te dhembeve jate procedureave te mjekimit
> te kariesit te thjeshte dhe te rderlikuet.

6/27

One of the grave problems facing this nation is its name—or rather lack of a name. "The United States" is an extremely generic name—every nation is a group of United States. Italy is a bunch of United States. What else would it be? "The United States of America" is misleading, since America is a huge area, comprising two whole continents, and this nation is not all those states united. A proper name would be "Some United States Of North America, Plus Hawaii", or S.U.S.O.N.A.P.H., for short. "The USA," of course, merely abbreviates this error, and "America" is so hubristic as to be nearly funny. Why not call ourselves "Earth"?

All these names are vague. Isn't there a word that describes something distinct in our nation, the way "France" seems to capture something French?

Hope arrives today in the form of a *New York Times* article, "Ancient Site Offers Clues to Vikings in America: Ruins Tell of a Norse Settlement": "Sometime at the end of the 10th century. .. [Leif] Ericson set out from the Greenland colony in his sturdy longboat with a soaring prow and a large square sail. . . . Here at, L'Anse aux

Meadows [Newfoundland], they established the base camp, their beachhead in Vinland. Said Tamara Ricks, acting supervisor of the National Historic Park: 'Over a period of about 10 years, we think, several Viking parties probably spent three to five years in total here, wintering over, hunting and fishing and repairing their boats.' Of Vinland, Adam of Bremen wrote in 1070, 'There grow wild grapes.'"

How succulent and true this name rings! We are Vinland, land of grapes and berries. Why, just this morning I stopped on my way across New Paltz to sample ripe mulberries—dangling, black, amid a tree's profuse leafage.

Sweet Vinland! This is the name I will now use forever.

6/29

Recently, looking through pages of my writings, I came upon this short essay:

> BOONE FEMALE?
>
> Was Daniel Boone a woman? New evidence
> buttresses this claim. Matthew Clease, a rab-
> bit trapper, wrote in 1811: "Boone wears . . .
> at all times . . . women's undergarments."
> Several sources remarked on "his" high voice.
> Danielle is the name on "his" birth records.
> And Kit Carson remarked (in 1823): "Once
> a month, Dan'l disappears."
>
> Scholars at Clark University are calling
> for Boone's body to be disinterred.

There is a politics to this essay. By questioning the masculinity of an American icon, I am suggesting that maleness is a buckskin garment, not an inner state. Men who have some contempt for women (as all men do) fear they themselves are hiding an inward female secret. "We are all secret women," this essay obliquely reassures.

7/1
New York City

Yesterday I called my friend Cliff. We were planning to spend the afternoon together.

"I wouldn't mind going to the Museum of Modern Art," Cliff offered.

"Is the strike still on?" I asked.

"I don't know."

We arranged to meet outside MOMA the next day. Meanwhile, I called the museum to ask about the strike. All I got on the phone was a menu, but ominously, option number six was: "If you are seeking employment in the museum . . . "

Today I rose up from the subway at 53rd Street to hear a drum beating and a bell. Six sweating strikers stood, or sat on crates, on the sidewalk in front of the museum. Barricades penned them in.

A woman handed me a leaflet: "DON'T SUPPORT A MUSEUM THAT WON'T SUPPORT ITS STAFF!"

"So the strike is still on?" I asked her.

"Nine weeks," she smiled, rueful. "And they refuse to negotiate with us."

"What is the strike about?" I asked.

"They could not guarantee our health plan. Right now we have a good health plan, but they said we might have to give some of it up. They weren't sure."

"They wanted you to just trust them?" I asked.

She smiled. "Right."

"And they're making money, aren't they?"

"Oh, yeah. There about to start a $200 million renovation."

"And they're just hoping you'll surrender?" I asked.

"Yes," she replied.

Cliff walked up. She repeated this information to him. "I found five dollars on the street today," Cliff said. He handed the striker the five dollars. "Thank you," she said. "And don't forget to write to MOMA's director, Glenn Lowry!"

Cliff and I walked off together.

7/1

Dear Glenn Lowry,

My friend Cliff and I were preparing to enter MOMA today, to visit the "Making Choices, 1920 - 1960" exhibit; however we noticed strikers standing before your building, beating upon drums. We spoke to them, and felt that we could not dishonor their vigil by entering the galleries of art.

So, I am writing you instead, to beg you to negotiate with these honorable women and men, forty of whom only earn $17,000 a year.

Yours in the triumph of Art,
Sparrow
Post Office Box 63
Phoenicia NY 12464
Sparrow44@Juno.com

7/2

Today I returned my daughter's book to the library (*Crazy Fish*). It was not yet due, but I returned it early, along with the tape of a Joseph Campbell lecture my wife has been enjoying. Also I renewed a book of interviews with Truman Capote (*Capote Revealed*).

I bring books back to the library early to lessen the work of the librarians—Debbie, Hilary, Susan— and to show fervid support for the integrity of libraries.

Why should one person own a book? Most of us simply read a book, then close its covers and never view it again. We are not scholars who pull down volumes to quote in our essays. And even if we are, why not allow one building in a town to hold all our volumes together? Why must we each buy our own copy? Let us save the destruction of wood pulp, and also practice sharing.

In Gainesville, Florida the library has paintings. For three weeks, you can possess a little Juan Gris still-life in a frame, for your house. You live with this painting—of a fish on a plate and two pears—for most of a month, then it moves on, to a new apartment house. A short woman named Allison, perhaps, will choose it.

I believe in the expansion of libraries until they include placemats, wrenches, chess sets—even food. Suppose a woman (let's name her Mrs. Culver) buys a box of oatmeal at the Boiceville Market. At home, Mrs. Culver opens the box—it's cinnamon-flavored! Mrs. Culver despises cinnamon oatmeal. So she brings the box to the Pine Hill library, and an elderly man—a Mr. Gormar—checks out the oatmeal. For 21 years, he has pondered whether he would enjoy cinnamon-flavored oatmeal, and now, due to Mrs. Culver's error, he can know. (He is too parsimonious to buy an extra box of oatmeal.) He *does* enjoy cinnamon oatmeal, he discovers!

This is the library I envision.

9/10

In the morning, as I await my bus (the 6:21 to New Paltz), the cold sometimes forces me into the ATM machine at the Key Bank. Today, three insects are crawling on the inside of the glass door. They are thin green beings, winged, considerably smaller than flies.

I watch their steps for a time, then gradually deduce that they are trapped in the ATM room. I open the door, to allow them flight. They do not escape.

So I blow on one. She falters, for a moment, then flees, by air.

I blow on the next. She too drifts off.

I blow on the third. She is freed.

FRUITOPIA: A CALL TO ARMS

We live in the age of Fruitopia: an era which combines the succulent taste of fresh fruit with a vision of the perfect human society. The Coca Cola Co., quite by accident, stumbled upon a new concept, a paradise that is edible, or rather drinkable. By linking two rather outdated ideas, fruit and utopia, they have revived both, giving us something utterly fresh and post-contemporary: Fruitopia. If one can remember back 6.7 months, to the era before we had seen the actual product, and only knew the busy, shimmering, chimeric posters, which decorated every subway, bus shelter, rooftop and college textbook cover, one recalls the elusive, tantalizing, yet familiar hope they offered. Fruitopia, a battering global rainfall of gladness.

At the time, we did not know, of course, that Fruitopia was really a treacly beverage that also fizzed; we didn't know that Fruitopia was a drink at all. We only knew that Fruitopia was . . . Fruitopia. And thus it remains for us mystics, cloud-warriors, power-activists and Catalysts Of The Future. We have heard the call of Fruitopia, we must only rise now and create it.

THE EAST VILLAGE MILITIA

In 1996, The East Village Militia was founded, to protect the East Village of Manhattan from natural disasters and capitalism. Sparrow held the rank of Specific Commander. In one of their daring escapades, the militia gave away books in front of Nobody Beats The Wiz, an electronics store on Broadway, to prevent people from buying televisions. The militia handed out this flier:

The Second Commandment says "Thou shalt make no graven image of anything that "creepeth" on the earth or "swimmeth" in the seas or "flieth" in the air." By emphasizing these verbs, God is forbidding us to show motion. Static art—paintings, drawings, engravings, etc.—are perfectly acceptable to God. It is television that God despises. TV is the idol of our age—and its heroes are commonly known as "television idols."

Repent ye!, before ye lose your souls. We offer free books to you, that your souls may be preserved. Read, look at paintings, listen to poetry, study modern dance! Do meditation! Pray! But buy no new TVs, and bury your present TV in the earth!

Love,
The East Village Militia

THE TRUTH ABOUT CHRISTMAS

The East Village Militia also traveled to Rockefeller Center to protest Christmas. They distributed this notice:

THE TRUTH ABOUT CHRISTMAS

The Pre-Christian World was economically depressed for 281 years, ever since Baal-worshippers (in 280 B.C.) outlawed the festival of Ktali, a yearly gift-giving celebration on Dec. 24th. A group of merchandisers in 1 A.D. created the myth of a child-god whose worship required numerous and expensive gifts, thus reviving the Mediterranean economy. Ironically, the historical Jesus (born 4 B.C.) opposed all spending—he was even against working! (See "The Sermon On The Mount.")

Defy the cabal of Capitalist gift-mongers! Give nothing on Christmas! Or if you must, give small gifts you make yourself *at no expense!* For example, cover a chicken bone with aluminum foil. Tie a string around it. This makes a lovely gift. (It can also be used in the game of *spotsa*, an Armenian tossing sport.) Or take a book you are tired of. Tear out all the pages. In their place, put three slices of bread. This too makes a jarring but simple present! There is no end to the human imagination. Put the "is" back in Christmas! Boycott stores! DO NOT BUY! For the love of Christ, give nothing for Christmas!

The East Village Militia

TO THE NEW YORKER WE GO, TRA LA

On December 7 (Pearl Harbor Day), 1994, Sparrow and other members of The Unbearables protested outside the offices of the *New Yorker* magazine. Sparrow distributed the following flier:

A PROCLAMATION

Generations of English-speaking magazine readers have asked themselves: "Why is there poetry in *The New Yorker*?" It's clear that no one reads—it or rather a few teenagers and some would-be poets read it, but none of them understand or enjoy it. The poetry appears to have fallen out of another magazine and landed in *The New Yorker*, like flakes of snow falling on a chilly November evening, as an ominous wind whirls. The question, "Why is there *New Yorker* poetry?" is as vexing as the theological question "Why is there evil in the world?" until one rethinks the query. Must everything in a magazine be entertaining or understandable—and must it be read at all? Perhaps certain sections of a magazine exist for the readers to pole-vault over, to give them a sense that they're making quick progress toward the final page. The poems in *The New Yorker* convince its readers that they're reading poetry, because they own a magazine which contains poetry, and they move their eyes past these poems as they turn the pages. It is wonderful to think of oneself as a reader of poetry; it gives one a sense of human dignity. And how much more wonderful it is to feel this dignity without actually having to read a poem! The question for true poets, then, is what to make of these phantom poems, usually found between page 29 and 78 of *The New Yorker* each week. Is there some way to reclaim these poems, to return them to the English language from which they presumably sprang? We, the members of this delegation, have translated a collection of *New Yorker* poems into English. We demand that they be published in the magazine, as the first Real Poems in the 64 year history of *The New Yorker*.

Also Sparrow led the singing of this song:

To The New Yorker We Go, Tra La

It's not easy
translating *The New Yorker*
into English.
It's more difficult
than shaving a camel.

But we tried,
we tried,
we tried,
and we have succeeded;

So now, to your office
we have travelled.

To *The New Yorker* we go,
tra la, tra la.
To *The New Yorker* we go,
tra la, tra la.

A small delegation of Unbearables visited the *New Yorker* office. Sparrow presented the secretary with an issue of his magazine, *Big Fish*, containing translations from *The New Yorker*. (Sparrow had been translating poems from the magazine into English for over a year.) Now, for the first time, these translations are being published:

PERFECTION WASTED

And another regrettable thing about death
is the ceasing of your own brand of magic,
which took a whole life to develop and market—
the quips, the witticisms, the slant
adjusted to a few, those loved ones nearest
the lip of the stage, their soft faces blanched
in the footlight glow, their laughter close to tears,
their tears confused with their diamond earrings,
their warm pooled breath in and out with your heartbeat,
their response and your performance twinned.
The jokes over the phone. The memories packed
in the rapid-access file. The whole act.
Who will do it again? That's it: no one;
imitators and descendants aren't the same.

—John Updike

Translation:

PERFECTION WASTED

The problem with dying
is you can't be funny anymore,
or charming.

Hands

Unadorned, they sat in our kitchen,
limp from the press of my mother's fingers.
All day she stood behind pedestals
of shoulders. I'd watch her
stand over them—elbows bent, arms
pumping lather. Eyes closed,
they willingly handed over their heads.
Hair was the one thing they could change.
In curlers they looked electric, pink.

Sometimes my mother was my customer.
The brush I held plowed its teeth
through her hair, turning the dark roots,
the magic oils that made it grow.
Silently I counted the strokes, waiting
for her to give up, lean
her head back into my expert hands.

A helpless customer, I pay strangers
to turn my hair light, lighter.
Soon I won't remember its original color.
If I could I'd go on counting the strokes,
backwards this time.
In the middle of our kitchen I'd tell you
it's no use
orphaned from your powerful, mothering hands.
                                        —Marianne Burke

Translation:

HANDS

My mother was a hairdresser.
Her customers came to our house,
and sat in the kitchen, as she
washed their hair.

I brushed my mother's hair sometimes,
hoping she'd appreciate it.

Now I go to beauty parlors
and get my hair tinted.
I miss my mother.

CRYSTAL ICE COMPANY

These grow beneath rusty plates, with brine
circulating and ammonia saturnine
in the nostrils. Slowly the brooding poisons calve
into substantial clarities. He moves
among submerged lights, which are weak,
as a low smoke or planetary cowlick
might fume across a lost explorer's lenses;
then in the acrid damp he stops, remembers

"Port Washington, a winter dawn, 1928":

"as he climbs Beacon Hill in the milkman's cart,
a plug of cream sucked from the broken foil top
of a bottle lights his face like a buttercup."

In the end, no airy pinions may remain,
no galactic rose at the center to lessen
the density with imperfections of surface,
no stalled titanium plume; and a steady pulse
of bubbles will insure this, ticking through.

"The last summer before the divorce, sixty years ago.
They are loading rock salt into the outer sleeve.
The crank turns, an unhurried passage of
Sunday evening into confections of cream and fruit."

It is time to vacuum the last impurities out
of the closing heart. Soon rusty chains will raise
three hundred pounds of perfectly gestated ice
in a shrieking transit, a crystal martyrdom
to the cutting floor, and ice will precede him
to the loading dock, bearded with excelsior,
to diminishment by the hand of summer air.

—Karil Kirchwey

Translation:

CRYSTAL ICE COMPANY

It is early in the morning.
He walks on ice.

He thinks of his father.
Then he vacuums air out of the ice.

A crane will lift the ice in 300 lb. blocks.

GARTER SNAKE

The stately ripple of the garter snake
in sinuous procession through the grass
compelled my eye. It stopped and held its head
high above the lawn, and the delicate curve
of its slender body formed a letter "S"
for "serpent," I presume, as though
diminutive majesty obliged embodiment.

The garter snake reminded me of those
cartouches where the figure of a snake
seems to suggest the presence of a god
until more flickering than any god
the small snake gathered glidingly and slid
but with such cadence to its rapt advance
that when it stopped once more to raise its head
it was stiller than the stillest mineral
and when it moved again it moved the way
a curl of water slips along a stone
or like the ardent progress of a tear
till, deeper still, it gave the rubbled grass
and the dull hollows where its ripple ran
lithe scintillas of exuberance
moving the way a chance felicity
silvers the whole attention of the mind.

—Eric Ormsby

Translation:

GARTER SNAKE

A snake moved through grass
and I watched.
It looked like an S.

When it stopped, it was very still.

The grass shook slightly when it moved.

HOUSE HOUR

Now the pale honey of a kitchen light
burns at an upstairs window, the sash a cross.
Milky daylight moon,
sky scored by phone lines. Houses in rows
patient as cows.

Dormers and gables of an immigrant street
in a small city, the wind-worn afternoon
shading into night.

Hundreds of times before
I have felt it in some district
of shingle and downspout at just this hour.
The renter walking home from the bus
carrying a crisp bag. Maybe a store
visible at the corner, neon at dusk.
Macaroni mist on the glass.

Unwilled, seductive as music, brief
as dusk itself, the forgotten mirror
brushed for dozens of years
by the same gray light, the same shadows
of soffit and beam end, a reef
of old snow glowing along the walk.

If I am hollow, or if I am heavy with longing, the same:
the ponderous houses of siding,
fir framing, horsehair plaster, fired bricks
in a certain light, changing nothing, but touching
those separate hours of the past
and now at this one time
of day touching this one, last spokes
Of light silvering the attic dust.

-Robert Pinsky

Translation:

HOUSE HOUR

A light is on, in
a kitchen, in a city, as the poet
walks by.
It's late afternoon.

The poet thinks of other
streets he's walked down
and feels old.

He attempts to use "soffit"
in a sentence.

IN APHRODISIAS

Here Homer's wine-dark sea is a deep,
bloody blue, like history.
Waves ride into Asia
with the fervor of Europe mounting a crusade.

This is Aphrodisias,
where the doves of Aphrodite still circle
the crumbling temple, the muddy spring.
I need no aphrodisiac.

I have come by speedboat with a pagan guide
from Chios, the island of dagger-bearing men.
We climb the slippery stairs while holding hands
in the frank Greek manner: we are friends.

The climb dizzies me. I fall. My guide
inscribes a message on a slip of paper
and sets it on fire on the leaning altar. Is it
a prayer for love? For war? He doesn't say.

The doves murmur on the broken roof.

He blows the ash away, and we scramble down
silently, no longer holding hands.
I smell the deadly oleander of a place
inhabited for over three thousand years.

We walk to the pier; the sea is churning foam.
A glint of Alexander plays in his eyes.
Which of us will bleed to death tonight?
                                        —Stephen Stepanchev

Translation:

IN APHRODISIAS

The water here is
blue, but reddish.

I am on Aphrodisias,
in March, and there are pigeons.
I'm horny.
I'm holding hands with my
  tour guide, climbing stairs.
On top,
he burns a paper he's written
  on, but I don't know
  what it says.

On the way down, we don't hold hands.

DISTANCES

The radio is playing downstairs in the kitchen.
The clocks says eight and the light says
winter. You are pulling up your hood against a bad morning.

Don't leave, I say. Don't go without telling me
the name of that song. You call it back to me from the stairs—
"I Wish I Was in Carrickfergus"—

and the words open out with emigrant grief the way the streets
of a small town open out in
memory: salt-loving fuchsias to one side and

a market in full swing on the other with
linen for sale and tacky apples and a glass-and-wire hill
of spectacles on a metal tray. The front door bangs

and you're gone. I will think of it all morning while a fine
drizzle closes in, making the distances
fiction: not of that place but of this, and of how

restless we would be, you and I, inside the perfect
music of that basalt-and-sandstone
coastal town. We would walk the streets in

the scentless and flawless afternoon of a ballad measure,
longing to be able
to tell each other that the starched lace and linen of

adult handkerchiefs scraped your face and left your tears
falling, how the apples were mush inside the crisp sugar
shell and the spectacles out of focus.

—Eaven Boland

Translation:

DISTANCES

The radio is playing downstairs in the kitchen.
It's 8 o'clock. It is winter.
It's a cold day and you are going out.
"Don't go," I say. "Don't leave without telling me
the name of that song." You yell at me,
"I Wish I Was In Carrickfergus."

The rest of the day it drizzles.

THE LETTER

Bad news arrives in her distinctive hand.
The cancer has returned, this time
to his brain. Surgery impossible,
exhaustion during the day.

I snap the blue leash onto the ring
of the dog's collar, and we cross
Route 4, then cut through the hayfield
to the pond road, where I let him run
along with my morbidity.

The trees have only just leafed out
and the air is misty with sap.
So green, so brightly, richly succulent,
this arbor over the road . . .
Sunlight penetrates in golden drops.

We come to the place where a neighbor
is taking timber from his land.
There's a smell of lacerated earth
and pine. Hardwood smells different.
His truck is gone.

Now you can see well up the slope,
see ledges of rock and ferns breaking forth
among the stumps and cast-aside limbs
and branches.

This place will heal itself in time, first
with weeds—goldenrod, cinquefoil, moth
mullein—then blackberries, sapling
pine, deciduous trees . . . But for now
the dog rolls, jovial, in the pungent
disturbance of wood and earth.

I summon him with a word, turn back,
and we go the long way home.

                                    —Jane Kenyon

Translation:

THE LETTER

I got a letter from my
mother about my father.
It says that he has cancer
of the brain.

I took my dog for a walk
because I felt bad.

It was spring, and
the sun was yellow.

Some trees were cut down.
The ferns still grew in between
  them.

The dog rolled around there,
and I felt a little better.

STONE VILLAGE

At the first sight of the old walls the rain
was over it was high summer with tall
grass already white and gold around
the somber brambles waves of them hiding
the house completely from the rutted lane
that ran among brambles and shadows
of walnut trees into the silent village
already it was afternoon and beyond
the barns the broad valley lay in its haze
like a reflection as it does long after
the house has risen dry out of the tide
of brambles and uncounted sunlight has crossed
the dust of the floors again all the fields
and the shoulders of the stone buildings have
shrunk and the animals have wakened in
the barns and are gone and the children
have come home and are gone and the rain
they say seems to have stopped forever

—W.S. Merwin

Translation:

STONE VILLAGE

I first saw the old stone houses
in the summer.
It was a hot, hazy day.

I moved into one, and
had children.

Now it is years later, and
it hasn't rained lately.

A Seated Demon
(After A Painting By Mehmet Siyah Qalem)

He sits, his black flesh deeply creased and rolled
  across forehead and chest, and holds, in one hand,

a golden figure. His neck and arms, gold-
  banded like his radiant ankles, tensile and

profane, strain with dignity toward the form
  he possesses. She is a headless, full-breasted,

heavy-thighed representation of warm
  life continuing, the sexual feast.

Naturally, she will soon pull away,
  leaving him demonstrably blacker. He'll rise,

adjust his scarlet trousers, turn to survey
  the dissolving form of his desire, train his eyes

on the slow vanishing of the painter's brush.
  His dark regard amplifies the drying wash.
                  —Sidney Wade

Translation:

A SEATED DEMON
(AFTER A PAINTING BY MEHMET SIYAH QALEM)

The demon is black, and fat.
He holds a small golden statue,
and wears gold bracelets and his wrists and
        ankles.
Next to him is a woman with big tits.

LOOKING LIKE OSAMA

Some people look like Brad Pitt or Sarah Jessica Parker. It is my fate to resemble Osama bin Laden.

Much of this resemblance is due to my beard. Actually, I never began "growing a beard." When I was seventeen, my father presented me with a new electric Norelco razor. Shaving for the first time, I enjoyed removing my few facial hairs.

The second time I shaved, I cut myself. I have never shaved since.

For many years, I had no beard—just some downy hairs on my cheek. Suddenly, when I was 24, these hairs coalesced into a beard. I continued growing my beard even after 1980, when most men began to discard or closely trim their facial growths.

At one time, great men had great beards. When I visited Rabindranath Tagore's house in Calcutta, I was impressed by the photograph of Tagore and George Bernard Shaw. The two philosophical writers sat together, pointing their long beards at one another. The greatest American poet (Walt Whitman) may have grown the greatest American beard.

Gradually, I noticed that no one else in American public life had a beard—particularly an untamed one. I observed this first on the cover of *Time* magazine. In 1981, in a supermarket, I saw a person who resembled me staring from *Time*. For an irrational particle of a second, I thought: "I have landed on the cover of *Time* for my achievements in poetry!" Instead, the photograph was of a wild-eyed terrorist.

In succeeding years, each time I saw a face like mine on *Time* or *Newsweek*, I would look hopefully—always to find an angry bomber.

It wasn't until after 9/11 that I knew the name of one of these men: Osama bin Laden.

Strangely, as Osama and I grew older, our beards aged in exactly the same manner. They both became streaked with white, and the streaks were identical: two long patches on either side of the chin.

Osama and I share other resemblances, besides our beards. We are both Semites. (Genetically, I am half Jewish.) We are thin. Also I meditate twice a day; Osama (presumably) prays five times a day. These contemplative practices give our faces an unworried look.

Here is a journal entry of mine, from 2001:

9/18

"It's him! Isamu Bin Laden!" a teenage boy says, pointing at me.* I am walking down the Main Street of Phoenicia. I examine the "Wanted Dead or Alive" poster of Bin Laden taped to Brio's Pizzaria.

Thank God I don't wear a turban!

Here is a selection from a letter, one month later:

I was in New York City for the first time since the disaster. The bars were full on Saturday night (I went out with friends, although I do not drink alcohol) and a very drunk Polish guy thought I was bin Laden, in the Homestead Bar on First Avenue and 3rd Street.

"I'm going to get my shotgun!" he announced. He marched to a corner of the room and returned with a sweatshirt bearing an image of an American flag. For a moment I thought I would be shot.

How strange to die for someone *else's* ideals!

One day in the elevator in my parents' house in Brooklyn, a woman walked in. "Oh, shit!" I felt her thinking. "Of every elevator on earth, I had to choose the one with Osama!"

But what could I do? If I say, "No, I'm not Osama," I sound insane.

People are obviously unaware that bin Laden is six feet six inches tall, and on a dialysis machine.

Soon after September 11th, I heard a news story about a Middle Eastern man who ran a restaurant in Texas called "Osama's Place." Suddenly, business had fallen off. I empathized with this man. He was punished for his name, I for my face.

The Easter of 2002, my family flew to Orlando. My wife, my daughter and I were all given the thorough, shoes-off search. On the plane, I felt everyone's eyes upon me. At one point, I stood up to remove my sweater, and several men prepared to tackle me.

Osama is about my age; he is 47, I am 50. We have had similar histories, actually. We both had a Western appearance as youths. There is a photograph of Osama with his family in Sweden, on vacation. He looks like a tall, uncomfortable teenager in a 70s-style paisley shirt—just how I looked at that age! Somehow we both decided to cash in our contemporary clothes for an ancient look.

What happened was that we began spiritual practice: I joined the Ananda Marga Society in 1974; Osama became an orthodox Muslim in 1978. Osama and I began to look like men did before capitalism, caffeine, and computers. Our beards connect us to saints and seers of an ancient world.

In the famous video where Osama speaks of the 9/11 attacks, most of the conversation is about dreams. Every morning, I lie in bed and remember my dreams.

Bearded men value their dreams.

It's difficult to hate someone whom you resemble. "An eye for an eye and a tooth for a tooth" applies less to someone with the same color eyes as you, the same crooked front tooth. I find myself seeing Osama as a not-too-smart, very religious guy who has been seduced by the radical allure of violence. (I must say I see Bush the same way.)

Of course, I personally benefitted from the invasion of Iraq. Suddenly, our public Villain was no longer Osama. Luckily, I look nothing like Saddam Hussein.

Still, each time I walk on an airplane, the stewardess at the entrance engages me in conversation. "How are *you* today?" she asks, usually in a Southern accent. (For some reason, nearly all stewardesses are Southern.) Her voice is hysterically cheerful, the way one is while conversing with a possible Islamic murderer. "I'm fine, very good," I reply, in my Manhattan accent, and she relaxes.

What if I muttered, "Death to the American infidels?" Would she refuse to serve me Sprite?

~Proverbs~

When one talks to a tree one tells the truth.

•

Women are men with better clothes.

•

A whole army can lose its way.

•

Karate can't hurt dew.

•

Antarctica awaits its hero.

•

The last generation will be female.

•

Hum a tune long enough and the radio will play it.

•

An ouija board can cross an ocean.

•

The best things in life are on sale.

•

A roof without a house is a floor.

•

To own something is to be puzzled by it.

•

Marriage works best for the blind.

•

The radio calls us friend.

•

The deepest hole is a tunnel.

•

Lunch is the hardest meal to poison.

•

Not everything that revolves is round.

Slaves are stronger than masters.

•

While I speak, I am a word.

•

Don't applaud a house of cards.

•

Armor hides one's age.

•

All cultures have dinner theatre.

•

The golden calf gives no milk.

•

Death is wise to come only once.

•

Some drink for the hangover.

•

Out of the mouths of babes comes fermented milk.

•

Mozart started on drums.

•

A nail can stand on its head.

•

After a snowfall crows are blacker.

•

Yeats' teeth are still here.

•

Where the weavers sing the cloth is finer.

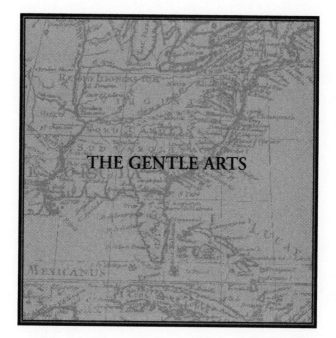

THE GENTLE ARTS

THE NEA AND ME

2/29

"I'm applying for a NEA," Emmy tells me, as we lunch on soup at the B & H Dairy Restaurant on Second Avenue, in lower Manhattan. (I have potato soup; she has borscht.)

These five words prove beguiling—and entangling, over time.

3/4

My National Endowment for the Arts Application Guidelines booklet arrives. I am not *certain* I'm applying; I'm just considering it.

3/5

Under "mission" the booklet writes: "The National Endowment for the Arts, an investment in America's living cultural heritage, serves the public good by *nurturing* the expression of human creativity, *supporting* the cultivation of community spirit, and *fostering* recognition and appreciation of the **excellence** and **diversity** of our nation's artistic accomplishments."

Since both "excellence" and "diversity" are in boldface, we can recognize what the NEA is hinting: if you are excellent but not diverse, you're only as good as someone who is diverse but not excellent—while the excellent *and* diverse have the best chance of all.

Well, I am certainly diverse. In any group, I represent diversity (except perhaps a group of Marxist old hippies). First of all, I am ethnically diverse. I am half-Pennsylvania Dutch and half-Jewish. It is very unusual for Jews to marry Pennsylvania Dutchwomen, partly because they never meet. And certainly, they rarely met in 1948, when my parents were first acquainted—where my father was a union organizer at the RCA plant my mother labored in. This was in Lancaster, Pennsylvania.

Besides, I am otherwise diverse. Religiously, for example, I am an agnostic, a devoted student of yoga, a Conservative Jew, an existentialist, a skeptic—plus I have converted to Christianity three times! Politically, I am anti-capitalist, yet my hobby is writing self-help books which will make me rich. Even my diet is mostly vegan, yet I am wildly indulgent in Wise Potato Chips.

3/6

Apparently you may not tell the NEA: "I want the money because I don't like working. I find employment a little tedious." Instead, you must invent some grand project the grant will help you achieve. Here is what I concoct:

> I live in a small town and have very little money for travel. I am interested in writing a book about Abraham Lincoln's brother. This grant would allow me to visit libraries in New York City and at SUNY New Paltz. Also I need to read to expand my literary education.

It sounds outrageous, but it is true. I was going to add other books I hope to write—one about the local Underground Railroad, one about George Washington Carver (and as I considered these, some evil Tempter said: "Maybe they'll think I'm black, and they'll *definitely* give me the money").

But would they believe I could write three books in one year? It doesn't sound very professional.

So I mention the one book I most believe I will write.

3/7

I struggle with the question—should I put a red-and-white striped paper clip on the three copies of my application form? Does it look too radical? Finally I decide, "I am a poet, goddam it. The least they can allow me is a peppermint-colored paper clip!"

3/8

To prove my eligibility I must submit "20 or more different poems or pages of poetry in five or more literary journals, anthologies, or publications which regularly include poetry as a portion of their format." But what exactly do they consider a "literary journal?" My most recent publication, *Emo 8*, for example (30 Colonial Ave., Lancaster, N.Y. 14086) is stapled together by Natalie Basinsky, who is 19. Besides, it contains my poem "Ton Anus":

In 8.2 years,
a ton of feces
passes through
the anus.

Finding a pile of unread magazines, I remember I have been published in *The Cafe Review* (c/o Yes books, 20 Danforth Street, Portland, Maine 04101) in the Fall of 1998—a nice, perfect-bound little journal (though a skeleton with a violin *is* on the cover). I turn to my entries, on pages 6 and 7:

CUM FORT
Out of my cum I built a fort.
Now I stand on the parapet, watching for enemies.

ZEN SEX KOANS, '98
1. As the Mayor closes topless bars,
   the President explains his blow jobs on TV.
2. "Sometimes a cigar is just a cigar" —Sigmund
Freud. True or false?
3. Who saves semen-stained dresses?
4. Imagine Linda Tripp's sex life.

(*My god!*, I think, as I read these. *I am a fucking pornographer!*) These are not the best poems, I decide, to submit to the George W. Bush administration while asking for funds.

Then I find *Mudfish 12* (Box Turtle Press, 184 Franklin Street, New York City 10013), a lovely, book like magazine that publishes John Ashbery. Within is my poem, "Giuliani Poem":

I hate
Rudolph Giuliani

And I fear
he will take revenge
on my wife, my daughter and me

if I sign this poem

So I will use a pseudonym: "Henry David Thoreau"

I hope Giuliani's face rots
under a subway

–Henry David Thoreau

"This is going to be more difficult than I planned," I ponder.

And what about *LUNGFULL!* magazine (126 East 4th Street, No. 2, New York City, 10003)? Does the NEA consider *that* a "literary journal?" Its most recent issue has 210 pages, with a glossy cover the editor (and my friend) Brendan Lorber describes as "entirely waterproof & stain resistant." Yet its name is mystifying, and it contains poems which begin

Who wouldn't resent this breathalyzer
on the middle finger of the occult
each photo finish a Shiite...

(I decide to include it.)

3/9

Triumph! I locate a cardboard box in the attic filled with literary magazines—including *Nexus,* a bona fide journal of the Ohio State University (WO 16A Student Union WSU Dayton, OH 45435) and *Verses That Hurt,* an anthology published by St. Martin's Press. I wisely decide not to submit "My Sexuality" from the anthology (in which I imagine seducing a sheep at the Duchess County Fair), but for some self-destructive reason I include "jargon" from *Nexus*:

cops are
happy with
jargon,

criminals

are angry
in jargon

Fuck you
say criminals

it's a 302
cops say

Having assembled my Proof of Eligibility, I must now compile my Manuscript Material ("clearly reproduced copies of manuscript samples of work that you have written between January 1, 1995 and March 11, 2002 and for which you have sole artistic responsibility"). In other words, a few poems.

Again, I avoid the word "shit" and insults to the Rich.

3/10
I worry about the following two pieces; should I submit them?

ZEN POEM
"   ," he said.

"   ," she replied.

ZEN POEM 2
"   ," she said.

"   ," he replied.

The problem is that the application guidelines warn: "No more than one poem per page." I don't want to waste two of my pages on these poems (I only have a maximum of 10 poems), but would the NEA believe me if I said: "These are two poems disguised as one"?

(I do not include "Zen Poem" and "Zen Poem 2.")

I finish my 10-page packet. Without politics and obscenity I am a romantic, with poems like:

PRAYED
Often I prayed—long nights, and bare,
dim mornings—for one face,

and now my prayers are unnecessary,
for you are here, in my room,

lying in bed with me —

and I can face God
without prayer.

A new fear: I don't have any return address labels with my actual legal name on them—all of them say "Sparrow." Will this disqualify me, after all my effort?

I walk into Phoenicia Hardware to begin my xeroxing. "I'm going to make a few copies," I tell Dave, the proprietor. "No, you're not," he replies, smiling.

I look to the back of the store—the xerox machine is missing!

"Dave got tired of everyone in town saying, ' 7 cents is too much,'" my wife explained, when I returned home. The nearest xerox machine is in Woodstock—and I don't drive!

"If you just help me with a little xeroxing, I'll split the $20,000 with you," I promise my wife.

She agrees.

How will I spend my $20,000? Certainly, I will give half to my wife. Then I will use $800 to arrange a grand banquet for all my friends I owe money to—who have paid for brunches and dinners for me, all these years. I'll hold this feast in Gandhi, an Indian restaurant in the East Village. Toasts will go around the table, over Golden Lion beer: "To Sparrow, whose gratitude is delayed, but never extinguished!" "To Sparrow, a truly Nationally-Endowed Artist!"

3/11
Violet takes my manuscript to Woodstock, to xerox.

"Did you read my poems?" I ask her, when she returns.

"Yes. I like them," she says quietly. "That onions one is ama.

That was the one I was most uncertain of—was it too weird for the United States Government?

ONIONS DIVINE
Cut onions into the shape of serpents. Soak in

1 cup vinegar
1 tsp salt
4 daisy petals

for two hours. Saute in canola oil. When onions are amber, remove. Serve on a sliced peach.

There is a bureaucratic pleasure in arranging the requisite pieces in order: the nine booklets of ten poems each, neatly stapled, the three copies of my Admission Form, my Application Acknowledgment Card, all smartly paperclipped together. Even if I lose—even if I receive a reply from a governmental agent, indicting: "These poems are pointless, and silly!"— I have succeeded, in some sense. I have proven myself an adult.

"Which corner do we staple them in?" Violet asks.

I search in the booklet, reading the same paragraph fifteen times. Finally I locate it: "It doesn't say which corner to staple them in. It only says the page numbers must be in the upper right hand corner."

There is something dispiriting about the address I send my application to: "Office of Information and Technology Management, Room 815." It is only after this, in parentheses, that the words "Creative Writing Fellowships" appear. Is that my fate, to be assessed by the Office of Information and Technology Management, in Room 815? Are my poems just "information" to be "managed"? Am I myself some human-looking piece of poetry technology? And how sad is the number 815!

Somehow I know that on my way to the post office tomorrow—in the one block between my house and the brick building the postal service administers—volcanoes will explode, earthquakes will erupt, fire will descend from Heaven to smite me. Something will stop me from mailing my masterpiece.

If only I could give the manuscript a title (which is disallowed)! I would call it *Boo-Boos Without Band-Aids*.

3/12

I picture all the poets across America—and even the squarest poets must wait until the last day to mail this—in their suede jackets, berets, bowties, sunglasses, bowler hats—and women poets, wearing long print dresses depicting pink orchids—all licking envelopes, sliding paper clips onto pages, borrowing five dollars from their mother for postage—all over America: atop mountains, overlooking bays, inside subways, hiking through the Painted Desert. God bless ye, American poets! God grant ye great poems, though He will deny almost all of ye $20,000!

I lick my own envelope, and place *Shelley's Poetical Works* on top to weigh it down—one last dose of good luck.

"Use Certified, First-class mail," advises the application guidelines booklet. "Do not use Special Delivery or Special Handling. We strongly recommend that you send material 'return receipt requested,' which will serve as your immediate notification (and postmark proof) that the material has reached the Art Endowment," the booklet continues.

I feel an urge to Battle The Status Quo, and *refuse* to send material "return receipt requested." But this anarchic moment vanishes, when I reach the postal desk.

3/13

What was I thinking? Will some panel of experts—there must be nine of them, because I made nine copies of my packet —all agree my anti-aesthetic poems deserve to be bathed in vast dollars? Oh, it is embarrassing, and impossible. For example, this poem:

FIX FIGS

I always
fix my figs.

If one tears,
I sew
the seam.

If a stem
is lost, I
make
another,
of
leather.

If a mouse
nibbles
one, I
fill the
hole
with wax.

Which nine people on earth would award this poem with 20,000 bucks?

3/22

I am composing a letter to our president, in case I win the coveted grant:

> Dear President George W. Bush,
>
> Although I despise you, your policies, and your dictatorial coup of our government, I sincerely thank you for the $20,000 you are sending me. In this case, you acted with discernment, kindness, and wisdom. Also, I really need the money.
>
> I will attempt to write a beautiful book about Abraham Lincoln's brother, in return.
>
> Love,
> Sparrow

WHAT IS POETRY IN THIS PRESENT DECADE?

How does poetry exist in an era where no reading occurs?

Let me began by saying that I know no one reads now. I visit my relatives, in their extremely large houses, and it is clear why no one reads. It is impossible to read. Middle-class houses in America now resemble discotheques, with music playing, flashing video screens, ringing bells. Reading in such a house is like performing the Zen tea ceremony at a rodeo.

Western culture has abolished interior thinking. Why? Because it cannot be bought or sold. Capitalism now must rent parts of our mind—fill our inner visual screens with amusement. You and I are the marketplace where the culture occurs. Ninety years ago, the Capitalists had huge steel mills, thunderous railroads, clouds of steam. Now they have sitcoms, "reality dating shows", teenage movies. They need our attention, like they formerly needed the Mississippi River and the iron ore of Michigan.

And we give them our attention. If we are intellectuals like myself, who have no television and never buy CDs, we read *Vanity Fair* magazine compulsively.

Vanity Fair is not reading. It is a movie that perches on your lap.

But poetry requires contemplation—it *is* contemplation.

Of course, poetry is still written, it is still published; it is simply not read.

By "poetry" I mean what Western culture has called poetry for 2500 years—words written on a page. If one includes all pop music as poetry, or all advertising, or the scripts of particularly appealing movies, or lost dog posters, there is much poetry. But I believe in using words as literally as possible. Perhaps this is why I am a poet.

Let us look at a particular lost dog poster:

My dog is lost.

She is white.
Answers to the
name "Sheba."

Half-terrier.
Call 607-1062.

Compare this to an actual poem, published in *The New Yorker*, by the famous poet W. S. Merwin (I will only include the first three lines of this poem, which is entitled "Net"):

> We were sitting along the river as the daylight
>   faded in high summer too slowly to be followed
> a pink haze gathering beyond the tall poplars

Now we can see why poetry is ignored. The lost dog poster is an infinitely better poem than the poem. Why? Its language is simple, not intended as beautiful, both amusing and sad, and it employs numbers to convey desperation. The interesting series of numerals, 607-1062, comes to mean: "Please call! I miss my pet!" It pleads to the reader, makes a demand on her: "Search for my dog!" Also the poster is literary; it refers to the biblical Sheba, wife of the wise King Solomon.

In comparison, "Net" is some private reminiscence, of some highly cultivated, self-satisfied nincompoops. Merwin's poem has the repetitive comfort of Prozac.

This explains why people read lost dog posters, but not poems.

THE SKIES OF THE CATSKILLS

Living in Phoenicia, the sky is my main cultural influence. I can't afford to go to the movies; we have no TV; I don't like trees and grass. Yet each morning, the sky appears with her curious, fresh ideas.

In Manhattan, where I formerly dwelt, only a partial sky occurs. Manmade buildings delimit her expanse. Here, Godmade mountains cut off the sky. I am grateful for these encumbrances. A total sky demands total attention.

What follows is my Catskill sky journal, punctuated by Tremendous Sky Facts. (I refer to the shapes in the sky without mentioning that they are clouds.)

June 24
1:08 p.m.
The sky is a uniform light blue—the blue of a pond, not of the sea—with, at the edges, a few smudgy Nike insignias.

4:18 p.m.
A faint picture of a bunny in the sky turns into a pair of pliers.

5:49 p.m.
Three abstract angels swooping down.

June 26
9:31 a.m.
A pale, diffident sky. In the center I see a sheep, then Ezra Pound, then nothing.

Woodstock 6:02 p.m.
The sky has grown paler and paler all day, until now it is white as an egg. To the north, Goofy, the cartoon character, swaggers.

June 27
5:38 a.m.
A low, watchful sky—a suspicious sky. I find myself moving through

the house surreptitiously, as if the firmament were a cop.

(Do skies remind me of cops because they both wear blue?)

INTERVIEW WITH A CELESTIALOGIST

I interviewed Zeke Blackmuir, a celestialogist (an expert on the sky) at Rembolt College.

Sparrow: What is the sky?

Blackmuir: Actually, there is no sky. What appears to be the sky is really four billion separate entities, called parms. These parms are nearly microscopic in size. Together they inter-refract—refract each other—creating the appearance of one sky.

Sparrow: Is the sky different in different locales?

Blackmuir: Absolutely. The vegetation of an area affects the sky directly. Plants give off oxygen and nitrogen. The exact percentage of oxygen and nitrogen in an area will affect the look of the sky.

Sparrow: What about the Catskills?

Blackmuir: The hemlock, spruce and maple forests emit gases which create a very high, bell-shaped sky.

Sparrow: How may we best see the sky?

Blackmuir: There is a great deal of research on this, and even experts disagree. I personally say that the morning sky viewed from very low—for example, while lying on the ground—is the most breathtaking sky.

June 29
8:31 p.m.
A giant impression of lips on the sky. Is God kissing us from above?

June 30
8:49 a.m.
A sensitive muted grey sky, reminiscent of Chopin's *Nocturnes* and Don Cherry's jazz solos.

2 p.m.
An exhaustive thunderstorm.

2:41 p.m.
The sky has cleared and I see distantly a demon from *Ghostbusters* wearing a baseball catcher's mask.

A POEM
In the book *Mountain Memories* (1921), edited by Alistair Oone, I found the following poem:

CATSKILL SKIES
O beauteous Catskills skies, whose glory is forever,
Where clouds float like pies, and hikers do endeavor
To climb your noble heights, and on a peak
For days and nights your colors do bespeak

The wonder that is locked in heaven above;
Poets cannot concoct to name this Love.
— John Ransom Crendaw

June 31
Woodstock 3:14 p.m.
A large elephantine shadow in the south, which appears to be defecating.

3:28 p.m.
A strong, alarming wind emerges from the elephantine shadow.

RADIO CHANGES CLOUDS
E. G. Sargent, an amateur aerialist in Chicago, noticed that clouds changed after the advent of radio broadcasting in 1921. Clouds close to the ground became longer and more ragged. Higher clouds were unaffected.

Sargent divided clouds into two main categories: radiolateral and radiophobic. Radiolateral clouds lined up parallel to the radio transmission. Radiophobic clouds avoided radio waves.

Sargent's findings were never corroborated.

July 1
A troubled sky, a sky that needs therapy.

July 2
7:38 a.m.
A bearded genie above Mt. Tremper, with arms folded.

July 3
2:15 p.m.
A bent drinking straw.

JAPANESE CLOUD DIVINATION
In Japan, one typically examines the sky early in the morning, and based on the number of clouds, augurs the tone of the day.

>One cloud: Danger
>Two clouds: Humor
>Three clouds: Softness
>Four clouds: Doubt
>Five clouds: Royalty
>Six clouds: Boredom
>Seven clouds: Fire
>Eight clouds: Theatre
>Nine Clouds: Courage

July 5
3:42 p.m.
High in the sky, almost directly overhead, a fissure in the clouds, resembling a vagina.

July 7
7:42 a.m.
A sky wearing a sky mask—an opaque expanse.

July 8
5:15 a.m.
The sky is white on the edges, as if the man painting the sky ran out of blue.

OUT THE WINDOW:
A LETTER FROM PHOENICIA

Dear Brian,

Here it is—the first gallery review in history in which the critic did not leave his house, because the critic (myself) can see the gallery from his house. It has taken the shape of a journal.

June 4

I moved to Phoenicia on Jan. 2. Before that I lived in Shandaken for six months. Previous to that I lived in the East Village (Manhattan) for a ten year period. I have lived four years in Gainesville, Fla., four months in Denver, two and half months in Calcutta. Never before have I lived in a town.

A town in an exercise in minimalism. Each human endeavor is represented by one example. From my house on Main Street I view the one video store (Phoenicia Films), the one ice cream parlor (Ice Cream Station) and the one pizza place (Brio's). From my daughter's room, I spy the one beauty parlor (Debra Jo's) and the one market (Kirk's Market). Phoenicia is lucky to have no supermarket, only a mortal market.

And now there is one gallery, also.

A number of trees interfere with my view of the gallery: a thirty-five foot sugar maple, a taller spruce, some branches of cedar, and a few low slippery elms. The gallery seems perched in the spruce tree, like a bird's nest—the art like little eggs in the nest.

June 5

Many times I have visited rock'n'roll nightclubs, and watched bands set up. The mustached drummer nervously drums, testing his kit. The singer tries out the microphone, sometimes glancing back at her boyfriend, the guitarist. The bass player stands at the rear of the stage, in profile. I watch from the crowd, with an aesthetic lust. Will this be the powerful rock combo I have always envisioned? For eighteen minutes I observe the band slowly gather together.

Then the song begins. After thirty seconds, I am bored. I turn and leave the Continental, or whatever club I am inside.

Have I stupidly wasted eighteen minutes? For a long time I thought so. Then one day I grasped the truth: what I love is the *theatre* of music, the drama of music being prepared. I love hope, and hot expectation. Only the best music is more superb than those pregnant minutes of possibility.

There is an analogous moment in art—when you see a gallery from across the street, or pass it in a bus. (In Manhattan, you first see the paintings through a glass door in the hallway.) The art is distantly small, and strongly colored. (Close up, I never notice colors in painting, but far away colors predominate.) How exotic and elated art is when you can't quite see it!

June 6

I just realized that if I can see into the art gallery, the art gallery can see into my house. (We have no curtains.) I can see the art, but they can see *me*. This is the danger of spying. Spies may also be observed.

June 7

A gallery, of course, is a work of art. I would say it is a work of conceptual art. Why? Because it never ends. Ordinary art can be finished. For example, Velasquez's *Duchess of Amadea* is finished. Velasquez finished it. But a gallery is never done. A gallery closes, and is still not complete. A gallery is never finished because it is a room that art moves through.

Sometimes a trace of the art remains—a few drawings, or slides, or reviews, in the back room. But some galleries save nothing. Bread Alone in Woodstock, for example, sells bread and paintings. The bread leaves, the paintings leave. Nothing remains of the bread or art.

I don't know about this gallery. I can't see into the back room. I don't know how much of the art will remain.

June 8

I must confess I know the gallery's name. Yesterday, on the way to the library, I peeked at its door. The name is Upstate Art. And here is a larger admission: I saw a painting, in the hallway behind the door.

But I immediately endeavored to forget it. All I recall is that the painting was nearly square, about three feet to a side, colorful, geometric, and not a portrait.

"Upstate Art" is certainly a general term. It does not link the gallery to Phoenicia, or even the Catskills. (Perhaps the gallerist wishes to move someday.) The name does, however, take a stand on the definition of "upstate." My friend Tom told me that in Plattsburgh "upstate" is defined as "above Albany."

Also the gallery does not call itself a gallery. It calls itself "art," as if the gallery were invisible, or were inseparable from the art—or were, as I have argued, a work of art itself.

June 9
Here comes the Hostess Cake truck passing the gallery. We are on opposite sides of the street. Traffic flows between the gallery and I!

June 10
Despite my best intention, I looked in the doorway as I passed Upstate Art today. The painting was gone.

What does this mean? Did I imagine the painting in the first place? Was the painting removed as some kind of message?

June 10, 11:33 p.m.
They turned on a light in the gallery, and I noticed suddenly a large painting I never saw before, with vivid pulling colors. I hadn't seen any of the paintings so clearly before. Normally, even during the day, they look like turned off TV sets. With the light on, this one looks like a *turned on* TV set.

I never noticed how similar paintings and television are. They are both screens that become animated by the presence of light.

Why is there no abstract TV?, I wonder. Why must video always represent some familiar object? Even Public Access Cable shows an unshaven guy on a couch shouting. I wish there were abstract TV, so that housewives and ironmongers could develop an untrammeled and exquisite inner mind.

Wait! I cannot develop abstract TV, but I can create abstract writing. Here it is:

d   cnl   c

o   l

                          t
                  dgh   dp   k

                              r
                  e   u

Kind reader, gaze for a moment on my abstraction, and meditate.

[Pause.]

So, how do you feel now? Are you more…abstract?

All art is abstract when viewed from a distance—even a portrait of George Washington 600 feet high. (Incidentally, it is a myth that the astronauts could see the Great Wall of China from the moon.)

I believe we stand too close to art. We think we know it too well. The best way to see a painting is from across the street—especially across a *Main* Street—to shyly glimpse it as we do a blond tennis player.

From nearby one can dismiss a painting by reciting its flaws. From a distance the flaws are virtues. The muddy brown is more of a purple. The skewed composition is a gentle blur.

And the paintings become much smaller from afar, as if they were the work of spiritual insects.

June 11

The gallerist has leaned one of the paintings against a window facing me. Thus I see the back of the canvas. This places me in a unique position as an art critic. Millions of pages have been written on the fronts of paintings. Nothing has been written on the backs of paintings.

Firstly I notice that the fronts of the paintings look dark from here; the rear of the painting is white. Paintings are dark on one side and light on the other, like the moon, which circles the sun, always keeping one face in light and one in shadow. Secondly, the rear of the painting has an industrial look—you can see it was made in a factory.

Paintings result from industrial processes. The canvas, the brushes, the paints are all created in factories. Because an individual combines these constituents, we imagine that individuals make paintings. Truly, artists only apply one factory-made substance onto another. Sadly, artists live in the same corporate world of manufactured goods that we do. They do not inhabit Renaissance Italy while we exist in 1999.

June 12, 10:04 p.m.
Some kind of meeting is occurring at Upstate Art. Folding chairs are arranged in rows, the lights are on, and someone is speaking. is this an art lecture, or a poetry reading? A Scientology meeting?

I wish I could go, but I am sworn to distance, for the duration of this essay.

Events at art galleries are usually distracted. There is a feeling that the paintings are behind the speaker, mocking him—because paintings speak without words, which is much more elegant than words.

June 14
(Flag Day)
Today the gallery seems darker inside. Each day it grows darker and darker. The more I look at it, the darker it gets. Am I somehow *consuming* the gallery's light?

> Yours in voyeuristic art criticism,
> Sparrow

~Proverbs~

Some gifts arrive opened.

·

The neck is the organ of forgiveness.

·

Buddhists don't pay ransom.

·

Seducers marry their mistakes.

·

A stopped calendar is right once a year.

·

If olives had wings martinis would fly.

·

The knot is wider than the rope.

·

Anything carried becomes heavy.

·

Poison is food for one meal.

·

You can't buy soap on the layaway plan.

·

Most politeness is paid for.

·

There is something foolish about toast.

·

Time zones don't have capitals.

·

Even a genius looks better from one side.

·

Know yourself—read your resume.

·

The Devil mostly waits.

Throw away the scale and you weigh the same.

•

Pride goeth before 3 A.M.

•

When it rains fish, hold out a net.

•

For pigs it's always Happy Hour.

•

When fate is exhausted politicians take over.

•

Missionaries know the best restaurants.

•

In time, anything on the floor becomes a rug.

•

Fire built the Great Cities.

•

In a coma one still earns interest.

•

Birds make their own breadcrumbs.

•

You can't blackmail a whore.

•

Anyone can get lost, but staying lost is an art.

•

Time waits for one man.

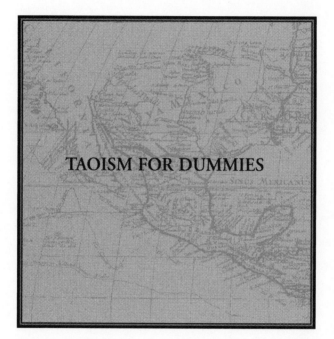

TAOISM FOR DUMMIES

A SPIRITUAL GUIDE TO MANHATTAN

I've been meditating fourteen years (not continuously, just twice a day) with the Ananda Marga Society—and this is the first time I've put it to use, except to relax when drunks driving 90 m.p.h. pick me up hitchhiking. Y'know how they have rainfall maps of nations, with colored sections? I wanted to do a "High Spirituality Zone," "Low Spirituality Zone" map for my nation, Manhattan.

This is simply what I did: visited major New York City venues, sat down, closed my eyes and performed meditation. I sat in a rattan Elysee Club chair (Bloomingdale's), on a tourist couch (U.N.), on a marble ledge (Grant's Tomb), on the floor. Depending on my guess about the proprietor, I'd ask permission. I'd sit at least a half hour; some sessions exceeded one hour.

Afterwards, I'd write my sensations fervidly on sheets of 8 1/2" x 11" scrap paper. I was surprised how distinct the images were. Perhaps every place *does* have a "vibration."

Anyone is invited to replicate my research. Please send your findings to: Manhattan Spirituality Survey c/o Soft Skull Press.

I began this as a joke on the New Age idea of "power places," but as my studies proceeded, I began to think Manhattan was one.

THE AMERICAN MUSEUM OF NATURAL HISTORY
77th St. Entrance
Tribal Life of N. Pacific America room

This is the room with the totem poles: a place one intensely wishes to take one's girlfriend—it's dark and sexy, and you can almost see the light bend around the wooden turtles. Also there are murals of Indians in what look like togas.

Between a bugeyed owl and a red-white-and-blue fox, on a wooden bench, I sat. Eyes closed, I felt a tutelary essence—the sense of being forced to learn. Children cried and shuffled, as stout women called: "Let's try to keep these lines together." Not much has changed here since 1904—an era of High Charity—and the charitableness of this charitable institution made me drowsy.

True, I sensed the secreted truth within the huge muskrats around me, but another force blocked it. Was it the spirit of Teddy Roosevelt, whose statue's in the lobby: that happy Imperialist who reached The River of Doubt in Brazil in 1913 and named it after himself?

BLOOMINGDALE'S
1000 3rd Avenue (at 59th St.)

This was only the second time I'd been there. The first time, perhaps because I'd gone with my old acidhead friend, Binks, it seemed like a funhouse: with multitudes of mirrors, and grinning men appearing, anxious to spray you with scents. On a landing of the escalator, a man in a dinner jacket played a grand piano, with the word OPIUM propped up on top. "My first subtitled hallucination," I whispered to Binks.

But this time, at 10:40 on a Tuesday morning, it all seemed tired and facile—even the fishnet stockings on the young purse saleswomen. "I don't like most of this stuff!" it hit me in the coat section. "It's boring!"

I picked the 5th floor because it had the most chairs and was out of harm's way.

I was directed to a heavy woman with a gorgeous telephone voice, Sharri Garvin, Customer Service Expert for the Furniture Dept., to ask permission. She had *The National Star* on her desk ("Hey, Look At Oprah Now!") and agreed easily to my request: "I tell you, people do a lot of things to our chairs—meditating will probably be one of the calmer ones."

Sitting down, I wondered, "What do people *do* to Bloomingdale's chairs?"

I closed my eyes.

Salespeople paced by at great speed, with the air of nearing someone on the phone with a lot of money.

"Is Mr. Subotnik on the floor?" came an announcement on the intercom, which reminded me of the famous Frank O'Hara poem:

and suddenly I see a headline
LANA TURNER HAS COLLAPSED!...
I have been to lots of parties
and acted perfectly disgraceful
but I never actually collapsed
Oh Lana Turner we love you get up

I'd been sprayed twice by cologne agents on floor two: both Obsession and Ralph Lauren; which was a distraction—or is there a piped-in scent at Bloomies?

"It's 66 inches, which only gives 6 inches to play with," a successful man said to his wife.

I had the sense of air streaming by, but not just air—some kind of happy moving molecules.

The strength of a store is that it's a receptive place. Like Lao Tzu says:

> The use of clay in molding pitchers
> Comes from the hollow of its absence;
> Doors, windows, in a house,
> Are used for their emptiness:
> Thus we are helped by what is not
> To use what is.

A store is an event waiting to happen; which gives meditation a chance to bloom.

Afterwards, I went to the bathroom—a surprisingly grim place, with a very lengthy wait for the stalls. five men were in longer than I have ever waited for five men. Perhaps Bloomingdale's has a constipating effect?

DEGAS EXHIBIT
The Metropolitan Museum Of Art
82nd St. and 5th

Did you know Degas visited New Orleans from October 1872 to March 1873—the home of his mother's family, the Mussons—and made "Portraits in an Office (New Orleans)," a breakthrough picture set in a cotton exchange? (Near it is "Woman Ironing" (1873)—one of those dark working class paintings—like early Van Gogh—suggesting that work, somehow, makes us gods.)

In this room, where Degas began to find his tune, I sat—and though the place was packed with Kept Women from Westchester, the Socially Secure (those on Social Security) and a few scruffy artists, I felt suddenly that no one was there, that I was in either a mosque or a bank, and a silver thread from some unseeable height descended to my head—as if I were the simplest kind of marionette.

Of course one *would* feel connected to Heaven and to no person in the Met. It's the one museum in New York City one never plans to pick up women in (It seems inevitable you wouldn't make it outdoors together—there's too many Babylonian Kings in the way.).

Nowadays, in the big exhibits, one is surrounded by voices emerging from people's earphones, as if the little machines they wear magnified their thoughts—the only problem being they all think the same thing.

A few human voices did speak—a Classical Music Announcer type: "It's so good to see this because I never knew their size;" a well-meaning Jewish relative: "Harriet, let me take your coat;" and a druggist from Ohio: "We should be through in one hour and five minutes..."

By chance, a real guru attended the show while I was there—Brahmananda Sarasvati, leader of the Ananda Ashram in Monroe, N.Y.—a man with quite a long beard and bright orange robery. He seemed to have suffered a stroke, judging from his speech. A woman who looked like a Born Again Christian pushed his wheelchair, and spoke quite loudly to him. (For some reason women with gurus always look like Born Again Christians.)

"Here's a woman in drapery," she said of "Standing Woman, Draped" (c. 1860-62) (graphite, watercolor, gouache).

"I, too, am draped," the guru joked.

BROWNIE POINTS CAFE
101 2nd Ave (at 6th)

I started coming here because I knew somehow, as moochers

do, that one can sit many hours and buy very little, perhaps by its large yellow plastic sign, with script letters. Or by the legend on each table:

FOOD & DRINK
PURCHASED ELSEWHERE
ARE NOT PERMITTED

This day I bought an almond ambrosia cookie for $1.20. It had three almonds, equally spaced and pointing to the center; the sign of an intelligence—either obsessive or idealistic—in its maker.

Meditating, I was immediately aware, feeling upward with a kind of antenna that comes to one in meditation, that "It's a cave." Then the warmth inside my coat, I realized, was not entirely physical; there was an emanation from my heart.

"This is one of the places that's saving New York!" I thought.

It peaked when Barbra Streisand came on the radio singing "There's A Place For Us." Lately I've noticed everyone in New York City thinks there's some other place they should be—Violet and I alternate between Senegal and New Mexico—a sense that This Is Not Our Real Home. But that's the greatness of this Immense Apple, that it gives you such yearning. And the way Barbra sings—with that somewhat insincere, but torrential, emotion—is just the way one thinks of that golden place: like Oregon, but with more angels.

"What's 'carob'?" a customer asked, looking at the glass case.

"Well, it's something like chocolate, but if you're expecting chocolate you'll be disappointed."

"Oh . . ."

"It's from the . . . what plant's it from?" the owner asked the other guy behind the counter.

"The carob plant."

"The carob plant. We're a wealth of information here."

Then the clock in my pocket started beeping and I went off to my therapist.

THE EMPIRE STATE BUILDING
Find it yourself.

It's quite an indelible fact that you walk down 34th St. past the thousand women buying Christmas cards that play "Jingle Bells," past the
Ultissima Beauty School, through the revolving doors, and you're in
the Empire State Building. I love this building, and it amazes me just
anybody can walk into it. It should be off on its own island like the
Statue of Liberty and take money to get to.

But where to sit? I rode down the escalator, to the basement, as a sax
playing "I'm Dreaming Of A White Christmas," piped in. Then, on a
blond bench near the ticket booth to the Observation Deck, I listened
to women gossip in Russian, and felt a *blanket* over me, or perhaps a 102
story building sitting on my head. I fell asleep and drooled in my beard.

THE STATEN ISLAND FERRY TERMINAL

I almost sat next to a man stooped over a shopping bag, but he had
that No-Home smell, and fearing I'd not be able to think of anything
else, coward I am, I climbed over the seat, closed my eyes and felt
immediately happy. "This place is like a birthday cake," I thought. "It's
got a round sensation. . ."

The boat came and an arm jostled me. "Maybe he don't want to
catch it. Probably prayin'," a guy said.

"That Napoleon Hill has very sound principles," a voice spoke, of
the author of *Think And Grow Rich*. "'Find your dream, and don't stop
until you reach it.'" Marcus Boon told me last Saturday, "The nice
thing about Midtown is the tides," and this room, too—this happy
room in which homeless live—is very much one of tides. Over fifty
minutes it emptied and filled, and the sound of thousands of Staten
Islanders standing is like a wind over alfalfa.

METROPOLITAN OPERA
Lincoln Center 66th St. and Broadway

I wasn't sure which building I was in: I *suspected* it of being the Opera, because I sensed the woman at the INFORMATION desk—gray-haired, German-accented and sympatico—was a volunteer. For opera, the aged will volunteer! This was the first time I had my letter from Kevin Kelly, editor of the *Whole Earth Review*, which I produced for her:

> January 2, 1989
> To Whom It May Concern:
>
> The bearer, Sparrow by name, is working on an article
> for our magazine. Please allow him to meditate in your
> establishment. His research is for a *Spiritual Guide to
> New York City*. Thank you for your assistance.
>
> Sincerely,
> K.K.

She looked at it wonderingly, as if she read Hesse in youth, stammered that the "chamber" was closed—and directed me to the security guard, who examined the note at greater length and pointed to a corner: "You may meditate there." Was he Italian? Were the Cultivated Races drawn to the Center, to aid spiritual reporters? Closing my eyes—by the glass window of the gift shop—I felt a wobbly thrumming giant harp within the building, making the sound of a bell before it rings. And I hate opera*...

It's the hollowness here I love (the hollowness of auditoria), I thought. Perhaps a great civilization builds great hollownesses. Certainly this was true of the Turks.

"Do I Hear A Waltz?" played in my mind as I looked up.

*OK, I like the French one about a girl who works in a cigarette factory.

THE PORT AUTHORITY BUS TERMINAL
42nd Street and 8th

There were three guys camped out by the escalator as I came in. "You want some potato chips?" I asked. The guy on the right took them before I'd finished the sentence.

Upstairs I saw they'd removed the seats to discourage drifters, so the drifters were sitting on the floor. I sat down near a pair of crutches and closed my eyes. "Is it possible to meditate with muzak?" I thought, and for thirty minutes the muzak continued—all songs I'd never heard of. They seemed to have been sung by Loretta Young in musicals of the 1950s. I knew the last one, though: "You Needed Me," the Ann Murray song:

> You placed me high up on a pedestal
> So high that I could almost see eternity

"This feels like a Woolworth's in Selma," I realized. It doesn't have a New York City sensation—possibly because it's a portal away from the city. I felt at one point that everything was leaning to one side: the left.

THE NEW YORK STOCK EXCHANGE
Wall and Broad Sts.

"Miss, would you step out, please?" the security guard asked.

"Ask her if she has a knife," the check-in man, who was dressed for a Presbyterian picnic, suggested.

"It must be my jewelry," the offending woman mused.

"Will you take your bangles off?"

"Sure." She passed through the bomb detector.

"Yeah, that did it," the guard noted. "Cameras are going to be checked in," he shouted at the new arrivals.

Finally, my curiosity overcame me. "Why aren't cameras allowed?" I asked.

"Because the flashes distract the brokers."

"You have probably seen the stock tables in your local newspaper. . ." a female voice began over New Age music. Bronze bull and bear bookends were $125 at the gift shop, I noticed. I walked out to the observation booth. Eyes closed, there was a sea-like surge. "Ah, this will be a good place to meditate." A push against my forehead.

Then it gave me a headache, and the voices from the floor sounded pained. There were shouts, as at a delirious revel. More New Age music came on, and, "What you are watching is the marketplace in action. . ." a friendly avuncular voice stated—then an explanation I heard fifteen times and still don't understand. ("If you look closely at the front of one of the trading posts you will see a discussion between a Specialist and a person employed by the broker. . . ")

This tape is a ploy to get people moving, I realized. At the end it suggests, "If you've heard this tape, please remove yourself so others may have a chance to see," plus a woman with a microphone repeated it, *live*. But the Stock Exchange is a paper tiger, reader. You can meditate as long as you like—or can stand.

Opening my eyes, I met a sociology student in a tie, taking notes. "There's more camaraderie than you would expect," he said. "I saw a guy giving a woman a massage. I wished I was down there."

"Who cleans the floor?" asked a Queens woman as I left.

PYRAMID CLUB
101 Ave A

Being here makes you love rock'n'roll. I have sworn off rock'n'roll a hundred times in my life—most recently an interview with Paul Morrissey, my favorite living director (*Trash, Heat, Spike Of Bensonburst*) suggesting that Rock is leaving us open to Soviet attack—made me decide, "I will try to listen to Tchaikovsky," which bores me to death absolutely.

But I compromise by playing songs of the Sami (Laplanders of Norway).

Now, though, hearing *Rank* (The Smiths' live album) as I meditate, I'm in a state of absolute grim delight:

> And if a ten ton truck
> Crashes into us
> To die by your side
> Would be a heavenly way to die.

"Oh, yes, it's supposed to be good to meditate in a pyramid," I thought—and remembered I'd meditated inside the Great Pyramid in Egypt. This was much better; Cheops appeared to have had a spiritual *lobotomy*.

Here, I sensed the familial warmth of beer and cigarettes—and I never drink beer *or* cigarettes—and a flight of stairs . . . no, a *tunnel*, leading down into Mysteries.

But I don't know the Pyramid's core—perhaps no one can. five years ago (1983) it looked like the club was going yuppie. It had the most heterogenous Good Dancers in NYC—Office Managers, junkies, hairdressing students—but yuppies, after flirting with the thought of taking it over, decided they'd rather eat dinner, so it's stayed ready-for-a-fight. If you can read lips, you'll hear good lyrics you'll remember at least one line of—for example, the Athens (Ga.) band, Oh, Ok, which sang, of a hairstyle:

> It's a permanent
> It won't last forever.

GRANT'S TOMB
122nd St. and Riverside Drive

"How large it is!" I thought. "Grant did pretty well."

Should I take off my hat? Thinking of Grant, the first President famous for corruption, yet so honest he became penniless and was forced to write his memoirs, which were the best of any Chief Executive, I went downstairs.

Two lurking caskets of stone held Grant and wife. "By a bust of Sherman I'll sit." (Up on a ledge—there are no seats.)

Luckily, the guards flirt and drink coffee all day, so they didn't chase me. And the white marble *warms* slightly to the ass after a while.

The place is the shape of a German WWI helmet—round with a tip—and the roundness holds a good silence; but the *tip* collects thoughts and keeps them from moving freely. I believed at times I could feel the heavy sensation of a man who lived behind a *beard* his whole life, and drank, and sent many thousands to die, and had to be *President*, but it may've just been imaginings.

Finishing my *guru puja*, I looked at Sherman. He seemed angry and vexed—because he's in *real* Hell now and finds that war was not so bad?

I met a black actor upstairs, and we conversed.

"Grant's quite photogenic," he said.

"I wonder what he'd look like without his beard."

"There's a picture in there. He shaved so his wife could have his picture taken."

I looked in the room he pointed to—and there was Grant with the center of his beard removed. He was utterly unrecognizable. This man we all think we know; we don't know him, we know his beard.

THE UNITED NATIONS
46th St. and First Avenue

On the plaza you pass a sculpture of a gun with its barrel tied in a knot: "Gift of Luxembourg, 1988."

Well, Luxembourg *would* be against war.

And the great neon Pepsi Cola sign across the river. ("Isn't there a committee to preserve the sign as part of our national heritage?")

Through the metal detector I went.

"Is it possible to use the meditation room?" I asked an INFORMA-TION woman resembling Mary Tyler Moore.

"No, it's indefinitely closed."

"Why is that?"

"Not enough security."

An ironic answer, I thought.

On my way to the MEN/MESSIEURS room I passed a little gift shop. A paper ball was fifty cents.

"Where are these from?"

"Tokyo," an old woman with a sari said tenderly.

It's like Star Trek here, I thought—so international.

Meditating beside a moon rock (from Apollo 14) in the lobby, I saw myself rise into the air, grinning, behind a desk—like in *Son Of Flubber*.

(Oh, I forgot to look for that rug—the Persian carpet that so impressed me in fifth grade, when the guide told our class, "There is one mistake here, deliberately, because Muslims believe only God is perfect."

I wish I'd spent my life looking for that mistake.)

APOLLO MEDICAL OFFICE
379 W. 125th St. (Harlem)

Walking 125th St., I pondered where to meditate.

Rogers Variety Candy Gum (409) looked good—full of old men sitting at tables or standing with canes. I knocked at the door.

"What do you want?" the man nearest the door asked.

"I want to buy a soda."

"No no no," he said, closing the door.

So when I peered in this "medical office," past a puddle on the floor, to see a narrow hall with 4 broken seats, I walked in.

A blonde woman and a black man were talking like they had just woken up.

"Are you waiting for the doctor?" a third patient asked me.

"No, I just want to . . . hang out."

"Sit down and be cool, he suggested."

I did. Lots of people came in, trying to give blood or use the toilet, but the toilet was broken ("Can I use your bathroom?"/"It will be fixed on Monday."/"Can I pee in your sink?"). And when no one was there, the medical personnel—all Indians—argued in English. Eyes closed, I felt someone right in front of me staring, hard. Or a bomb about to ignite.

"Excuse me." A hand touched my shoulder. I looked up to see a green sweater with WALKDON CRICKET CLUB on it.

"Can I help you? Are you waiting for the doctor?"

I showed him my letter, from Kevin Kelly.

He looked at it a long time.

"You have to bring this to Social Security, before you come here," he said.

CAVE, FT. TRYON PARK
(near Bway and 193rd St. entrance)

The Navajos believe your soul stays in the land where you were born. "My soul is here," I felt, leaving the subway at 190th St. (I grew up in the Dyckman Projects, six blocks away.) Still I was terrified of my cave, where Max Seinert and I first smoked pot, and found bags of glue, all stiff, from neighborhood sniffers, inside.

Is it gone? I worried, then remembered rocks don't move.

I climbed the hill, fifty yards.

Hello?, I called into the crevice, standing over an old man's hat. No answer.

Inside was a carpet—I'd *forgotten* the carpet! I sat on it damply, first laying down *The New York Times*. (It *had* to be *The New York Times*— the way Don Juan tells Carlos Castenada, "It must be a branch of mesquite.") A shaft of sunlight fell from a chink. *Plants* are growing in my cave!

I heard dripping water, closed my eyes and thought, "I'm the Prodigal Son," because the cave seemed to say: "You may always return."

"The peace that passeth understanding" came to me. Then I left, afraid someone would knife me.

Outside: "I did it! I finished this article!"

A cop was on the roof of my cave. "Don't worry, I'm not looking for you. There's a policeman missing," he said.

"He's not in that cave," I volunteered.

"What's in there?"

"Just a carpet."

The cop continued descending the hill—a young-faced guy, looking worried and trying not to.

I'll read the papers tomorrow, I thought.

FIRST IMPRESSIONS OF THE THIRD WORLD

As soon as you leave Israel the window gets more tempting to look through. Israel, it is true, has made "the desert bloom," but that's more interesting to say than to see—it looks like Arizona. Over the border, houses are no longer made of concrete, but of piled up five gallon aluminum cans, burlap, palm fronds—and everything has too many colors. It's the Third World.

How do you know you're in the Third World? The Australian next to me on the bus said "by the smell," but the first smell I had was my hotel room in Cairo ("The Lotus"): the same musty furniture of the 1920s that was in my grandmother's house.

In the Third World women carry things on their heads—even huge water jars on a coiled-up white cloth. A man passed me in Cairo wearing a tangle of chicken-cases the size of a jungle gym. This is something "progress" has destroyed. A citizen of Washington Heights can grow to maturity having seen nothing more than a thirteen year old girl balancing a Math book to improve her posture. To him this yoga of carrying seems uncanny, like someone walking on fire.

There are *animals* in the Third World, and not on leashes. Roosters start crowing in the middle of Marmaris at 4 A.M. (their tune reminds me of the theme from *The Odd Couple*) and donkeys wander. A city of men is also a city of horses—balding horses, horses beautiful as Brooke Shields. Cars kill more people, but relieve us of the sight of beings whipped on our streets.

The Third World is *cheap*. In Alexandria, a falafel costs two cents; so does a ride on the tram. A movie, with newsreel, is forty-five. (The Third World has bad taste in movies—the same taste as 42nd Street, in fact: Kung Fu and Arnold Schwarznegger. *After Hours* succeeded only because it affirmed a popular conception about America—that all women come up to you and ask you to sleep with them.)

Everyone in the Third World believes in God, and at three hour intervals the whole place rings with antirhythmic chanting from three hundred mosques at once, which either lifts you off the ground or gives you a headache, depending on your mood. Theological conversations always begin and end with: "How can you look at the world and think no one made it?" and after a while it's hard to remember what everyone in America is so *worried* about.

You can have the sidewalk to yourself in the Third World, because people prefer to walk in the gutter, with the garbage. Theft is rare and violence of the type we attribute to "human nature" almost unknown. Everyone you meet seems to specialize in being *kind*, the way we specialize in cotton futures or air conditioning repair. Men can be twenty-five years old, not have sex, and still be happy.

Being American in the Third World is like being Clint Eastwood; people stare at you wherever you go; and while they don't exactly ask for your *autograph*, they all want your address, to be your "pen-friend," and eventually come to America, so they can walk down the street and all the women will ask to sleep with them. (And if your name is Michael, every time you give your address the guy says, "Michael Jackson, heh heh"—which isn't even funny the *first* time). After a while you understand why Frank Sinatra punches reporters.

In Egypt I realized my ambivalence about the Third World was formed in my tenement in Manhattan: it's too noisy, too dirty, you never have a moment's *peace*, but when you leave it you feel you've left the Real Life. Why is it the longer I stay in the Third World the younger I look?

HOW THE NEW AGE BEGAN

The New Age was started by April Furshwitz of Oronco, Ca. on April 17, 1974. April taught occasional workshops in Berkeley entitled "Wishing Your Life Around," under the name April Faith. These classes integrated self-hypnosis, breathing techniques and a series of affirmations ("I am the jewel at the bottom of the sea; I am the first ray of sunrise; I am the milk that flows from every mother's breast"). She charged only $3 for these sessions, as she lived in a hut on State land and subsisted on berries, food stamps and a part-time job in an ice cream parlor.

On April 13, however, a misprint occurred in her ad in *The Berkeley Beacon*, an alternative weekly, stating that the class cost $300. Instead of her usual halfdozen students, 150 people showed up on April 17, eagerly offering their savings.

The New Age was born.

TAOISM AND ME

PART ONE

The story of my life is the story of the *Tao Te Ching*. I first discovered this book, by Chinese philosopher Lao Tzu, when I was twelve years old. At that time I was in the smartest class at P.S. 152 in Manhattan. In fact, I was one of the smartest youths in the smartest class. I commonly received grades of 98, 99, and 100. I was also president of the class and captain of the Monitor Squad. I planned to become a doctor.

But then, in my grandmother's house on Fifth Street in Philadelphia, I found a copy of the *Tao Te Ching*. (My Uncle Jimmy had read it in college.) This was the Mentor edition, of R. B. Blackney's translation. The price was 35 cents.

I read:

> On tiptoe your stance is unsteady;
> Long strides make your progress unsure;
> Show off and you get no attention;
> Your boasting will mean you have failed;
> Asserting yourself brings no credit;
> Be proud and you never will lead.

Suddenly I changed my mind. I would not be a doctor, but a quiet, humble soul— perhaps a streetsweeper. I would become what we call in America "a failure."

PART TWO

English-speaking people must read the *Tao Te Ching* in translation. The first thing a reader should know is: translation is impossible. This is a secret known primarily to translators.

In clothing design, no one translates a sari into a three-piece suit. No one says, "I am presenting this garment—a kimono—as if it were a sundress." Why do we believe words may be translated, when clothing cannot? Because long ago writers tricked us into accepting that translations exist. Why did they trick us? Because writers are audacious and busy.

I know what you're thinking. The writers *you* know sit in cafes all day long drinking coffee and staring at the waitresses. But it is the *other* writers who are audacious and busy. You do not meet them because they are constantly in their rooms, writing three-part essays, revising plays, and in their spare time "translating." They translate books from whatever language their girlfriend knows. (Translation, being impossible, requires collaboration.)

In the introductions to their books, translators admit, in a circumspect way, that translation does not exist. "I have attempted to stay as close to the tone of the original as possible," they remark. This is just what a hobbyist who has built a replica of the Eiffel Tower out of sugar cubes will say.

Let us recall, as we read the *Tao Te Ching*, that we are reading not a book but a replica of a book built from sugar cubes.

Part Three

My daughter Sylvia recently received a Groucho Marx CD (*Here's Groucho!*) for her birthday. She has been playing it constantly, and also singing along. Compare this selection from the *Tao Te Ching* and a song by Groucho:

> They call it elusive, and say
> That one looks
> But it never appears.
> They say that indeed it is rare,
> Since one listens,
> But never a sound.
> Subtle, they call it, and say
> That one grasps it
> But never gets hold.
> These three complaints amount
> To only one, which is
> Beyond all resolution.

• • •

Hello,
I must be going.
I cannot stay,
I came to say
I must be going.

I'm glad I came,
but just the same
I must be going.

I'll stay a week or two;
I'll stay the summer through,
but I am telling you
I must be going.

Groucho Marx and Taoism may be two parallel paths to a single Truth.

PART FOUR

In 1977 I read an interview with a Taoist farmer in the *New Age Journal.* He said: "In the spring I walk to the lower part of my land, near the creek. I throw some rice seeds in the ground. Then I return to my daily life. Sometime in the fall, I notice the rice is growing. I go down and harvest it. I thresh the rice and bring it to market. Then I continue with my life. Years go by, and I forget I'm a farmer."

Reading this had too large an effect on my life. This was the fate I wanted. And now it is the fate I have. I do my meditation every day, twice a day, and don't think I am planting seeds. Later, something grows in my mind. I write it on a page. The page is sent, via electronic mail, to another person. That person places it in a newspaper or magazine. Years go by, and I forget I'm a writer.

I don't feel that I'm writing. I feel that I'm avoiding writing. And I *am* avoiding most of the writing in the world. I don't write novels. I don't write sonnets. I don't write articles for *The New York Times.* Mostly I don't write at all. The only time I'm writing is when I'm writing.

Part Five

One forgets that in the *Tao Te Ching*, Lao Tzu was speaking to a king. Isn't that strange? No one recalls this. People picture Lao Tzu saying to everyone: "Make no effort. Avoid the world." Yet he speaks to a monarch, a man who rules a vast nation. For some reason, I never noticed this. If I had, my whole life might have been different. I might have become a king.

The One Hundred Thousand Biographical Notes of Sparrow

Sparrow has worked in a sheet metal factory, a natural foods store, a cherry orchard, a train station, and a marketing research firm.

Sparrow is the first member of his generation to understand the musical *Annie*.

Sparrow was in The Inwood Little League, where he played right field for Pizza Haven.

Sparrow does not know the difference between right and wrong.

Sparrow is bewildered by soda machines.

Sparrow was recently alarmed to learn that ice no longer exists. All the "ice" commercially available in today's supermarkets is actually "chlontizide," a synthetic icelike substance. Sparrow will no longer buy such "ice."

Sparrow enjoys overhearing conversations, the most notable of today's being: "A ghostbuster? You mean like some people are doctors and lawyers, you want to be a ghostbuster?"

Sparrow plays silverware and plastic lids with the band Foamola.

Sparrow has been self-published on three continents.

Sparrow is currently at work on an issue of *Big Fish* (his literary magazine) where each poem is in a different language (with no translations).

Sparrow is wondering if he'll ever learn that the left knob turns on the *back* burner.

Sparrow is the first person to be published in *The New Yorker* as a result of protesting against it. He and a group of his cronies, known as The Unbearables, demonstrated against the magazine on Pearl Harbor Day, 1993. While his comrades filibustered in the *New Yorker* offices, Sparrow quickly wrote eighteen poems, including:

More Poems

I have written
more
poems

than you
have ever
published.

Alice Quinn, the poetry editor, rejected the poems with a warm note, and Sparrow continued to submit to the magazine. He has now had four poems accepted by *The New Yorker*.

Sparrow has also had five poems in *The New York Times* (in "Metropolitan Diary") though he was later barred from the newspaper when eleven readers noticed the similarity of one of his poems to a piece of doggerel by Lord Ewen, a 19th century English aristocrat.

His poems appear frequently in such publications as *Rant, Reptiles Of The Mind, Cute Alien, Uno Mas* and *Headveins*. A poem of his also appeared in the October *Vogue*. The poem is:

Poem

This poem replaces
all my previous poems.

Sparrow ran for President in 1992 with the Pajama Party, and was the first candidate in history to beg his supporters not to vote for him. (They obeyed.) He is also responsible for the levitation of Tompkins Square Park, and founded the One Size Fits All Movement, which Allen Ginsberg joined.

He also organized the first rally against Nature, which was covered by *The New York Observer* and *Outside* magazine.

Sparrow has read at Mona's, The St. Marks Church, Tompkins Square Park, The Community Garden, The Gas Station, CBGB's Gallery, Limbo Lounge, ABC No Rio, Cafe Nico, Paddy O'Reilly's, No Bar, Chez Rollo, Biblio's, Eureka Joe, Anseo, 92nd St. Y, New Museum, Nuyorican Cafe, Medicine Show Theatre, The New School, Flamingo East, The Fez, Cedar Tavern, Washington Square Church, Westbeth Theatre, The Charleston, Sun Mountain Cafe, Deanna's, Canio's Bookstore (Sag Harbor), Borders Books (Albany) and on the Poemphone.

The band he is in, Foamola, has played at Wetlands, Brownies, Siné and Irving Plaza.

Sparrow is running for President again, this time seeking the Republican nomination. He is the only GOP candidate currently espousing revolutionary socialism.

Sparrow is often mistaken for Jesus Christ.

On the week of May 20, Sparrow was in *The New York Times*, *The Wall Street Journal*, and his band Foamola played "Balzac Prozac" at Lincoln Center.

Sparrow is reading back issues of *Architectural Digest* from 1984, for no apparent reason.

Sparrow is currently running for President, with the slogan "Forgive All Debts, Free The Slaves." He has purchased a stovepipe hat for this purpose. Sparrow is also inventing folktales of the Manhattan Indians, and writing a New Age self-help book entitled *How To Become A Playwright, Dancer, Poet, Water Ballet Choreographer, Opera Singer, Sculptor, Architect And Photographer—The Easy Way!*

Sparrow recently invented performance science, the left-brain equivalent of performance art.

Sparrow has founded the East Village Militia, which has been handing out free books in front of Nobody Beats The Wiz, to prevent people from buying TVs.

Sparrow was a TV star for 56 seconds (Channel 13) in 1996, and was interviewed in *TV Guide*. He has been recorded on four CDs, but unfortunately no one bought any of them.

Sparrow has been questioning the values of Western Culture, recently.

Sparrow is a conceptual artist. For example, he sees this biographical note as a work of conceptual art.

Sparrow is currently organizing the world's first temporary religion.

Sparrow has a small greying beard and a pot belly.

Sparrow's plans to run for Mayor in 1997 are detailed in the current *Machete* newsletter.

Sparrow is currently mourning Jerry Garcia.

Sparrow is planning a beer march down the Bowery, where thousands will protest the laws against public drinking.

Sparrow is the author of the first self-help book written in verse: *Power Poetry*.

Sparrow is living on unemployment in Olive Bridge, N.Y., near the largest kaleidoscope in the world.

Sparrow is spending the autumn making soup. Soft Skull Press published *Republican Like Me: a Diary of My Presidential Campaign*. In addition, he has two chapbooks: *Test Drive* and *Wild Wives*.

Sparrow bought the record *Flower Drum Song* (the Rogers and Hammerstein musical) at a garage sale for 5 cents, and became obsessed with the song "Chop Suey."

In stray moments, Sparrow imagines himself a cartographer.

Sparrow enjoys reading *Alpha Force* comics and Sumerian religious poetry.

Sparrow is a terrible squash player, and dislikes squash the vegetable, also.

Sparrow was recently kissed by Allen Ginsberg.

In the face of catastrophe, Sparrow is fearless.

Sparrow voted for Clinton, anyway.

Sparrow is currently learning to feed pigeons.

Sparrow loses his glasses every two years.

Sparrow rarely buys books. The last book he bought was the oral history of Ed Wood.

Sparrow is trying to solve the problem of urban poverty—his own.

Sparrow is working on a new book, *How To Live In America.*

Sparrow recently protested New Gingrich's speech in Manhattan by carrying the sign NEWT G(ETT)INGRICH.

Sparrow loves to cook papadams.

Sparrow is recovering from hernia surgery and reading Robert Browning's novel-in-verse, *The Ring And The Book*.

Sparrow is listening to The Dirty Three, Banco De Gaia, and Puerto Rican rap music this month.

Sparrow is a Marxist and amateur paleontologist. He or she lives in Shandaken (New York), in the shadow of Mt. Wellpayet. Sparrow draws with a pencil in a foot.

Sparrow is a substitute teacher at Onteora High School. His new band, The Tinsel Apartment, is rehearsing.

Recently Sparrow journeyed to Washington, D.C., to protest our current military government, and its "president," George W. Bush.

Someone has been sending Sparrow *Vanity Fair* each month.

Sparrow lives in Phoenicia, New York, a hamlet seated among the Catskill Mountains. He is working on a new book, *1001 Ways to Lose at Chess*.

Sparrow regrets that he stopped collected stamps when he was twelve. In fact, he no longer remembers *why* he discontinued this valued hobby.

Sparrow is a poet, a philosopher, and a novelist. He is also a cook, a policeman, an insurance salesman, a doctor, a thief, a Senator, a dog, a book, a tablecloth, a Baptist minister, a submarine captain, a tango instructor, an aerobics coach, a professional sandalmaker, a shepherd, a clown, a landlord, a real estate agent, a gymnast and a cowboy.

Sparrow is a firm believer in Boyle's Law.

Sparrow enjoys hiking, long hot baths, and sex.

Sparrow is currently reading G. K. Chesterton (*The Club of Queer Trades*) and losing weight.

Sparrow is delighted with the new Madonna album.

Sparrow is a substitute teacher, palindrome scholar, poet and theologian. He lives above a children's clothing store in Phoenicia, New York, with his wife (Violet Snow), daughter (Sylvia) and rabbit (Bananacake). His favorite musician is Ornette Coleman.

Sparrow is hard at work on his new book, *How To Keep A Secret*.

Sparrow's daughter Sylvia (age ten) has recently discovered Barbara

Streisand, so their Catskills apartment fills often with "Absent Minded Me" and "My Lord and Master." Outside, the summer tourists seek omelettes.

Sparrow's favorite color is pale brown.

Sparrow has been a Presidential candidate, a carpet laborer, telemarketer, substitute teacher, fig packer, magazine salesman, and cook.

Sparrow lives among 3 mountains and listens to drum'n'bass.

Sparrow is currently reading Francis Bacon's *Essays, Civil and Moral.*

Sparrow is a gossip columnist for *The Phoenicia Times*, also he writes "Quarter To Three," a monthly feature for *Chronogram* (www.chronogram.com) and art criticism for *New Renaissance* (www.ru.org).

Sparrow is studying the inventions of Thomas Paine.

Sparrow's poetry and writing have appeared in *The Village Voice*, the *Daily News, Mudfish, LUNGFULL!, The New York Observer, The Sun* and *Monster Trucks*. Articles about him were in *Rolling Stone* and *The London Times*. His band, Foamola, was quoted in *Time* magazine. He has been in thirteen anthologies, including *Verses That Hurt, Aloud: Poetry from the Nuyorican Cafe, Mondo Barbie, The Exquisite Corpse Reader* and *Stubborn Light: the Best of the Sun*. He was featured in the PBS documentary *The United States of Poetry*, and also in the HBO film *Best Man*.

Sparrow is reading his third book about the Shroud of Turin.

At his thirtieth high school reunion, Sparrow danced to "Play That Funky Music, White Boy" with a criminal lawyer.

Sparrow has been visiting colleges (Bard, Haverford, York) encouraging students to love their parents and destroy the government.

Sparrow studies French every day, for about nine minutes. He is currently reading *Le Petit Roi D'Ys (The Little King of Ys)*, a voyage to a lost kingdom undersea. He also reads one page of Ezra Pound (*Personae*) each day. While doing dishes at night, he listens to Cuban salsa. Sparrow's proverbs are available on www.bonney.org/proverbs.

Sparrow invented the bumper sticker DON'T BLAME ME—I

VOTED FOR BRITNEY SPEARS.

Responding to our current political crisis, Sparrow is writing *The Dick Cheney Joke Book* (with Lawrence Fishberg). (I believe this is available at www.hungryghost.net.)

Sparrow enjoys *Spidergirl* comics and agitating against the war in Iraq. On a recent visit to Las Vegas, USA he played the slot machines and lost 35 cents.

Sparrow has now seen all three movie versions of *The Great Gatsby*. His favorite state is Nevada. His favorite meal is vegetable lo mein. He lives next to the Esopus River, in the Catskill Mountains, in a double-wide trailer.

Sparrow is slowly writing a cookbook of Catskills cuisine. (His most recent recipe is "Mustard Oats.")

Sparrow reads one page of *Das Kapital* by Karl Marx each day. He is afraid to ride in a convertible.

Sparrow has begun keeping a list of every Chinese restaurant he visits.

Sparrow was born October 2, 1953 in Manhattan. He grew up in the Dyckman Projects with Kareem Abdul-Jabbar. Sparrow flunked out of Cornell University in 1973, and studied with Allen Ginsberg, Philip Whalen, and William Burroughs at the Naropa Institute in 1976. He received a master's degree from the City College of New York, where he studied with Ted Berrigan. Sparrow has been in twenty-two anthologies. He has run for President four times.